Friendly Fire

Friendly Fire
THE ACLU IN UTAH

Linda Sillitoe

SIGNATURE BOOKS
SALT LAKE CITY
1996

Jacket design by Julie Easton

∞ Signature Books titles are printed on acid free paper and composed, printed, and bound in the United States of America.

© 1996 Signature Books. All rights reserved.
Signature Books is a registered trademark of Signature Books, Inc.
2000 99 98 97 96   6 5 4 3 2 1

Library of Congress Cataloging-in-Publication Data
    Friendly fire : the ACLU in Utah / by Linda Sillitoe.
      p.   cm.
    Includes bibliographical references and index.
    ISBN 1-56085-076-0 (cloth)
    1. American Civil Liberties Union. 2. Civil rights—Utah.
I. Title.
JC599.U5S543   1996
323' .06'0792—dc20   96-18400
                                                  CIP

Utah-ALCU Directors and Presidents

EXECUTIVE DIRECTORS
Stephen W. Cook, 1972-73
James H. Joy, 1974-75
Shirley Pedler, 1976-86
Robyn Blumner, 1987-88
Michele Parish, 1989-92
Carol Gnade, 1993-present

BOARD PRESIDENTS
Spencer L. Kimball, mid-1950s
Adam Duncan, 1958-60
Steven Smoot, early 1960s
Ben Roe, 1960s
Bill Lockhart, 1970-71
George Grossman, 1972-73
Michael Rudick, 1973-76
Bill Procasey, 1980-82
Wayne McCormack, 1981-82
Ross Anderson, 1982-84
Jeffrey Montague, 1984-86
Gerald Nichols, 1986-90
Boyer Jarvis, 1990-91
John Morris, 1991-92
Bill Orchow, 1992-93
Elizabeth Dunning, 1993-1996
Gregory Williams, 1996-present

Contents

Sources and Resources . . . . *vii*

1. The Long View 1
2. Conception in Utah 13
3. Coming of Age 39
4. Welcome to Utah 63
5. To Pray or Not to Pray 89
6. Guns Blazing 117
7. The Scarlet Issue 145
8. Scene Change 169
9. The Prison Medical Ward the ACLU Built 191
10. And Justice for All 209

Notes *245*

Index *255*

Sources and Resources

When the files of the Utah affiliate of the American Civil Liberties Union were deposited in Special Collections at the Marriott Library, University of Utah, the numerous boxes of correspondence, newspaper clippings, legal documents, minutes, videotapes, and other data represented nearly forty years of struggle, conflict, and change.

Within this paper hillock lay evidence of contrasts in ideology and social action, for Utah—despite its roots in civil disobedience—showed little in common with the eastern civil libertarian mindset. A book drawn from these files would naturally explore the public interface of the ACLU in Utah, from the earliest days of a struggling ad hoc group in the 1950s and 1960s to its occasional moneyed victories in the 1980s and 1990s. Issues involving the separation and interaction of two prime powers, the Church of Jesus Christ of Latter-day Saints (Mormon) and Utah state government, emerged with the greatest continuity.

The public record amply papered the way, augmenting the sometimes incomplete fragments of correspondence and minutes. For the ease of readers, the styles of diverse manuscripts have been standardized (including omitting the repetitious use of courtesy titles) except in a few instances where meaning might be affected. Also, local director Michele Parish was known as Michele Parish-Pixler during part of her directorship. Here her shorter and current name is used throughout to avoid confusion. Also, the national ACLU is referred to as "National" within state affiliates; that term is capitalized as a substitute title in context.

Due to privacy issues, as well as their irrelevance to the book's focus, individual complaints, donor lists, and memos dealing with routine office matters were disregarded. On the other hand, correspondence spanning a forty-year period proved interesting and helpful. For instance, U.S. Supreme Court Justice Ruth Bader Ginsburg had risen to the nation's highest court when a letter she penned decades earlier to the Utah ACLU surfaced, quite forgotten in the files. The extensive clip files of civil liberties attorney Brian Barnard also yielded interesting and much appreciated information.

Interviews with more than a score of people involved with the ACLU proved invaluable. Some were interviewed at length or repeatedly, and all deserve appreciation. Throughout the narrative, the integrity of each viewpoint is preserved, including the contradictions and disagreements expected in hard-fought battles of policy and conscience. Missing, regrettably, are the perspectives of the political emissaries of the LDS church, who interacted with ACLU leaders but were not permitted to give interviews. It should also be noted that numerous individuals who contributed to the work of the ACLU are mentioned briefly or not at all. This is due to space and scope limitations, not because their gifts of time, effort, or money were insignificant. The interview notes now join the other materials in the ACLU Collection.

In addition, Samuel Walker's book *In Defense of American Liberties* proved helpful in placing the Utah affiliate within the national context, for the American Civil Liberties Union was organized in 1920, preceding the Utah affiliate by more than three decades. *In Our Defense: The Bill of Rights in Action,* by Ellen Alderman and Caroline Kennedy, also proved useful, particularly the introduction. Here the authors describe how the ACLU frequently defends "not very nice people" in order to preserve for all the liberties delineated in the Bill of Rights and interpreted since in the courts. Utah histories also influenced this work's context; specifically cited are Ronald Coleman's essay "Blacks in Utah" in *Peoples of Utah*, edited by Helen Z. Papinikolas, and John S. McCormick's *Salt Lake City: The Gathering Place.*

All these and other sources are listed by chapter in the bibliographic notes at the end of the book. Also helpful were a variety of ACLU events including a biennial conference of executive directors held in 1992 in

Santa Monica, California. Local groups whose issues engaged the ACLU's attention lent perspective on occasion, including a visit with leaders and members of the Gay and Lesbian Youth Group of Salt Lake City. Notes, studies, or clippings pertaining to the events or groups described are included in the collection.

Throughout the years of research and writing, the Special Collections directors and staff offered valuable assistance. Executive director Gregory Thompson provided essential support, encouragement, and guidance, augmented by the advice and assistance of Manuscripts director Nancy Young and the skillful expertise of Mark Jensen, who catalogued the collection. Finally, the Utah ACLU's executive directors, other leaders, attorneys, and staff all exhibited a spirit of cooperation, openness, introspection, and humor that made this project not only interesting but thoroughly enjoyable.

1.
The Long View

Before first light *Salt Lake Tribune* reporter Christopher Smart drove down Parley's Canyon toward a dirty fleece of winter smog. Once in the city he would breathe the grayish air like everyone else without thinking much about it, too focused on the morning's interview.

For some time he had seemed to breathe the story itself, one he knew—when he took the long view—was the story of his career. The American Civil Liberties Union was battling the Utah Department of Corrections over medical conditions, overcrowding, interception of legal mail, and inmates' access to religion. Over the last couple of years, Smart had blasted article after article onto the *Tribune*'s front page.

As he drove to work, copies of the *Tribune* were slapping on to subscribers' porches, scooting down driveways, banging storm doors like wake-up calls. This morning's newspaper reported a search for a new corrections chief.

Pursuing the prison story implied criticising a state department head, Gary DeLand, who was strong-willed, articulate, and backed by the governor. It meant questioning a state department that, a few years back, was considered an unassailable bulwark. It meant relying on sources such as Michele Parish, executive director of the Utah-ACLU, who not only led out on the prison lawsuits but was embroiled in other controversies as well.

In conservative Utah, a battle between the man who locked up bad guys and the woman who defended their rights didn't require a poll to determine which way the public leaned. By the time an editor had growled, Stop quoting Parish, Smart had developed a network of sources in the prison—inmates, guards, staff. He had good sources among them, but most talked without attribution. Only ACLU-types were likely to speak forthrightly on-the-record when it came to prisoners' rights.

Smart could never write the texture of the scenes that filled his head. He never described to readers how DeLand and his aides marched into the *Tribune* office to protest its coverage. The corrections men had seemed in uniform, Smart noted as he joined the meeting. They all wore sport coats, golf shirts, jeans, and cowboy boots, and DeLand had eased his jacket back as he sat down to display his hip pistol.

Nor did Smart describe Parish in her downtown Boston Building office that was layered everywhere with paper—lawsuits, posters, correspondence, memorabilia. Soft-voiced but acerbic, Parish was as hard-hitting in print as DeLand. Readers didn't see her bustle through the office in stocking feet with runs climbing the backs of her legs, tossing wisecracks over her shoulder as she photocopied documents.

He hadn't told readers how he angered Governor Norm Bangerter at a press conference, or how the governor had called the *Tribune*, demanded an apology, and gotten it. Smart just quoted these news makers, thrust for parry.

Straight reporting offered no way to describe the tension that hummed over telephone wires between the newspaper and the prison when he talked to sources at the Point of the Mountain. Some days it was more than tension, and the outright fear boosted his own adrenalin, coursing through his hands to the keyboard, rattling out the lead for the next article.

Of course the ACLU was known for championing unpopular causes. In the same edition with one of Smart's prison stories, Parish was quoted in other articles, on topics just as sensitive. Turn to the editorial page, and her caricature would appear in the morning's cartoon. The framed cartoons hung on her office wall like trophies.

Parish's willingness to anger local authorities to get things done was unusual and outrageous in Utah, where problem-solvers paid deference to traditional authority—church and state. Even the media chided itself for being too docile, willing to let newsmakers and their public relations people define the news. Yet the pattern was ingrained, and controversy tended to cost all who became involved.

In early 1991 that held true for DeLand as Smart reported his departure. A year earlier the media had covered the firing of DeLand's inspector general. Conditions were changing at the penitentiary. What Smart couldn't know was that the media would soon report the departure of others now at the heart of the fray. Michele Parish would pack up her activism and leave Utah; Governor Bangerter would decide not to run for a third term; and, well before the ACLU and Corrections resolved their differences in court, prison administrators would ensure that Christopher Smart would no longer work as an investigative reporter at the *Tribune*.

Controversy and the American Civil Liberties Union lived as conjoined twins, not only in Utah but elsewhere. Born and bred in New York and infused with eastern liberalism, the ACLU and the conservative Utah mindset stood at opposite poles. "The ACLU is a four-letter word in Utah," the affiliate's first staff lawyer would observe. Never had that been more evident in the public arena than early in 1991.

The Utah legislature had recently passed the Criminal Abortion Law, which posed the strongest threat yet from conservative states to legal abortion. Bangerter said the state would spend a million dollars to defend the bill, if necessary; and the ACLU would accommodate with a lawsuit.

In addition, northern Utah's editorial pages were filling with letters about prayers in public schools. This, like abortion, was a national issue with a local twist. The Rhode Island ACLU had filed suit on a similar case, and now controversy raged in Utah while litigants kept an eye on the United States Supreme Court.

Prisons, abortion, and public prayer were issues the ACLU took on nationwide. But in Utah, with a population that remained nearly 70 percent Mormon—members of the Church of Jesus Christ of Latter-day Saints—almost every issue seemed colored faintly or vividly by religion. The abortion statute, for instance, closely resembled the Mormon church's policy on abortion and was passed by an overwhelmingly white, male, Mormon legislature who, as lay clergy, led neighborhood congregations. Prayers in public schools were almost always LDS prayers, offered by students taught from childhood to pray spontaneously alone and in groups. And within a population whose lives centered around religion, who lived a rigid health and moral code, and who believed the Kingdom of God must be established by the righteous on earth as well as in heaven, prisoners, who had committed not just sins but crimes, prompted little sympathy.

Despite its peculiarities, Utah's majority politics at the onset of the 1990s fit securely into the nation's mainstream as U.S. presidential candidate George Bush called Democratic candidate Michael Dukakis a "card-carrying member of the ACLU." Thus the ACLU had become a pejorative buzzword among conservatives nationwide and certainly in Utah. Bush's administration, like Ronald Reagan's before it, legitimized the outrage Utahns felt toward an organization that helped prisoners, litigated for reproductive rights, and wanted prayer out of schools.

As the membership and resources of the national ACLU grew during the Reagan-Bush years, so did those of the Utah affiliate. Americans were beginning to perceive the enemies of one civil liberty or another as residing in the White House and ensconced in Congress. Locally, Parish had a theory that donations came in direct proportion to the number of minutes the affiliate captured on news broadcasts. People listened to sound bites and then opened their wallets.

Controversy had made the ACLU the power it had become, but controversy had nearly broken it more than once. As Samuel Walker would write in his book, *In Defense of American Liberties:* "The history of the ACLU is the story of America in this century." Walker called it "one of the most unpopular organizations in the country."

In Utah, the briefer history of the ACLU similarly capsulized the state's history, not in years as much as in highlighting the culture's torments, triumphs, and trials of conscience. Principles lay at the core of each conflict, deeply rooted, where social and individual conscience formed. Such principles found expression in both secular and religious ways, whether over the pulpit, in the legislature, or at ACLU board meetings.

"Critics often charge the ACLU with arrogance," Walker wrote. "Who, they ask, gave it license to say what a civil liberty is? Who gave it authority to impose its will on the rest of the country?" In fact, the ACLU holds no special license. "The ACLU," Walker explained, "has no greater authority than any other advocacy group has had. It has argued its point of view in the courts and the arena of public opinion along with every other group. . . . "

But the ACLU reached into the heart of crucial issues including pornography, separation of church and state, and the rights of lawbreakers. Repeatedly, Walker asserted, the ACLU asked itself and the nation, "What is the nature of freedom in a democratic society? Where should the lines be drawn in determining the boundaries of individual rights?"

Founded in New York in 1920 by Roger Baldwin, the ACLU announced itself as the first public interest law firm dedicated to the Bill of Rights: to preserving freedom of speech, freedom of the press, freedom of religion, freedom from unreasonable search and seizure, freedom of assembly, and eventually to preserving implied freedoms such as privacy.

Preceded by the National Civil Liberties Bureau that Baldwin and Crystal Eastman organized, the ACLU drew its founders from three main groups—social workers such as Baldwin and Eastman; Protestant clergy, including socialist leader Norman Thomas; and conservative lawyers who idealized the Constitution.

The concern in the early twentieth century coalesced even as the nation succumbed to the fever of World War I. To pacifists such as Baldwin and Thomas, the government's treatment of dissidents and conscientious objectors graphically illustrated the practical absence of civil liberties in the United States. Not only were the times inspiring charismatic leaders like Baldwin and organizations like the ACLU, they simultaneously propelled young J. Edgar Hoover into power, largely to quash the dissidents, immigrants, and workers the ACLU would learn to defend.

Essentially, free speech did not exist before World War I, for it was supported neither by legal precedent nor by public tolerance. "The glittering phrases of the First Amendment were an empty promise to the labor movement, immigrants, unorthodox religious sects, and political radicals," Walker wrote. In order to cope, dissident groups simply relocated within the vast geographic area claimed by the United

States. In a nation that stretched from sea to sea, people could live apart rather than learn to live together.

Mormons, for instance, had traveled westward in increasing numbers as their communities struck discord with their neighbors. From the church's inception in New York state, the Saints had built and then abandoned one city after another, including the second-largest city in Illinois, then fled to Mexican territory and claimed it as their Zion. Unlike their sojourns in various states during the westward exodus, Mormons found on the western side of the Rocky Mountains time to grow and prosper before their enemies caught up with them. With their collective memory stained by battering, rape, and bloodshed, their need for a stronghold was as intense as their determination to provide one.

Other groups, differing from the core of white Anglo-Saxon Protestants by race, ethnicity, class, or belief, had clustered as well. When the ACLU took root in 1920, it did so in a nation that seldom questioned discrimination on the basis of race, gender, or social position. Women were just receiving the vote after a bitter struggle, and racial segregation remained the law and custom of the land. The Supreme Court had never upheld a free speech claim under the First Amendment. The fledgling ACLU immediately fought for the right of the Industrial Workers of the World and other trade unions simply to hold meetings. Baldwin would speak prophetic and often-repeated words when he said, "No fight for civil liberties ever stays won."

The very controversy that made the fledgling ACLU known throughout the nation—the Scopes "monkey trial" and organic evolution in public school curricula—ended inconclusively but popularized the notion of variant ideas and free speech. In the decades that followed, the question of Bible study in public schools returned perennially. Walker wrote, "In the 1980s, fundamentalists pushed a new theory of 'scientific creationism,' and the Supreme Court again sustained the ACLU in 1987 by declaring unconstitutional a Louisiana law requiring its teaching." The day that decision came down, a journalist asked ACLU executive director Ira Glasser "how long the ACLU had been fighting the case. 'Sixty-two years,' he replied."

Baldwin was dead right, said law professor Nadine Strossen in 1994. As the first woman president of the American Civil Liberties Union,

Strossen quoted Baldwin in an interview with *The Progressive*. When asked whether the Bill of Rights could be passed in the nation's current climate, Strossen replied, "Every now and then someone does an opinion poll in which people are told what the Bill of Rights is. The pollees always seem to say, 'Let's get rid of that.'"

Such public sentiment prompted authors Ellen Alderman and Caroline Kennedy to write the book *In Our Defense*. They noted that a 1987 newspaper poll showed that 59 percent of Americans could not identify the Bill of Rights. In introducing fundamental principles of the Bill of Rights, the authors "decided to begin with the people, traveling the country to meet with them. Because the law evolves in tiny increments of *Plaintiff v. Defendant*, we decided to tell the stories of their cases."

The cases were chosen for the "majestic principles of liberty and justice . . . played out in the lives of ordinary Americans, some heroic and some malevolent." The authors quoted a Supreme Court justice who wrote: "It is a fair summary of history to say that the safeguards of liberty have frequently been forged in controversies involving not very nice people."

The authors concluded, " . . . as the Bill of Rights enters its third century, it is only by fighting for those rights, win or lose, that they will continue."

Defending "not very nice people" was, in fact, an ACLU hallmark. The ACLU prided itself on championing the unpopular—prisoners, minorities, troublemakers, misfits who did not flow with the mainstream. In preserving itself and its institutions, society offered such people its indifference at best, and its force of will at worst. The Bill of Rights had been written, after all, to abridge the power of the majority.

In fact, as Alderman and Kennedy explained, it was not until after the Thirteenth, Fourteenth, and Fifteenth amendments were enacted following the Civil War that the U.S. Supreme Court even began to protect citizens against the states, using the Fourteenth Amendment as a doorway. Judicial debate then commenced over which and how many guarantees of the Bill of Rights applied federally and should be incorporated against the states. The debate continued for decades. The incorporation of most rights during the 1960s prompted an increase in constitutional litigation and propelled what the ACLU would call the "rights revolution." That social unrest would strike—in Americans who dwelled comfortably in the majority—a chord, a sense of "their" society losing control.

The goal of preserving civil liberties would frequently become contradictory, as the ACLU veered from libertarian stances to liberal positions, then back again. Interpreting complex questions often raised internal debate. Would the ACLU support the vanguard freedom of the press or would it resist pornography as part of its Women's Rights Project? Should the ACLU defend a woman's or a couple's implied right to reproductive privacy or defend the unwritten rights of the unborn?

Such internal conflict rarely impeded the organization's health, however, for the ACLU and its people thrived on discussion. Twice every year the executive directors of the ACLU convened to discuss budgets, fund raising, current politics, and issues. At every gathering these affiliate directors proved themselves politically savvy and suspicious of authority, as they refused to rubber stamp any agenda without thorough consideration. Even behind closed doors the ACLU tended to model the diversity and freedom of expression it advocated within the public arena.

The national ACLU celebrated thirty anniversaries before it was conceived in Utah. True, women voted and schools and parks were integrated, but the roles for both women and racial minorities remained firmly circumscribed in many ways. In addition, workers' rights were comparatively nonexistent, and resistance to unions ran high. Most pervasively, Utah enjoyed a racial and religious homogeneity that automatically magnified the will of the majority as appropriate and preferable.

In Utah, church, family, and government formed a trusted triad; generally the same men led and shaped all three. Industry and loyalty to those in authority carried the promise of prosperity and peace. This seemed the just blessing of the descendants of Mormon settlers, many of whom had eked out a hardscrabble existence; prosperity also felt fine in a state hit particularly hard by the Great Depression. Not surprisingly, the seeds of civil libertarianism sprouting elsewhere in the nation between 1920 and 1950 fell on crusty soil near the Great Salt Lake. For decades after the Utah affiliate took root, it would be viewed by pioneer stalwarts as sprouting obnoxious weeds to infest the grain of an orderly society.

An orderly society had been shaped in Utah territory as an element of survival, for colonizer Brigham Young's concept had depended upon a fierce sense of loyalty that allowed people transplanted from greener climes to impose their vision on the fertile but arid valleys. Below that practicality lay an even deeper vein of unity—testimony that the leader spoke God's will, not his own, and gave God's counsel.

Historian John S. McCormick described the Mormon vision of a western utopia in *Salt Lake City: The Gathering Place:* "A religious impulse would infuse every activity, so that it would be difficult or impossible to draw a line between the religious and secular aspects of life." Church leaders would extend their edicts into political, social, and cultural realms as well as the religious. "For Mormons, only a society that God designed and closely directed could endure and provide peace and justice on the earth."

The vision of nineteenth-century Mormons depended on a strong central organization backed by an obedient people. Furthermore, in capitalist America this "would be a cooperative, rather than a competitive society. The emphasis would be on group consciousness and activity, not on the individual," McCormick wrote.

"Kingdom," for Mormons, meant God's civil authority on earth, a concept at once spiritual and literal. The binding words of a prophet, "Thus saith the Lord," were not spoken often in pioneer times and rarely in the corporate church of the late twentieth century. Yet the implication of inspired authority in both eras sped along an intricate priesthood network from the church hierarchy to the neighborhood bishop and permeated every LDS home, ideally headed by a father holding the priesthood. Thus "the gospel" interfaced with every aspect and level of living.

Most importantly, perhaps, territorial Utah's temples, cities, and farms symbolized an enormous improbability—the triumph of a people and a religion that very nearly had been quashed by the majority. After all, no ACLU had existed to protect beleaguered nineteenth-century

Mormons driven from state to state. No ACLU had marched to free their founder and first prophet, Joseph Smith, from the Carthage Jail where he was killed by a mob. Once the Mormons founded their community beyond the Rockies, no ACLU defended polygamy to the federal government as an aspect of freedom of religion. When the United States confiscated Mormon property, canceled voting rights, and jailed citizens who obeyed all laws except monogamy, the cries for justice under the Constitution went unanswered. In defiance, on one July 4 Mormons flew the American flag at half mast.

Before Utah became a state, it was forced into compliance with the majority values of the country—capitalism, monogamy, and representative government, though belief in communalism, polygamy, and inspired leadership burrowed deep but did not die. Not surprisingly, a century later the cultural memory of strife and persecution found expression more in solidarity with like-minded people, in civic order, and in prosperity than in dissonance. The community sense of having triumphed over an ungodly world rarely bent toward those currently considered radical.

In fact, by the time Baldwin founded the ACLU, Utahns were determinedly mainstream American. In 1925, as the ACLU defended John T. Scopes, Utahns, like many other Americans, opened public meetings and classrooms with prayer. As the ACLU litigated for workers' rights, Utah remained an anti-union state where labor uprisings were squelched and labor activist Joe Hill was executed for murder. As the ACLU protested the internment of Japanese-Americans during World War II, Utah hosted a prison camp in the desert.

After the wars, Utah entered a slow but persistent curve toward Republicanism and dependence on military industry. The ACLU seemed distant, offensively eastern, and relatively small. Its local legal department of one attorney was more likely to file an *amicus curiae* (friend-of-the-court) brief than undertake litigation. Utahns might read about the case in the newspapers. But as the 1960s approached and television-borne social issues seized the heart of American society, organizations devoted to civil liberties swelled as never before, even as the LDS church and the State of Utah each assumed a strict stance favoring the status quo.

As ACLU influence was channeled into the civil rights movement, Little Rock, Memphis, and Birmingham seemed distant. Minority communities in Utah were small and thus far timid, and the Utah legislature resisted civil rights measures well into the 1970s. As controversies tended to, the issue of racial equality swarmed around the powerful yet vulnerable Mormon church which withheld its lay priesthood from African-American men. The church drew fire, ranging from criticism of LDS presidential candidate George Romney to protests and boycotts of sporting events involving church-owned Brigham Young University.

The ACLU opposed the Vietnam war, but Utah's economy depended on military industry. Often semi-annual LDS general conferences urged Mormons to support the war, though many young people avoided service by filling church missions or seeking educational or marital deferments. As the ACLU called for the impeachment of President Richard Nixon, Utah offered him a small but steady stronghold. As the Christian right absorbed the backlash of the liberal and libertarian tendencies of the "rights revolution," Utah offered itself in the late 1970s, 1980s, and early 1990s as the hallmark of "family values."

Nevertheless, despite these general trends, the changes that swept the U.S. after World War II reached Utah, too, including increased employment among women and a surge in higher education. For the first time the LDS church was led by a college-educated prophet, David O. McKay, who brought other educators into church service and encouraged education in both church and secular formats. The defended border between religion and academia faded, and by the 1960s knowledge in both arenas seemed possible and desirable. And so, as the nation emerged from the Cold War to wrestle with its conscience and its young, the blowing seeds of libertarianism caught hold in the minds of a few in Utah and began to grow.

History would show that the polarity between the power structure and the ACLU's insistence on civil liberties ultimately forged the two into a synergistic relationship both nationally and in Utah. The resistance the ACLU encountered in its crusades lent energy and resources to the organization as it unfurled its banner across the public consciousness. Conversely, the outrageous efforts of the ACLU in opposing mainstream opinion bolstered the confidence of the conservative majority. While many—perhaps even most—conflicts were resolved without litigation, winning in court would underwrite the meager coffers of the fledgling Utah affiliate and guarantee its challenges to the establishment in the future. Taxpayers often paid not only for the armistice but for the battle.

In any war involving the ACLU, the gains and losses have included barrages of "friendly fire," an oxymoron coined by the military for casualties inflicted by comrades-in-arms rather than foreign troops. The relationship—not the intent or the damage—gave rise to the term, for those sending and those receiving fire were undeniably linked.

Linked too are the Utah ACLU and the community in which it thrives and wars. Thus the questions of who won, who lost, and how civil liberties fared in the fray inevitably require interpretation.

2.
Conception in Utah

The idea to organize a Utah affiliate of the ACLU was conceived in the fertile environment of the University of Utah Law School in the mid-1950s. Professors there, like many nationwide, were alarmed by the activities of Senator Joseph McCarthy and the congressional investigation of American citizens. In addition, they were keenly aware of the civil rights issues beginning to smolder in the South.

World War II had left Americans vulnerable to insinuations of an enemy within—communism—but simultaneously people of all races, ethnicities, and genders were determined to claim full citizenship. People of color had fought in the war, people previously unemployed had gone to work, and the GI bill had made higher education a reality for working-class people. All in all, Americans' vision of themselves was changed, and the change demanded expression.

Author Samuel Walker wrote of the decade between 1954 and 1964, "These were great years for the ACLU, as it played a leading role in virtually every major Supreme Court decision, and, in several, directly influenced the court's thinking. . . . " During that decade the ACLU's membership soared from 30,000 to 80,000 backed by staffed affiliates in seventeen states. "A new sense of freedom was in the air: An increasingly educated public expected the freedom to read without restrictions imposed by religious moralists," Walker wrote. "The sexual revolution challenged censorship in the arts and restrictions on birth control, eventually leading to a new concept of privacy. And in 1960 the sit-ins gave political participation a new personal dimension."

The impetus was hardly lost on those who formed the nucleus of the Utah ACLU. A few years after its inception the affiliate would receive its national charter and, decades later, become self-supporting. By the time the chapter declared financial independence, it would be embroiled in complex, heated lawsuits involving national issues.

In some respects, the Utah ACLU deviated from the national course. Some issues never blossomed in Utah, or they took a different form, such as in the early 1990s when Utah resisted the national campaign to challenge the religious right. Utah's own church/state patterns dominated. Nor would the national drive for workers' rights find much resonance in a state where these were essentially undeveloped.

In Utah two issues provided continuity: prisoners' rights and church/state issues. In fact, the propensity to square off with the LDS church left Utahns bemused, since the first person to lift the ACLU banner in Utah was the oldest son of a Mormon prophet.

Spencer LeVan Kimball, professor and acting dean of the University of Utah Law School, became, in the mid-1950s, the first ACLU representative in Utah. Kimball's father, then Apostle Spencer W. Kimball, would later become one of the most influential of all LDS church presidents. By that time the Utah ACLU was firmly ensconced and the younger Kimball had left the state. However the potential irony played out on a larger scale. Under President Kimball's leadership, the LDS church would play a crucial role in defeating the Equal Rights Amendment nationwide, despite the vigorous efforts of the national ACLU's Women's Rights Project to achieve ratification.

In the 1950s, all of that still lay in the future. Spencer L. Kimball and others found initial impetus in a notorious murder in southern Utah in which the defendants received woefully inadequate representation. The case was championed by Salt Lake City attorney A. Wally Sandack who became interested in the embryonic issue of defendants' rights. Kimball, Alfred Emery, Ben Dykstra, Sandy Kadish, Adam Duncan and others sought such allies as Sandack while the ACLU was still coalescing. Kimball, for instance, signed *amicus* briefs for civil rights lawsuits as a law professor rather than as an ACLU representative.

Kimball left Utah with mixed feelings in the summer of 1957, lured by a tenured professorship at the University of Michigan Law School. He had considered running for political office, probably the U.S. Senate. "I would have felt a little uncomfortable trading on the family name running for office, although I know it's done all the time," he said later.

Besides, he reasoned at the time, the seat was held by Senator Arthur Watkins, a Republican considered unbeatable by the disorganized Democratic Party. And Kimball would have to beat Frank (Ted) Moss in the primary. But when Moss unexpectedly triumphed, it left Kimball wondering if he had missed a chance. Resettled in Michigan, he helped organize the ACLU in Ann Arbor, though in later years he left the organization, discouraged that it pursued issues he considered frivolous, including that of public prayer.

In 1957, according to Adam (Mickey) Duncan, Kimball had a parting request: "I want you to do something for me, Mickey. I want you to take over my ACLU post." Duncan agreed. He and Kimball felt that the civil liberties banner should be carried by "at least a nominal Mormon," as Duncan identified Kimball—or better yet by an active Mormon, as Duncan was. An "insider" would know the customs and the parlance peculiar to Utah and could work from within cultural assumptions "outsiders" tended to bypass or misunderstand entirely.

Duncan's family was of pioneer stock. He had filled a mission to South Africa, which, in fact, fired his lifelong interest in civil rights. While preaching the LDS faith, he and other missionaries were instructed to avoid African and "mixed blood" men. Even in the 1940s Duncan "realized the vicious folly of that policy."

While working his way through law school, Duncan taught at the LDS seminary adjacent to East High School. He mused later that his liberal views separated him from the norm. His teaching contract was not renewed after he convinced students to "squander" their graduation party fund by replacing the vandalized stained glass windows in a nearby Baptist church.

As a leader, Duncan perpetuated, perhaps unconsciously, a policy toward conservative Mormons similar to Brigham Young's touted philosophy toward native peoples in Utah Territory: "It's better to feed than to fight them." Given the number of LDS church members versus ACLU members, that policy of conciliation and education would remain strong in the Utah affiliate.

Nationally the ACLU was split internally on issues of tactics. One group, led initially by Roger Baldwin, Norman Thomas, and Scott Nearing, favored direct action and heightened rhetoric to sway public opinion. The other group, which included attorneys Walter Nelles and Walter Pollak, believed in litigation. The former group placed the ACLU on the map of public awareness. The latter group, Walker wrote, "patiently carried test cases to the Supreme Court, establishing the ACLU tradition of legal craftsmanship."

In Utah minority issues became a primary concern for Duncan, knowing that minority defendants fared poorly within the legal system, especially those who did not speak English fluently or understand the courts and legal rights. But Duncan insisted on appeals to reason and respectability. He pled with national ACLU officials for local autonomy, arguing, "You don't slap a Mormon in the face. You try to talk him out of what he wants in a reasonable way. You don't try to bully him."

In another state such sensitivity to religious homogeneity might seem excessive. In Utah it scarcely needs articulation. The ACLU was formed to confront government not religion, but here contending with judges, legislators, and politicians implies suing bishops or stake presidents. Raising issues meant opposing church authorities. Virtually every confrontation with civic authority would, by extension, thumb its nose at the unofficial collective authority—the Mormon church.

When Duncan accepted Kimball's spot, he believed that his people's "loving side" would surface. Utahns believed in goodness, industry, and volunteerism. At church they sang, "All is well," and tended to believe that all should be well. Idealism was often salutary, for when problems were acknowledged they were quickly solved.

In 1958 the Utah affiliate was awarded its first charter. One civic-minded businessman, Ben Roe, recalled the formal organization in his autobiography, *A Blend of the Two:* "I had been a member of the national ACLU for many years before a chapter was organized in Salt Lake City. During that time I worked with Reverend John Wade of the Campus Christian Center on a very similar organization . . . called the Citizen's Organization for Civil Rights. . . . "

He continued: "One Sunday morning in the fall of 1958, I saw a little note in *The Salt Lake Tribune* that an organizational meeting for a Utah chapter of the ACLU was scheduled to take place Monday night . . . in the rotunda of the Utah State Capitol Building." He immediately arranged to attend. "I was elected treasurer," he wrote, "which became a seventeen-year obligation."

Finances were, of course, critical. Duncan lobbied national headquarters to be able to keep most of the local dues within the state. Every affiliate leader to follow Duncan would juggle twin concerns—the unique lay of the political landscape and limited funds.

The Campus Christian Center dealt with minority issues, as did the National Association for the Advancement of Colored People. In 1948 the local NAACP successfully protested the City-County Building's refusal to serve African Americans at its lunch counter. Meanwhile Duncan lobbied ranking Utahns, never accusing anyone of racial prejudice but rather reporting a "perception" that injustice occurred. He appealed to Utahns' desire to be viewed as decent, mainstream Americans rather than as survivors of a radical, evangelical sect. In fact, David O. McKay, current LDS church president, was the first Mormon prophet never to have practiced polygamy. Also, Utah was a small state in population and the LDS church tiny among world religions. Utah's cultural memory of antagonism from outside aroused an immediate reaction of feeling outnumbered or even persecuted.

Quick to shine a positive light where he could, Duncan honored those who publicly supported civil liberties. When Utah Supreme Court Justice Alan Crockett wrote a dissenting opinion on the treatment of indigents, the ACLU presented him with an award at its annual banquet, beginning an enduring tradition.

Nationally the civil rights movement simmered under a lid maintained by the Dwight D. Eisenhower administration. In Utah the African-American population was so proportionately small that many residents disregarded local implications. A century earlier African Americans had been among the earliest explorers and settlers (the latter both slave and free) of the Great Basin. Slavery was legalized in the Utah territory and continued for a decade. Although the Saints proclaimed their loyalty to the Union, they viewed the Civil War as the proclaimed apocalypse preceding the reign of Jesus Christ and stood ready to lead at his second advent. More practically, they had their own gripes with the federal government, which had sent an army to keep watch on them.

Nor did many Utahns in the twentieth century think twice about barring African Americans from hotels and restaurants. Segregation operated in common aspects of everyday life. Decades after the civil rights movement brought change, Utahns hardly noticed the scarcity of black retail clerks, schoolteachers, government officials, or police officers even along the populous Wasatch Front.

Striking the battle against prejudice, Mickey Duncan did not realize the resilience of this indifference. He was elected in 1956 as a Republican to the Utah House of Representatives. The same year, he chaired the Utah Advisory Committee to Eisenhower's United States Commission on Civil Rights. As an attorney and the youngest House member, Duncan also served on the judiciary committee, which, among other tasks, set the standards for paying judges. In those days no one chided him for talking informally to various judges and law enforcers about minority rights.

Whenever a petty crime occurred, Duncan remembered, the police tended to bring in Hispanic, Native American, and African-American youth for questioning. "It was like [the movie] *Casablanca* when the police chief says, 'Round up the usual suspects,'" Duncan reminisced. He dropped in on the police chief to discuss the "sweeps" of minority neighborhoods. "I told him the police were at least perceived as doing this even if it wasn't true. 'If you have to round people up, at least don't do it by race,'" he urged, and the chief agreed.

Heartened, Duncan then visited city court judges Maurice Jones and Paul Grant and discussed the dilemma of suspects who didn't speak or understand English. Did the court call in translators or advocates for such people? "Bend a little bit when you get a defendant like this," Duncan encouraged. "Help us stop the sweeps." Conditions seemed to improve, and at the next ACLU banquet awards went to the police chief and the judges for their sensitivity to civil liberties.

Despite such efforts, discrimination was ingrained. Blacks and Asians had trouble buying houses; Jewish people were excluded from club membership; businesses double-charged American Indians, especially near Utah's reservations; and minority citizens could not rent a motel room.

"Again ... we find that Negroes encounter more offensive discriminatory practices and of greater severity than any other ethnic group," Duncan and his committee wrote in one report. "They are accorded unequal treatment in opportunities for employment, public accommodations, and, most severely, in housing."

In both Salt Lake and Weber counties "the vast preponderance of the population live in 'ghettos' or poor, overcrowded areas," they wrote. "A Negro must pay a higher down payment, higher purchase price, and accept less favorable terms than a non-Negro in purchasing a home outside of his district . . . ," the report continued. In predominantly Caucasian neighborhoods, "virtually none of the apartment houses or other rentals are open to Negroes." When public accommodations served African Americans, the report claimed, they charged them higher prices than others.

Although Utah's schools had never practiced racial segregation, the report explained that a "Negro teacher will have an extremely difficult, perhaps impossible, task in finding employment. . . . " A 1960 graduate of the University of Utah was refused a teaching position because he had not scored an A average in college. "Similar academic standing has never been required of white teachers," the ACLU noted. Despite this injustice, a few blacks were employed as teachers in Ogden, and several Japanese in Salt Lake City and elsewhere. "The employment of Japanese teachers invariably requires extra or exceptional justification."

In both 1957 and 1959 Duncan threw his energy behind a "toothless" civil rights bill in an effort to begin changing attitudes. The bill stated that people seeking public accommodation could not be unlawfully discriminated against. It sustained what had already become federal law.

Toothless or not, Duncan knew his bill would be seen as a shark. He needed clout from some established authority so the bill could at least pass the Senate rules committee, which included several Mormon bishops. Duncan regarded a fellow attorney, Marion D. Hanks, an effective public speaker. Under David O. McKay, Hanks had been ordained to the LDS First Council of Seventy, a tier just below the

Quorum of Twelve Apostles, and Duncan knew of Hanks's sympathies toward civil rights.

"I called Duff Hanks at home and explained the bill," Duncan related. "Duff said, 'What do you want me to do?'"

"Come up and talk to this committee and just say what you've said at your firesides," Duncan urged. "Let people see this is the right thing to do."

"I'll be there," Hanks assured him.

Before long Duncan was hand-delivered what he called a thumbs-down letter on LDS church stationery with the designation, "Dictated but not signed." The letter began "Dear Mickey," and ended with "Duff." Hanks wrote that he had delivered a copy of the bill to the First Presidency. "President McKay's secretary, upon my inquiry, told me that the president had talked with her about it and felt it could conceivably be very embarrassing to some church institutions." He continued, "I did not talk with President McKay or any members of the First Presidency about the matter, although I had hoped they would invite me to do so and explain our difficulties."

He added: "Independently of the president's thought, I had come to the conclusion that while I am entirely in sympathy with your purposes in introducing the bill, it could well be a matter of grave concern to the church and of real damage should any crusading 'liberals' assail us through our institutional establishments." He used the Hotel Utah as an example. "The thought of a dozen visitors making repeated demands upon the hotel, for instance, leads one to consider some grave possibilities." The Hotel Utah was a grand showpiece, owned and operated by the LDS church. Duncan further reflected on the possibility of integration at the Deseret Gym, a tax-exempt club segregated by gender and frequented by high-ranking LDS leaders.

Decades later a boyhood friend of Hanks recounted the atmosphere in Salt Lake City during this period. Myron Q. Hale, who would become a professor of political science at Purdue University, worked as a teenager and college student in the lobby of the Hotel Utah prior to the year 1951. Hale wrote in a letter: "Perhaps the awakening for me was the treatment of blacks by the Hotel Utah. As a night desk clerk at the hotel, I was told that blacks were not to be given rooms should they attempt to register." Hale recalled that African Americans would be directed to the recently integrated Hotel Newhouse, a traditional competitor with the Hotel Utah. "The words were, 'I am sorry but we are filled to capacity, but I could attempt to obtain a room for you at another hotel.'"

Painfully Hale recalled a scene during the patriotic years of World War II. "I'll never forget the night sometime in 1942 that an army captain, who was black, with one arm missing, and on his uniform a chest full of ribbons, attempted to register at the Hotel Utah," Hale wrote. "I was ashamed, but I said, 'I am sorry, I cannot lie to you. Hotel policy prohibits my assigning you a room. . . . I will, however, call another hotel and try to obtain a room for you.' The captain said nothing, and I made the call." The Hotel Newhouse was full that night, so the captain spent the night sitting in the hotel lobby.

Hale recalled another incident that would become infamous. "I was at the Hotel Utah desk when [singer] Marian Anderson was forced to use the freight elevator after her performance in the Mormon Tabernacle." During her stay at the hotel, Hale said, "the rooms were 'blank'— no name—and no information was to be given to the newspapers or anyone else. . . . She took meals in her room."

Despite this climate of ingrained prejudice, Duncan believed that by 1959 his bill's chances of success had improved over its failure in 1956. This time, however, he could not get another legislator to co-sponsor it, and so the ACLU chief presented it alone.

"On March 14, I gave the best speech of my life," Duncan recalled. He pleaded for an end to all inter-racial rancor including the bitter feelings toward Japanese Americans left over from World War II. The bill passed the House of Representatives with an overwhelming 80 percent, then sailed on to the Senate.

University of Utah political science professor J. D. Williams credits Duncan's fiery speeches and astute politics. "If it hadn't been for Mickey Duncan and the ACLU, progress would have been dreadfully slow in this state," he told *The Salt Lake Tribune* in 1993. "'Mickey had a way of getting people to see the light,' Williams said. 'I consider him one of the most important civil-rights leaders this state has ever had.'"

At the time, Duncan's triumph in the House of Representatives was short-lived. To get his bill through the Senate, he approached Sherm Lloyd, a future U.S. congressman who was then Senate president. "I want that bill debated on the floor of the Senate whether it can pass or not," Duncan told him.

"Well, the majority and minority leaders don't want it on the floor," Lloyd said.

"I talked with Clyde," Duncan insisted, referring to Governor George D. Clyde. "He'll sign it."

The bill perished quietly in committee. Despite Duncan's stout belief that a lot of good resided in Mormon bishops and the other lay churchmen filling the legislature, he concluded bitterly that if "by their fruits ye shall know them," his fellow Mormons had proven themselves unenlightened.

Duncan was especially unhappy with one man, despite the House victory. House speaker Sheldon Brewster, a Democrat, headed the "sifting committee" which directed legislative business to the floor. If Brewster didn't approve a bill, only a two-thirds vote of the body could bring it to the floor. Brewster fought Duncan's bill vigorously.

Brewster was a motel owner and realtor who resisted accessibility for African Americans. As a Mormon bishop in 1939, Brewster initiated a petition, gleaning 1,000 signatures, to relocate African-American residents living just south of the city center to a ghetto farther from downtown. This district, wrote historian Ronald Coleman in *Peoples of Utah*, "would be located away from the City and County Building where visitors to the city would not come in contact" with them.

According to Coleman, "Brewster employed a local Black in the attempt to persuade other Blacks to sell their houses and agree to be colonized in one location, but he failed to secure their cooperation." To the contrary: "Blacks rose up in indignation and marched to the Capitol to protest Brewster's action." Though denied, Brewster's petition to the Salt Lake City Commission reflected the current state of the housing market in Utah, for restrictive covenants in deeds and contracts limited options. The area Brewster wanted to purge lay within the LDS Liberty-Wells Stake, where Brewster later served in the stake presidency.

Near one session's end Duncan decided he should resolve his disagreement with Brewster and paid his office a call. "Sheldon, I don't want this session to end with me feeling so angry with you," Duncan confessed to the older man. "Let's just part friends."

"Sheldon was unctuous," Duncan reminisced, "and said, 'Mickey, I'm glad that in your heart you know I'm right.'

"'That's not what I said.'

"Sheldon pointed to a spot on the carpet and said, 'You know, Mickey, every morning I kneel down right here and pray about the bills that are in the hopper. Then I call President Moyle [LDS first counselor Henry D. Moyle] and tell him, 'These are the ten bills that will be submitted today.' I ask him for his suggestions. We talk a little bit, and those bills he suggests are the bills that I call out of committee. So you see, Mickey, the Lord's work is being done here.'"

This did not fall happily on the ears of the ACLU president. "I said, 'Sheldon, I'm sorry I came in here.'"

Nearly forty years later, white-haired and still practicing law across South Temple Street from the LDS Church Administration Building, Duncan would retell his experiences. "The legislature is probably better than we deserve," he mused. "I look at my religion as a heritage; my grandparents walked across the Great Plains. But the domination of religion in Utah is as bad or worse now as it was then, maybe a little more subtle."

Although Duncan found church and state locked in a solid fist over civil rights, he also found the fingers beginning to loosen. Duncan would lead a civil rights commission for Utah's new Democratic governor, Calvin L. Rampton, elected in 1964, as well as the local federal commission, all the while becoming impatient with sluggish process.

The national advisory committee met in various areas of the state to accommodate its diverse and far-flung membership. The Reverend H. Baxter Liebler in Bluff, near the northern border of the Navajo Nation, always brought his dog to meetings. Following one meeting in Bluff, Duncan went into a cafe in nearby Mexican Hat and ordered a beer. He noticed four or five Navajo men there and realized that the bartender was charging the Native Americans $1.00 per drink to his own thirty-five cents per drink. He confronted the bartender, who explained that these men were Navajos and were getting drunk, so he charged more.

Duncan told him about his anti-discrimination bill. The bartender was not impressed. "He said, 'Get the hell out of my bar,' which I did."

Although the national advisory committee worked hard, Duncan came to doubt that President Eisenhower took their work seriously. The fifty committee chairs and their spouses were invited to a lunch in Washington, D.C., at which the president was scheduled to speak. However, Eisenhower, clad in golf attire, arrived half an hour late, "clearly snatched off the links," in Duncan's opinion. "He said, 'You people are doing good work, and I encourage you to continue. Thank you very much,' and left. I thought it was a brilliant way of saying, 'I don't give a damn about you people and what you're doing.'"

Similarly, Duncan said, when the state civil rights commission inquired too vigorously into employment hiring and firing practices, the "word came down that we were going to embarrass the governor." Although Duncan found his three-pronged effort for change painfully slow, the national ACLU was picking up momentum. National staffer and Mountain States director Dorothy Davidson later recalled that during those years money and memberships poured into the ACLU. The running joke was that they could send out a piece of toilet paper with the words ACLU on it, and a certain amount of money would come in.

Despite difficulties, Duncan and his colleagues built the Utah ACLU into a genuine, though subsidized, affiliate. On July 15, 1959, Duncan issued a "Dear Member" letter on official letterhead announcing the chapter's national recognition. The executive committee, consisting of Stephen P. Smoot, Barry N. Sigel, Charles Edwards, Pat Coontz, Leon Ward, Allen L. Hodgson, Albert Fritz, and William G. Fowler, met in September to plan the annual meeting. The affiliate celebrated on October 27, 1959, at the Young Women's Christian Association building at Third South and Third East streets.

Before the year's end a "bird dog" committee was formed with Steve Smoot as chair. "Snoopers" were assigned to monitor the NAACP, city hall, police station, newspaper columns, police court, bail bondsmen, and juvenile court to spot issues. Although no major litigation developed, the chapter hoped that the very presence of the ACLU would promote fair play and civil liberties.

Meanwhile Duncan and others continued their informal education program. "I talked to the owner of Lamb's Restaurant," Duncan recalled, "and said, 'You don't need a statute to let anybody in here, do you?' He said, 'No, I don't.'" The better hotels and restaurants integrated first, Duncan recalled.

In 1961 he introduced the "toothless" civil rights bill again only to find that this time the bill faced even more vicious opposition. "Whereas no one had spoken against the bill itself in 1959, except to suggest that it was not needed, in 1961 critics at the House public hearing spoke openly of the Negro as 'a thorn in the side of America': and civil rights legislation was labeled 'Communist inspired.' The bill received only thirty yes votes and died in the House," Duncan's 1961 report read. By then, juggling the ACLU presidency, legislative work, civil rights efforts, and a law practice was too much for Duncan. In 1960 he passed the ACLU torch to Steve Smoot, who became the second affiliate president.

Like Kimball and Duncan, Stephen Smoot had deep roots that extended into pioneer soil. As a political science major at the University of Utah, he had paid dues and received the national ACLU newsletter unaware that an affiliate had sprouted in Utah. He was concerned about Utah's "own little microcosm of McCarthyism" and, like his predecessors, tried to influence the state powers without launching a frontal assault. He too was an active Mormon.

Smoot's great-uncle Reed Smoot was once a powerful U.S. senator who established Republicanism in Utah with the backing of then LDS church president Joseph F. Smith. Another conservative LDS leader, J. Reuben Clark, later solidified "the aura of the church into conservative politics," Steve Smoot observed. His direct line of Smoots came from an equally political but Democratic background, and young Steve thought that liberal issues raised Christian sensitivities that the LDS church, which "brought up the rear" in terms of social policy, could benefit from.

Smoot was offended by a local McCarthy-like effort to label liberals as communists. The smear came from the vocal former Salt Lake City police chief W. Cleon Skousen who had worked for the FBI in the 1940s and received a *de juris* law degree in the East. Smoot observed that connections between prominent FBI officials and prominent Mormons in Washington were tight. Ed Brossard, who chaired the U.S. Trade Commission and was a friend of J. Edgar Hoover, was Skousen's LDS stake president. Brossard's wife, Laura, was the sister of Samuel Cowley, involved in the arrest of gangster "Baby Face" Nelson. Former U.S. Secretary of Agriculture Ezra Taft Benson attended the same LDS stake. He had become a lobbyist for a powerful agricultural group. Benson later would become an LDS church president, and his sons would appear prominently in rightist politics such as the John Birch Society and Skousen's organization.

When Skousen first moved to Utah, he became a popular speaker at Mormon gatherings. As such, his impact was significant. Associated first with the Birch Society and later leading his own ultraconservative Freemen Institute, Skousen wielded political clout that was hard to trace but equally hard to miss in the state's electoral dynamics. Years later Smoot would watch Orrin Hatch, formerly a Pittsburgh lawyer, glean the backing of the Freemen, then astound the local populace by eliminating several popular Republican candidates in convention, win the primary election, and topple tenured Senator Frank Moss. As Steve Smoot led the ACLU in the 1960s, he and Skousen clashed when the latter discussed the communist threat in seminars, tarbrushing the ACLU in the process.

Operating virtually without a budget, ACLU members carried on their activism as best they could. Legal matters were directed to William Fowler and other volunteer attorneys. Civic-minded housewife Pat Coontz was "my Michele Parish," Smoot would recall. Harriet Brewster served both on the board and as its president, and downtown merchant Ben Roe played an active role in fund raising. The dollars returned by national headquarters from new memberships and dues went to the volunteer attorneys to cover costs.

Meeting frequently at the Jewish Community Center or the Unitarian Church, the group continued to address racial inequalities. The minutes of a 5 January 1965 board meeting were typical: "Hershel Saperstein introduced the three lawyers responsible for drafting the civil rights legislation which Governor Calvin Rampton will present to the Utah legislature." A fair employment bill, drafted by A. Wally Sandack, defined "a series of unfair labor practices by employers, labor organizations, vocational schools, and agencies forbidding exclusion on the basis of race, color, religion, national origin and sex. . . . " The bill directed grievance claims to the Industrial Commission and a "special civil rights coordinator."

Alfred Emery, who served as interim president of the University of Utah, lifted Mickey Duncan's torch in drafting another public accommodations bill. The bill would make the state attorney general responsible to "investigate and conciliate" cases of discrimination. There was "no criminal liability but an individual may bring a private action in the courts."

William Lockhart introduced a public housing bill which prohibited owners from refusing to sell, rent, lease, or advertise property on the basis of race, color, religion, or national origin. Discrimination complaints would go to the attorney general. While the first two bills proved successful, Governor Rampton was shocked to see the last defeated by a real estate lobby.

The ACLU board considered internal matters at their January 1965 meeting, beginning with some good news. One hundred people had attended a recent meeting, and they had forwarded more than $1,000 to the national headquarters. The board passed a motion to contribute 10 percent of its annual income to the Southern Regional Office for civil rights defense. The board also decided to launch a letter-writing campaign to legislators.

Correspondence between Smoot and national membership director Marie M. Runyan depicted the status of the Utah affiliate. In September 1961 Smoot reported one new member who contributed $100. This member, Smoot wrote, "helps the cause considerably. He joined one of our promotional mailings." At the year's end, the seven-month intake had reached $484, with three renewals in October gleaning $20 each. There was a $500 annual operating budget.

In February 1965 the board was told: "Our financial status makes us the smallest affiliate in the ACLU. In 1964 we attained $1,183 of a project goal of $2,000." The next year's goal was lowered to $1,700, to be shared by national and local coffers. Still, the 10 percent tithe to the Southern Regional Office would continue.

Despite a skinny pocketbook, the ACLU was instrumental in forming a Salt Lake Legal Defender Association, based on a three-year grant from the National Legal Aid and Defenders Association. The affiliate promised to raise one-third of the costs and to recruit volunteers. The affiliate helped make court proceedings more accessible to working people. In April 1965 Hugh W. Gillilan, who followed Smoot as board president, urged the Salt Lake City courts to hold sessions at night and on weekends.

The early, under-funded efforts were sincere but not overwhelmingly effective. Still members took heart in the organization's sweeping successes nationwide. Toward the late 1960s the increasingly controversial Vietnam crisis became a compelling issue. Stanford University law professor Daniel J. Dykstra chose the "Right to Dissent" as his topic when he addressed the 1966 annual affiliate meeting.

The war compelled the Utah ACLU to join a national effort in 1967 to sue the U.S. Selective Service. Draft boards were punishing war protesters by reclassifying students who participated in the protests. In fact, the University of Utah *Chronicle* reported ACLU support for Henry Lowell Huey, a junior whose draft status was altered following a memorandum issued by General Lewis B. Hershey who told draft board officials: "There can be no question that an individual who is engaged in violating the very law that deferred him can not very well be acting in the national interest."

Huey had participated in a sit-in outside the local Armed Forces Induction Center doorway six days before he was reclassified. The *Chronicle* explained: "The cooperation of ACLU affiliates in filing suits across the nation on the same day was done for dramatic effect," quoting law professor and ACLU board member John L. Flynn.

"We thought it was necessary," Flynn told the newspaper, "because the impact of this kind of action by the Selective Service is rather drastic." Flynn said the reclassification violated freedom of speech despite the appeals allowed within the Selective Service Act. "It's had an ... effect on our campus, and college campuses all over the country, to silence any kind of dissent. ... "

Utah participation represented a small part of a massive litigation effort. By 1971 the New York ACLU juggled more than 200 such cases, nearly all of which were won. Lawyers in other areas of the country triumphed frequently. Author Samuel Walker explained "the key to their success [was] the archaic and lawless selective service system. ACLU lawyers convinced prosecutors and judges that the selective service system officials had violated their own procedures." The ACLU victory, Walker claimed, constituted a "legal revolution," one that "introduced principles of constitutional law into a bureaucratic apparatus previously untouched by law."

Such a triumph against the national government was heady, and by the early 1970s the Utah affiliate was ready to hire a part-time executive director. Steven Cook, with a brand new law degree in hand, assumed that role for $250 per month, with Curtis Oberhansley acting as legal director. Cook had served on the board of directors while attending law school. He was drawn to this activism by his "firm belief that civil and constitutional rights in Utah were seriously abused."

The ACLU remained closely tied to the University of Utah; Cook would schedule meetings in the law school's conference room. He offered on-campus support to the war resistance movement, which resulted in several "love-it-or-leave-it confrontations." After several individuals were arrested during one sit-in, Cook and another attorney, Dennis Olsen, went to the Salt Lake County Jail to visit their clients, and the jailers refused to let them in.

"I remember pounding my fist on the table and threatening to have a federal judge down there in a matter of minutes—our office was right across the street, and we could have issued a subpoena," Cook recalled. "After a number of phone calls, they decided maybe it would be okay for us to see our clients. That incident happened because the jail personnel and the police supported the war, and the protesters were considered the scum of the earth." A future ACLU board president, John Morris, remembered a court hearing where university administrators were called to testify and spoke against the right of students and faculty to protest.

In 1971 an anti-communist meeting in Salt Lake City included epithets hurled at the ACLU. Pat Coontz, then executive secretary of the Utah affiliate, protested to Senator Moss, who replied: "I regret to hear that libelous attacks are being made upon the American Civil

Liberties Union. Unfortunately, in times of hysteria people can be stampeded to demand suppression of criticism and stifling of free speech." Moss endorsed the principles of the ACLU but stopped short of offering a solution.

The ACLU continued to extend low-key influence, objecting to the termination of a teacher over her pregnancy, the jail sentence of an individual who was found with a roach clip but no marijuana, and the imprisonment of a convict who was mentally ill. In addition, meet-the-candidates evenings and other educational services flourished.

Questions surrounding decency, pornography, and censorship arose. Let public standards be manifest through public attendance and purchases, the ACLU argued. But Supreme Court Justice William Brennan had set the legal obscenity standard in the *Roth* decision, writing, "Obscenity is not within the area of constitutionally protected speech or press." He offered this test: "whether to the average person, applying contemporary community standards, the dominant theme of the material taken as a whole appeals to prurient interest."

In 1972 the Salt Lake County Commission passed what the LDS-owned *Deseret News* referred to as a "smut law." George S. Grossman, by then ACLU board president, denounced the law to the commission and the media, claiming, according to the August 19, 1972, *Salt Lake Tribune*, that the law "could ban such movies as *The Godfather, Midnight Cowboy, MASH,* and *The Last Picture Show.*" The *Deseret News* reported consideration also of "an anti-hardcore pornography ordinance which would give the city better control over magazines and books displayed in local stores and grocery stores." In this instance Maurine Brimhall, head of the Citizens for Decency Committee, and psychologist Victor Klein spoke in favor of the ordinance. Stewart Hanson, Jr., an attorney for the magazine distributor Bonneville News, opposed it. Grossman spoke against controlling books and magazines, citing censorship as a "very dangerous weapon," according to the *Deseret News*. "He said it has become one of the weapons against our greatest literature."

Grossman passed the ACLU board presidency and free speech baton to University of Utah English professor Michael Rudick. Criticizing the *Deseret News's* coverage for editorial bias regarding "moral pollution," Rudick privately chided *Tribune* publisher John Gallivan, as well, for refusing a Gay Community Center advertisement. Rudick reminded Gallivan of the responsibility the press bore to avoid censorship and represent all sectors of the community, but to no avail. It would be some time before Salt Lake City newspapers would accept ads from homosexual groups.

The social issues of the early 1970s established a bedrock belief in civil liberties among young people. This restless generation came to consider the ACLU an ally. By 1972 over 50 percent of the national ACLU membership was under forty years of age, with 30 percent in their mid-twenties to mid-thirties. Roughly half had joined within the previous three years. Profession-wise, educators accounted for around 30 percent; business people 15 percent; and government workers, attorneys, and physicians nearly 10 percent. Eight of every ten members were college graduates, and over half of those had graduate degrees. Most were urban—63 percent—and a majority were male—60 percent.

"The preponderance of youth may augur well for future recruiting and financial support," the affiliate newsletter noted, including a cautionary line about a "disturbing" appeal "among those not members of a well-educated, professional, and financially well-off segment of the population."

At the end of 1972 the issue of prison rights came to the fore of Utah ACLU concerns. It decided to investigate the Salt Lake County Jail following complaints and rumors. The county had investigated and found no proof of abuse by jailers, but the affiliate launched its own probe and invited any who felt they had been abused to come forward.

In September 1973 the Utah group also filed a class action lawsuit in federal court challenging "unconstitutional practices in the treatment of inmates at the Utah State Prison." Named as defendants were Warden Samuel Smith, Director of Corrections Ernest Wright, and other members of the board. The complaint alleged that the plaintiffs had been denied their rights to due process in disciplinary proceedings, to adequate medical care, to uncensored and unsuppressed mail, and to freedom from cruel and unusual punishment.

The issue would endure, but this particular lawsuit waned. Steven Cook filed a number of lawsuits against the jail or the prison, but, without funds for litigation, was forced to resolve conflicts amicably. The courts would not award attorney fees even if the ACLU won, Cook said, and so replenishing the affiliate's coffers was difficult. More than once Cook and other attorneys paid the filing fees out-of-pocket and counted the money as a donation to the ACLU. "It was an exciting time, though" Cook said, "involving a lot of hard work and a lot of dedicated people. It was personally very rewarding. Even though our victories were few, they were very sweet."

"Why is it necessary to impeach President Nixon. And how can it be done?" This headline on a full-page ad in the 14 October 1973 *New York Times* made the ACLU the first national organization to call for Nixon's impeachment. Walker wrote: "The Watergate crisis was the most serious constitutional crisis in American history, turning on the fundamental question of whether the president of the United States was accountable to the rule of law."

In Utah an ACLU-sponsored rally for impeachment indirectly attracted the affiliate's next part-time executive director. In December, James H. Joy, a doctoral candidate in political science at the University of Utah, accepted the position of part-time executive director for the same salary Cook had garnered, $250 per month. He was recruited after his next door neighbor attended the rally and heard about the search for a director. "He woke me up and said, 'Jim, I can't imagine a better job for you,'" Joy recalled.

This time training for the position included a flight to headquarters in New York, "where I wandered around the ACLU office for two days talking to anyone who had time to talk to me," Joy said. Thereafter, he depended on the large brown envelopes National sent containing directives, newsletters, and circulars, which arrived at his downtown office on Monday mornings. The office contained a small desk and a contrary printing machine. "Every time I'd print anything, everything would be covered with ink, and I was covered with ink."

Despite these humble beginnings, about ten days into his directorship Joy addressed the Salt Lake County Commission to oppose a pornography ordinance that would ban X-rated theaters. The *Salt Lake Tribune* reported that Joy "agreed that minors and those who don't know they are going to a dirty movie should be protected," but he also felt that "laws must be written so the average merchant can understand them. What's patently offensive to these ladies wouldn't be to me," he said. He added that the "community standards" rule was "so vague it won't be enforced at all." Roselee Norwood, representing the Catholic Women's League, said, "You're almost saying 'don't do a damn thing—let nature take its course,'" to which Joy agreed.

Two days later a *Tribune* editorial paired Joy with television western star Roy Rogers. Titled "Different Outlooks, Same Approach," the editorial observed that Rogers was "so strait-laced that he has often been accused of shaking hands with the girl and kissing his horse. . . . " Yet Rogers had recently offered the same argument as Joy, that economic sanctions should be allowed to control movie content. The paper commended both for supporting a "reasonable and proper" way to "get 'dirty' movies off the screen" through "economic pressure rather than resorting to liberty limiting laws of dubious constitutionality and doubtful enforceability."

Joy continued the impeach Nixon drive, lobbying Utah's new Democratic U.S. congressional representative Wayne Owens, who sat on the House Judiciary Committee. When Joy organized a public forum on the topic, he recruited Owens to speak. But, said Joy: "We could have a press conference and nobody would come. The *Deseret News* would never cover us. The *Tribune* would if we pushed them hard enough." He talked local radio stations into running sound bites from his speeches.

After Nixon's resignation and pardon, Joy issued a press release criticizing President Gerald Ford's decision to allow war resisters to be prosecuted. Joy claimed, "Involuntary servitude is punishment, whether called compensatory service or slavery, and is a denial of equal protection of the law." The case-by-case review Ford proposed would "lend itself to terrible abuse," probably "on grounds of race, class, and religious affiliation," and would "preclude consideration for the poor, uneducated, and bilingual population who had the courage to resist the war" but no means to articulate their position in court. Joy's concluding sally: "It is sad that President Ford could not have given the same consideration to these young men as he did to the man who made him president."

Throughout the 1970s the national organization promoted women's rights as a top priority. It had long supported full emancipation by applying the 14th Amendment to women. Future U.S. Supreme Court Justice Ruth Bader Ginsburg, then a law professor, became one of three lawyers to write a historic ACLU brief, *Reed v. Reed*, in which she challenged the automatic preference of men over women as administrators of estates, which she said violated the equal protection clause. The triumph of this case in the Supreme Court proved to be a major breakthrough for the women's movement.

As the ACLU mounted its campaign, it checked its own procedures for gender bias. Susy Post, of the women's rights national steering committee, asked for a report on the Utah affiliate's efforts "to increase the participation of women in the work of the ACLU." On August 18, 1973, Michael Rudick responded: "If we have no codified affirmative action proposal, it is because we have never been accused of discrimination against women in affiliate affairs in the past." He listed women in responsible positions, including two recent board presidents and five women serving on the board.

Rudick mentioned the local committee which was affiliated with a coalition of women's groups. He listed discrimination cases the ACLU sponsored, including "a hearing before the state anti-discrimination committee (won) and a suit to insure adequate budget for women's intercollegiate athletics at the University of Utah (in process of settlement)."

The Utah affiliate joined National in promoting ratification of the Equal Rights Amendment. The requirement that three-fourths of the state legislatures approve the amendment seemed attainable. However, in 1973 a Utah group backed by the John Birch Society launched a surprise attack and effected defeat in the Utah Legislature. Supporters rallied to try again with the 1975 legislature. Success seemed likely. Just three months before the legislative vote, a poll showed that a majority of Utahns supported the amendment, a figure that was reflected in the legislative make-up.

However, ten days before the House vote, the *Deseret News* editorialized against ERA passage and objections on the part of the LDS hierarchy were read from Sunday pulpits. The next poll revealed that a majority of Utahns now opposed the ERA—which predictably failed in the legislature.

A political scientist, Joy was impressed to the point of shock. Those working for ratification had expected that if the LDS church opposed the ERA, it would cost votes, but they had not imagined "a poll reverse by twenty points within ninety days." "Well," said Joy, "I knew I was witnessing power."

As the decade waned and the ERA approached a photo finish, the LDS church's Special Affairs Committee mounted a massive lobbying effort in crucial states, linking with other conservatives such as the Birch Society and Phyllis Schlafly's STOP ERA. In Virginia, Arizona, North and South Carolina, Illinois, Missouri, and Florida, Mormons were recruited in worship services, anti-ERA petitions were distributed in church foyers, bishops raised funds and sometimes laundered them, missionaries canvassed key areas with brochures, and Relief Society women were bussed to rallies. The power Joy witnessed in Utah became manifest in other states, though it was not unleashed as effortlessly.

Simultaneously the case of *Turner v. the Department of Employment Security* was making judicial history as it first ruffled feathers in Utah and then climbed to the U.S. Supreme Court. This resulted from a tip from Joy to Kathleen Peratis, director of the national ACLU's Women's Rights Project.

Mary Ann Turner had contested a Utah policy that lost her her job and denied her unemployment benefits due to her pregnancy. The local ACLU filed a brief. The Utah Supreme Court told Turner that she should contest her female nature rather than the law—i.e., "the great creator organized the differences between men and women." Joy alerted national headquarters.

On November 8, 1974, ACLU attorney Ruth Bader Ginsburg wrote to Joy from Columbia University's School of Law listing several precedents the Utah Supreme Court had contradicted, adding, "I would strongly recommend a supplemental brief if time has not run out. One of my students is preparing a memo which should be ready in about ten days. I will be glad to mail a copy...."

Several months later Joy wrote again regarding "an amended brief" that incorporated "suggestions from Kathleen Peratis and Ruth Bader Ginsburg." He continued: "As you will see, the Utah Supreme Court is not exactly a bastion of legal scholarship or objective justice. Nonetheless, *Turner* is now the law of the land in Utah." He then popped the question: "Do you think that this case is worth appealing to the U.S. Supreme Court?" Joy had not discussed this possibility with Constance Lundberg, Turner's attorney who had moved her practice to Washington, D.C. He closed with, "Please let me know where we should go from here."

The answer came in a March 4 letter to Joy from Peratis, who began: "In spite of the fact that the best argument, the due process argument, was not raised . . . and the time to petition for a rehearing has passed, we have decided to petition for *certiorari* in the Supreme Court." In the following paragraphs Peratis made it clear that National would take the case and would not welcome the original attorney's assistance. "Because you don't have staff counsel," she continued, "I presume there is no Utah [ACLU] lawyer's name we should put on the papers. . . . I drafted the petition this morning, and we'll probably be ready to file in a week or two. I'll keep you advised."

In November 1975, a year after Ginsburg's letter, the U.S. Supreme Court overturned Utah, ruling that states may not refuse unemployment benefits to women required to leave their jobs to have a baby. The *New York Times* called this "a substantial victory for the women's movement," affecting laws in twenty states.

Two days later the *Tribune* carried a response from Utah Supreme Court Justice A. H. Ellet who insisted that the high court erred and was "entering into affairs that are not its business." Utah Attorney General Vernon Romney called the ruling "offensive," saying that the federal judiciary should not "presume to decide something that is much better left to our own court." Despite the naysayers, nothing could dampen the celebration for this milestone, spirited by the ACLU from defeat in Utah to success in Washington and altering employment laws for all American women.

During his tenure, Joy encouraged the growth of ACLU chapters beyond the Wasatch Front in Moab, Ogden, and Logan. In addition, cocktail parties and issue-oriented dinners in Salt Lake City drew over one hundred people. One event, at D. B. Cooper's private club, was oversold, and Joy and the board of directors found themselves on the outside looking in.

"The liberal human rights community hung together in those days with a minimum of infighting," Joy reminisced. "You'd see all the same people everywhere you went, a lot of collegiality. We'd all support each other's events." With help from volunteer attorneys, the affiliate nipped at the impervious Utah establishment by filing lawsuits every few weeks. For instance, they defended a University of Utah student from Greece who had been snagged during finals week in a drug sting in the dormitories. The student pled guilty to a minor charge, then found himself facing deportation. The ACLU persuaded the judge to set aside the conviction and the Immigration and Naturalization Service not to return him to Greece where he would be the target of repercussions for his political views. A compromise landed him in Canada instead. During this time, two young boys also escaped from a private reformatory in Provo Canyon and found their way to the ACLU office where Joy agreed to initiate an investigation. His successor would continue this task.

Colorado's executive director, Dorothy Davidson, was meanwhile appointed regional director to offer support to western affiliates. Davidson encouraged Joy to apply for the Colorado position she vacated. He was hired, but found that affiliate nearly as broke as the Utah office. Nevertheless, it was a full-time position with a full-time assistant, and on July 1, 1975, he began a long tenure. He left the Utah board a short list of people to consider for his position.

With the end of the Vietnam war and major civil rights battles, donations and memberships began to decline nationwide. By the mid-1970s, Davidson recalled, "There was no Bull Conner on television with dogs and whips and fire hoses. People didn't feel the same moral imperative to do something." But the nation now held elevated expectations of the ACLU, and the ACLU had acquired a heightened assumption about its own future.

In Utah the issues that had gripped the nation for decades were just beginning to gain currency. The state that had voted overwhelmingly to re-elect Nixon had seen him fall. People who had supported the war through the bitter end saw veterans return to disillusionment rather than parades. Those who had endorsed racial segregation now found it was socially unacceptable and unlawful. The ACLU, all the while, had gained a quiet but tenacious toehold in the granite of Utah's power structure.

3.
Coming of Age

"My initiation was simple and, frankly, a little brutal," wrote Utah's first full-time director, Shirley Pedler, in the program for the 1984 annual dinner. "I was given the keys to a disordered little office on Third South, vacated some weeks earlier by the previous director, Jim Joy...."

She described how she "struggled to make some kind of sense and to bring some kind of order out of the confusion of papers, unopened mail, and ringing phones," but admitted: "The executive director was scared, and more than a little in over her head." She added, "Executive director: pretty fancy title for a young woman just graduating from college. Pretty fancy title for anybody running a little store-front operation on next to nothing."

By the time ACLU members read this description, Pedler was in her tenth year of directorship and the Utah affiliate had come of age. It had acquired in Pedler an "inbred agitator," nomenclature she stumbled on while explaining to the *Salt Lake Tribune* how her local upbringing had produced anything but the "outside agitator" critics liked to picture haunting the ACLU office.

Pedler brought a number of "firsts" to her leadership but also continued many traditions. She was the first woman at the helm, the youngest executive director, and, unlike most of her predecessors, was not an attorney. Like most of those before her, she was affiliated with the University of Utah.

She had a degree in anthropology and would pursue a master's degree in philosophy while serving as director. During her last year as an undergraduate, she participated in the university's Year for Action program, working with the Coalition for Criminal Justice and sometimes with the ACLU. Thus when Joy turned his eyes toward Colorado, he recommended that Pedler apply for his job.

Despite the fact that she was full-time, her gross salary was under $600 per month. Members passed the hat at one board meeting to meet her semimonthly wage. This was Pedler's first "real job," she said, and "had the affiliate been better developed in those days, I wouldn't have been qualified."

Despite her youth, Pedler had possessed strong feelings about civil liberties since childhood. "I remember sitting on a bus and feeling outrage hearing some children talking," she told a reporter in 1978. "They were making jokes about the fact that a black family had moved into the neighborhood. Their parents said it would lower the property values."

She recalled: "I was always angry, too, in school because there were all those records on me, without my consent, that were open to lots of people. I think I was offended young."

That "level of outrage," as Pedler called it, combined with her hometown sense of how Utah worked. During her tenure of a dozen years, the Utah affiliate would achieve some significant landmarks, including important church/state cases. Less successfully, but in the glare of the national attention, they would join national headquarters and other civil libertarians in resisting the first execution in more than a decade, as the nation's death penalty caught its second wind in Utah. Young, female, articulate, and outraged, Pedler embarked on what would become an eventful ACLU career.

When board president Michael Rudick updated the *Salt Lake Tribune* in August 1975 on the status of the Utah affiliate, he mentioned that the membership had almost doubled in the past two years, now reaching 750. Rudick commented on the ACLU's recent support of draft resisters and war protestors. "There are a great many public stereotypes of the ACLU," he told the newspaper. "One example is that it's a left-wing organization; that we are entirely devoted to keeping radicals out of jail. People who say that," he continued, "forget that we had, for a number of years, also defended the rights of southern segregationist governors, such as George Wallace or Ross Barnett, to a fair trial while at the same time disagreeing with their views."

In Utah, Rudick explained, conflicts differed from the norm. "Utah's history, given the role of the LDS church in founding the state and in maintaining the state for so many decades, has eventuated a serious church/state problem, which is always a delicate problem. . . . "

Other issues surfaced, too, the article added. Currently the affiliate was involved in court cases involving unemployment benefits for pregnant women; protecting the rights of juveniles from expulsion from high school without due process or parental notification; disciplinary practices at the State Industrial School; and nondisciplinary transfers and polygraph tests without due process for certain prison inmates.

The affiliate was to become increasingly noticeable as well as busy. "When I started the job, the ACLU had a half-time director, but the organization had not been visible," Pedler said in an interview near the end of her tenure. "When they hired me I could literally feel the shock wave go through the community because the state was so accustomed to being able to do the things that we litigate against."

Like many in her generation, Pedler had been influenced by the social movements of the 1960s and early 1970s. As director, she adopted a confrontive style modeled after the ACLU staffers she met nationwide, who were the most aggressive people she knew. "I was doing what I thought I was supposed to do," she said later. "I felt that was our role."

In retrospect, she wonders whether a conciliatory approach would have been more useful at times. This hindsight followed her tenure with the ACLU affiliate in Louisiana where "the pretention to niceness is more pronounced than in Utah and the meanness underneath is worse."

Pedler's administration began typically enough. She moved the office from Third South to Main Street's venerable Judge Building. She held an organizing meeting in Moab in southeastern Utah. "They have many immediately apparent problems there," she wrote in a newsletter. "The local sheriff collects returned checks for the local merchants. The county jail prisoners are kept without sufficient food." She added, "They routinely harass 'hippies' with sanitation and vagrancy laws that are almost surely unconstitutional. The school expels students without a proper hearing" and had fired one teacher who was too outspoken.

Another chapter was being considered in Dugway, as well, on the western side of the state. While the Logan and Ogden chapters maintained a steady presence, most tended to flare and then dissipate when individuals ran short of time and energy or when a particular issue lost momentum.

In the capital city censorship issues continued to erupt. The city toughened its stance, and in the latter half of 1975 a theater operator was arrested, tried, and convicted on obscenity charges for showing the film *Deep Throat.*

City court judge Paul Grant handed Lee Harper, proprietor of the Palace Theatre on State Street and Broadway, a maximum sentence of six months in jail, a fine of $299, and an additional $249 in court costs. He suspended five and one-half months of the jail sentence on six months' probation, requiring public restitution to charity in the amount of $5,000, and released Harper on $1,000 bond. Harper vowed to appeal, adding, "It's a shame the city prosecutor's office is being run by [Citizens for Decency Committee leader] Maurine Brimhall...."

Decades later a news clipping surfaced in the ACLU files, flagged by a typed note at the top that read: "Shirley—the ACLU should get involved on the [Harper] appeal and file an *amicus* brief saying the ordinance is unclear. brian." The lower case "Brian" was Brian Barnard, who became a cooperating attorney for the affiliate. Pedler announced that the ACLU would support Harper's appeal. The *Tribune* quoted Pedler, "The ordinances on obscenity are so unclear that no one knows what is against the law. An obscenity ordinance must make perfectly clear what is obscene...."

Barnard's brief contended that the vagueness itself stifled free speech and due process. The judge failed even to define "obscenity performance" and "obscenities in accordance with United States Supreme Court decisions." Barnard argued that since the same movie was taken to trial in Magna, in southwest Salt Lake County, and found not to be obscene, it did not violate community standards. What was essentially a second trial in Salt Lake City, he said, constituted double jeopardy. (Despite Barnard's defense of the film, he quietly declined an opportunity to view it with prosecutors.)

Meanwhile, the *Deseret News* hailed the judicial decision with an editorial headlined, "Bravo, Judge Grant." It praised: "A penalty that stiff ought to cause other movie house owners to think twice before trying to turn a fast buck by pandering to mankind's baser instincts." The editorial continued: "Moreover, while smut's damage can never be entirely undone, a fine that must be donated to charity can help repay some of the harm."

Late in 1975 assistant city prosecutor Ted Cannon was given free rein to increase legal action against theaters and bookstores. Cannon's campaign would help get him elected to the office of Salt Lake County Attorney. But despite the effort to suppress erotica, the ACLU's effort saw results. Roy City paid more than $8,000 to the ACLU after losing its attempt to censor cable television, and North Ogden was forced to pay $1,400 in a similar case.

Barnard and the ACLU teamed up on another case. By October the Utah ACLU was threatening court action regarding an excessive force suit brought against two police officers. The suit was brought by New Yorker Lynnell Parmer who was arrested in April 1974. The officers were found guilty in U.S. district court of using unlawful force and were fined $4,000 each in general damages and $2,000 in punitive damages. Salt Lake City backed the officers by saying it would pay the punitive damages, and city insurance would cover the liability damages.

The *Deseret News* reported the ACLU's criticism of the city's plan on October 2, 1975. "Cities can spend money only for public purposes under the Utah Constitution," a spokesman said. "The payment of punitive damages for individuals is not a public purpose . . . . "

The article continued: "The ACLU announcement came more than a week after Brian M. Barnard charged that the city's paying punitive damages for the policemen would place them and other officers above the law. . . . " Quoting the ACLU: "The City Commission should support the police to the fullest extent, but when officers are in the wrong, and have exceeded their authority, those officers should be held responsible."

While such cases were relatively small, they were harbingers. Barnard's impact on the ACLU would be significant but immeasurable, since he most often gave behind-the-scenes advice and filed separate but complementary lawsuits. After twenty years of association, he joked, "I don't know whether I should claim the brickbats aimed at the ACLU but meant for me, or charge them a fee for building their practice."

Barnard had moved to Utah from southern California in 1971 and began working at what became Utah Legal Services, a non-profit organization representing those who could not afford private attorneys. His tolerance for boards and committees was as low as his enthusiasm for bucking the system was high. During law school he worked evenings in a university program to orient high-risk high school students. When students voted him the most helpful counselor, as Barnard told it, one-third of the daytime staff responded with, "Who is he?"

Barnard's legal emphasis became financially feasible in 1976 with the passage of the Civil Rights Act, which made attorney fees collectible. From then on he found he could afford to do what he did best—impress the importance of individual rights on government.

"One of the fun things about civil rights litigation is teaching the other side," he would say years later. "My fee is their tuition payment." The opposition, whether city, county, or state government, seldom viewed its education so rosily. But Barnard and the Utah affiliate would remain natural allies.

Roughly between 100 and 200 complaints per month entered the affiliate office during Pedler's term. Her first high profile case would be called the "Terrace Ballroom incident." Salt Lake County's Hispanic population enjoyed gathering for parties and celebrations, sometimes in homes or businesses, but often in rented halls. In June 1976 a large group held a party in the city's downtown Terrace Ballroom. As the evening progressed, and revelers became high-spirited, the party was broken up by Salt Lake City police who charged in with police dogs. Several people were bitten, others arrested. Within hours the telephone of ACLU cooperating attorney Judith Wolbach rang with complaints of racial prejudice and excessive force.

As riots, racial issues, and police actions had filled television screens during the last decade, some downtown businesses had removed streetside windows to riot-proof their property. The police were on the watch for disruptions. The Terrace Ballroom party seemed such an outbreak on a small but alarming scale.

In June Michael Rudick began a letter to affiliate members: "By now you're surely aware of the ACLU's engagement in the legal aftermath of the Terrace Ballroom incident in Salt Lake City earlier this month," he wrote. "The more we learn, the more convinced we are of the substantial civil liberties implications."

Rudick continued: "Ordinarily, the ACLU of Utah does not undertake police abuse litigation . . . [but we] argue for an accessible civilian review board to deal with such cases." However, he wrote, the "Terrace affair is an exception. The ACLU has been widely criticized for what is considered its haste in announcing its position and undertaking legal defense of the victims." But this was based on "extensive interviews with witnesses and with persons who were arrested and who were injured by beatings and dog bites." The letter requested financial support for the five volunteer attorneys preparing legal action against the police department and the city.

The Terrace incident dominated discussion at the 1976 annual dinner, which featured assistant Salt Lake County attorney Gerald Kinghorn. He called for an independent investigative agency to handle citizen complaints against government and police officers. He said, "Unless such an agency is created, brutality and official misconduct will likely be repeated."

The flare of publicity around the Terrace incident ended in a legal fizzle. Several of the volunteer attorneys were transferred to other work situations, leaving Judith Wolbach overwhelmed. With the affiliate unable to financially muscle the effort, cases were quietly resolved by private attorneys. In retrospect, however, Wolbach believed that the ACLU's stance and resulting publicity influenced the police's future reluctance to use dogs in crowd control and heightened sensitivity to ethnic issues.

Although the Utah ACLU was gaining a higher profile, the need for follow-through volunteers illustrated a larger problem. Pedler's annual budget requests to National totaled around $6,000. For the first several years she had no support staff. Later CETA (Comprehensive Employment and Training Act) workers assisted in the office, and finally an administrative assistant, Steve Francis, was hired on a part-time basis.

"We were seriously broke a lot of the time," Pedler said. "I was not a skilled or trained fund raiser and National was not dealing effectively with that concept either. The board didn't recognize a responsibility for fund raising. It didn't enter our heads."

In the latter half of the 1970s National encountered a financial crisis after it protected the rights of Nazis to march in Skokie, Illinois, the home of many Holocaust survivors and other Jewish citizens. The backlash from within and without the ACLU shook the organization.

According to Samuel Walker: "Skokie was a struggle in keeping with the highest traditions of the ACLU. As its president, Norman Dorsen, had explained, the 'ACLU had preserved its honor by keeping faith with our principles.'" Walker continued, "In the face of ferocious public hostility, it had defended the First Amendment rights of the unpopular. The victory for the First Amendment had extracted an enormous price...."

The loss of memberships and contributions following the Skokie controversy plunged the ACLU into a half-million-dollar debt by 1978. Ultimately, Walker concluded, "Skokie was a blessing in disguise, exposing a host of organizational problems and forcing the ACLU to overhaul its operations."

During those years of organizational stress, the Utah affiliate "limped along," in Pedler's words, running more on gritty idealism than on cash. In late August the Utah ACLU declared pornography ordinances passed in Woods Cross north of Salt Lake City (Davis County) and in Utah County's Orem to the south to be unconstitutional. Pedler and Barnard issued a press release quoting letters they had sent to the respective city councils regarding "unconstitutional and otherwise illegal and unenforceable" ordinances. They advised the cities they would "defend anyone convicted under the ordinance and . . . challenge its constitutionality in a court of law."

The Woods Cross law made illegal "the use of abusive, menacing, insulting, slanderous or profane language." The clause was so broad that "almost any expression or opinion could be a possible basis for arrest, and it gives authorities an incredible amount of discretion in deciding who may say what."

Other local skirmishes continued, but these were soon upstaged by events drawing the attention of the nation. The State of Utah was poised to execute convicted murderer Gary Gilmore. By doing so, this would reinstitute the death penalty which had been ruled by the U.S. Supreme Court to be unconstitutional as then practiced. To prevent the execution, the national ACLU sent attorneys and support to Utah. The national and local media, book authors, film makers, and a storm of controversy also arrived independently.

Gilmore was a sociopathic client of virtually every social program devised, from foster homes to juvenile detention to prison. While on parole, he killed two Utah County men in separate robberies. Then he refused to appeal his death sentence, though his attorneys did for him.

The case mobilized civil libertarians and death penalty opponents nationwide. For the ACLU, Gilmore's attitude, his crimes, and his guilt were all beside the point. The organization considered the death penalty a barbarous example of cruel and unusual punishment prohibited by the Bill of Rights.

In mid-November the battle intensified. With the execution date of December 6 quickly approaching, the Utah Supreme Court, in a four-to-one decision, voided the stay of execution. New appeals enjoined one jurisdiction after another to halt the firing squad.

Shirley Pedler watched as the Utah State Board of Pardons reviewed the case, then voted two to one not to commute Gilmore's sentence. She called the board's decision "very unfortunate" and criticized the hearing as contradictory and subjective. She praised the dissenting vote cast by Harriet Marcus. ACLU attorney Jinks Dabney was quoted by the *Tribune* on December 3 that, when the United States Supreme Court received the case on appeal, "they're going to look at it and say, 'My God, this is a circus.'"

With less than seventy-two hours to go, the U.S. Supreme Court did, in fact, order the action delayed until appeals could be heard. Gilmore was "not very happy." He and his attorney released the following statement to the *Tribune:* "I wish my mother, the niggers [the NAACP, involved due to the number of African Americans sentenced to death] and sons of bitches would butt out of my life. It's none of their business. They are a bunch of cowards." He continued: "If I have a right to a speedy trial, why don't I have a right to a speedy execution? I am being held with a sentence of death not a sentence to do time. My sentence expires December 6."

Despite Gilmore's frustration, appeals traveled to a three-judge federal court, to the Fourth District Court, and, at Gilmore's mother's request, to the U.S. Supreme Court. Chief Justice Warren Burger denied the appeals, commenting that the "case may be unique in the annals of the court" since Gilmore "not only was not asking for a stay of execution, but has asked for execution." On December 30 *The Salt Lake Tribune* published an open letter from Gilmore blasting the organizations and individuals trying to preserve his life, the "ACLU, legal defense funds, sundry assorted lawyers for cowardly condemned criminals." Gilmore particularly asked Shirley Pedler to "lay off": "I wouldn't be so presumptuous as to presume I could impose any unwanted thing on your life. Get out of my life, Shirley."

Pedler wrote to Gilmore to explain why she was involved. Similarly the national ACLU wrote an open letter to Gilmore, carried in an Associated Press report: "Sorry, but we won't let you turn us into killers—of you or anybody else." They continued: "Someone sentenced to death, like you, is to be executed 'in the name of the people,' and we believe that the killing of human beings is an act so appalling that we would not have the state do that in our name."

Michael Rudick told the *Tribune* he felt certain that an appellate review would declare the state's capital punishment law unconstitutional. But the ACLU decided not to file its own lawsuit in preference to an *amicus curiae* brief to accompany any other lawsuit.

An ACLU flyer called for a mass meeting on Saturday, January 15, in the auditorium of the State Capitol Office Building. The Very Reverend Robert Anderson, dean of St. Mark's Episcopal Cathedral, state senator Frances Farley, and Lalo Delgado, Chicano educator and poet, were listed as speakers. The flyer said, "Join us in protest against capital punishment and the scheduled execution of Gary Gilmore. If our protests are unsuccessful the coalition will hold a silent pre-dawn vigil at the state prison on the date of the execution."

Judicial gymnastics continued throughout Gilmore's last night. At 1:00 a.m. on January 17, U.S. district judge Willis Ritter halted the execution. Before dawn, however, Ritter was overruled by the U.S.

Appeals Court in Denver. Gilmore was executed by firing squad before first light.

Gilmore absorbed Utah's young ACLU executive director completely. She recalled later, "I had no real preparation for it, either for the affiliate or myself to be at the center of a major national controversy. It was absolutely consuming from the time we became involved in November until he was executed January 17," a date that remained fresh in her mind more than a decade later. "It was my life for that period of time," Pedler continued. "I was young, new, and idealistic, and I thought we were going to win, that we could prevent the execution. I was personally devastated when we didn't."

Gilmore's execution not only altered the history of civil liberties in the United States, it became a landmark for establishing media rules and state laws governing literary rights and profits. Following a moneyed battle on several fronts, eastern author Norman Mailer landed the story, writing *The Executioner's Song*. In it he profiled Pedler and the Utah affiliate:

> Five or six Salt Lake attorneys volunteered their time on a regular basis, and as many as twenty might help once a year. It was small stuff and, right now, beleaguered. In Utah, belonging to the ACLU was like being a Bolshevik.
>
> Once the ACLU got into the Gilmore case, Shirley Pedler began to receive a lot of hate mail and crank calls.... She knew it would continue until Gilmore was dead. She was living by herself, and sometimes after a long day, she would dread going home to hear the phone ringing.... "I hope you get shot with Gilmore,"... [a] caller would say. Sometimes the men were obscene. One remarked that since she was good looking and single, he was ready to do this and that to her.
>
> They usually hung up quickly. By now, these days, she was tending to flare up. Didn't hesitate to tell her callers off. Her nerves had never been well insulated, but with the loss of sleep and the loss of weight, she had nightmares about... Gilmore. A man would kick a platform out from under him. As he hung in the air, they would release gas pellets. Some of the dreams were bloody.
>
> Raised to be active in the church, she was no longer a practicing Mormon. All the same, these callers were like people she had grown

up with. She didn't feel betrayed so much as unable to believe what was going on. . . . It had been a travesty, and in the middle was Gilmore, a terribly pale and quite attractive young man, Shirley Pedler thought. His [hunger strike] had made him look ghastly, but unforgettable. He was so pale.

Afterward, she became personally self-conscious about the fact that this man's life, due to the maneuvering going on, was in very uncertain circumstances. He did not know his fate from day to day, and yet she was part of those maneuvering.

So she wrote a letter to Gilmore. She told him that she regretted the discomfort that the ACLU was causing him and the terrible uncertainty. . . . She thought that if she could speak to [him], she would say that she was not personally out of sympathy with his wish to commit suicide . . . but his execution would touch off others, for it would demystify the taking of life by the state. The real horror was people lining up to blow somebody away with a lack of passion, a methodical, calculated turning of the machinery of the State against the individual.

"I never resigned myself to Gilmore's death," Pedler would tell the *Tribune*. "When the last appeal was denied, my gut level feeling was that he would die. It had not been there before."

The lawyers, the media, and the civil liberties groups quickly vanished after the execution. For a time Pedler went through the motions of her job but felt shellshocked. Although she had been under fire figuratively, the intensity had dominated her life and the backlash was a further shock.

"Not only was everything anti-climatic," she recalled, "but I felt separated out from the rest of the universe. My experience had been so acute, so audacious, and in some ways, painful." Nevertheless, she learned that following such an experience, "you learn to regroup and carry on."

Two years later Pedler criticized Florida's governor for refusing to stay the execution of convicted murderer John Spenkelink. Gilmore's execution set a precedent, just as she had feared.

"Of all the ACLU positions," Samuel Walker wrote of the director of the capital punishment project, "Henry Schwarzschild's most closely resembled the lonely role of the ACLU leaders during the 1920s." He "faced overwhelmingly hostile public opinion and found little support in the courts. . . ."

Schwarzchild and the ACLU nationwide despaired as the number of death-row inmates increased steadily, reaching 1,900 by early 1988. After Gilmore's death broke the *de facto* moratorium in 1977, the "pace of executions steadily increased: two in 1979, five in 1983, and more than 100 in 1988." Walker added, "No other area of the ACLU's programs seemed to offer so little hope."

Regrouping and carrying on would bring the Utah affiliate a variety of issues and cases as the 1970s became the 1980s. It would protest the fingerprinting of juveniles, involuntary commitment of mental health patients, abuses in juvenile programs, and the state's exclusion of third party candidates from the ballot. In 1979 cooperating attorneys Brian Barnard and Kathryn Collard filed lawsuits against the Salt Lake County Jail based on overcrowded cells and lack of a mental health facility. The lawsuits would take years and a new county attorney to resolve, but ultimately a mental health facility would be provided and limits on the maximum number of jail inmates would be negotiated.

Soon after Gilmore's execution, Pedler had another high profile battle on her hands, although this one drew attention mainly within Utah. For years the LDS church had provided religious instruction for high school and college students in seminaries and institutes that the church located near the campuses. Not only were students excused from high school classes to attend seminary during the school day, some classes counted toward graduation.

This was not unique. Other communities combined religious and secular instruction in a variety of formats. A Champaign, Illinois, program allowed students to take religion classes taught by privately paid clergy but held in the school building, but these had been ruled unconstitutional by the U.S. Supreme Court. However, the court's attitude had been mixed. In 1952 the court refused to hear an ACLU challenge to Bible reading during class time and upheld a released-time program in New York which allowed students to attend religion classes off school property.

In May 1977 cooperating attorneys Collard and Steven Cook filed a lawsuit in U.S. district court against the Logan, Utah, School Board and district officials for granting graduation credit for seminary courses in Old and New Testament. The plaintiffs, Ronald Lanner, Harriet Lanner, and Jack Sherting, all lived in Logan. The ACLU attorneys claimed that the courses were primarily religious instruction, and therefore could not be granted graduation credit. The LDS church maintained that the courses were not particularly Mormon but simply taught students Judeo-Christian tradition.

Rabbi Abner Bergman, leader of Congregation Kol Ami in Salt Lake City, testified for the plaintiffs regarding "racial overtones" in the instructional material's portrayal of a Jewish man named Kahn who converted to Mormonism and survived the Holocaust, apparently due to his conversion. The *Salt Lake Tribune* quoted Bergman: "I don't want my children to read this. Am I to believe that if we had a Holocaust here we would be spared by converting to Mormonism?"

The defense attorney objected to use of the word "Holocaust" due to a television series by that name. Bergman replied, "The Holocaust I was referring to is not a television show, but a reality, something that occurred in history. A lot of members of my family, I wish, could view the television show, but unfortunately they are now glue." Bergman objected to LDS depictions of marriage, sabbath observance, and alcohol.

Cook remembered the release-time case as significant and challenging. Both he and Collard received death threats. "We took a lot of heat," he said. "We were challenging the very foundations the state stood on, that is the LDS church's right to educate children as part of the school system."

Ultimately release-time religious instruction was upheld provided that it was an option for all churches. However, the days when students received graduation credit for LDS seminary classes were gone. But the State Board of Education and school districts scurried to adjust graduation requirements and scheduling so that students could attend LDS seminary and still earn enough credits to graduate.

The Lanner case represented a significant victory for the ACLU, since it had challenged the state power structure and dominant church and won. Pedler told the *Tribune*, "For years we had calls questioning the LDS seminaries granting credit to students. That was the origin for the suit and an example of a problem that affects many."

Regional director Dorothy Davidson commented later on attorney Collard's involvement: "Kathy gave the ACLU in Utah a big boost. She won court-awarded fees, which she turned over to the ACLU, and she raised the profile of the ACLU as a litigator." In 1984 board president Ross Anderson praised Collard: "The financial condition of the affiliate is greatly improved, due primarily to the award of substantial fees . . . obtained by Kathryn Collard in the *Lanner* case and in the Provo Canyon Boys School case . . . ," adding, "the Utah ACLU will always be deeply indebted."

By the time Shirley Pedler reached her third year as executive director, she felt like a veteran. The *Tribune* portrayed her as "bound to her cluttered desk, unable to be out and about." In times of crisis such as before the Gilmore execution, "the office becomes her home," the *Tribune* said.

Church/state issues continued to generate tension. Pedler heard from various parts of the state that prayer in the public schools was common: prayer in classrooms, prayer before assemblies or school plays, and prayer before football games or other athletic events. Invariably non-LDS students felt excluded or insulted.

Despite the complaints, no lawsuit developed. When the callers realized "we can't wave a magic wand and make the problem go away, but had to represent them as plaintiffs and calculate damages, usually they were not willing to go forward," Pedler recalled.

Nevertheless, Pedler sent a letter to school principals and superintendents objecting to prayers as part of the school day and reminding the officials that it violated federal law. One Utah County principal, Brent Milne, ordered the practice stopped. He told reporters the school had no written policy regarding prayer but understood that if the prayers in classrooms were challenged, they would then cease.

Asked about her letter, Pedler told reporters that she was attempting to save school districts trouble and taxpayers' money. She added that school prayer was illegal and that the ACLU was prepared to sue if necessary. Eventually school prayer would become a bitter battle, but not yet.

Pedler's enthusiasm for her work was evident in her interviews. "That's why it's so nice to have this job," she told the *Tribune*. "I'm earning my living doing something of personal concern." Asked to trace her bent toward civil liberties, Pedler said: "I don't see the issues as that hard to grasp. It's a matter of treating a person unjustly on the basis of race, sex, sexual preference, age, etc. We don't want to force our philosophies on anyone. We just work to change the system."

She added: "It seems antithetical to the American way that anyone bucking popular prejudice is labeled a threat to democracy. That's why to be discredited as a radical or communist is so devastating."

The affiliate would successfully settle a lawsuit based on age discrimination, brought against the University of Utah after a fifty-one-year-old woman was refused admittance to a doctoral program. Defense of a woman's right to promotion took a different turn.

On June 27, 1983, the affiliate filed a class action lawsuit in U.S. district court against the Jordan School District, in the southwest Salt Lake Valley. The majority of the administrators in that district, as in most others, were male and usually Mormon. *Marianne Van Avery v. Jordan School District* alleged violation of Title VII of the Civil Rights Act by promoting less qualified men.

Pedler issued a press statement outlining the case. Van Avery, she said, spent five years as an elementary school teacher interested in promotion to principal. Accordingly, she completed an administrative intern program, served as an intern-administrator under several principals, and obtained an education specialist degree, an elementary administrative certificate, and received consistently high ratings. Nevertheless, the district appointed and promoted "an overwhelming predominance of males notwithstanding the large number of qualified female applicants. . . . "

Worse, after hearing that Van Avery had filed charges with the Equal Employment Opportunity Commission, one school administrator "told her that if she pursued her charges, she was finished in the Jordan School District," wrote Pedler. "Such threatening behavior constitutes unlawful retaliation."

The lawsuit requested retroactive promotion, back pay, $100,000 in compensatory damages, and $200,000 in exemplary damages. It further asked the court to enjoin the Jordan School District to correct its discrimination. However, U.S. District Judge J. Thomas Greene rejected the teacher's claims, writing, "There was no direct evidence of any discrimination because of sex." Pedler disagreed, telling the *Tribune* that the "Equal Employment Opportunity Commission found that there was not just discrimination against her, but that there was a [broader] pattern of discrimination...."

Religious issues wore several guises and filled many days in the Judge Building office. In 1983 Pedler showed *Wall Street Journal* reporter Ken Wells material from a public school in rural Utah. The topic was ancient Indian rock carvings, but Pedler pointed out that the accompanying explanations were "all tied to the Book of Mormon. This stuff is being passed on as authentic history."

Wells noted that the ACLU generally sent letters rather than filed lawsuits, since the incidents were too prevalent for the affiliate to litigate. A recent newspaper survey, he wrote, "showed that prayer was practiced in about a third of forty-five school districts polled. And school prayer in Utah means Mormon prayer...."

Pedler told the journalist that in this "crisis area," the ACLU wrestled more crucial issues. "The right to abortion and even contraception is constantly under attack; the specter of sex-discrimination is ever-present; Utah's small homosexual community is often the object of abuse...." Pedler admitted that these were not overtly church/state but said they stemmed from the same source.

"New Right crusaders of all stripes are at work here, often cloaking themselves without sanction in the Mormon banner...," Wells wrote in his article. "... the Mormon insistence on conformity, its absolutist, aggressive moral posture is the medium in which the New Right ferments."

Richard Lindsay, spokesman for the LDS Special Affairs Committee, offered Wells the positive side of the church's influence, stressing that Utah had less violent crime, less welfarism, fewer deaths caused by drunken drivers, and lower cancer and heart disease rates than most states. He did not claim full credit for this, Lindsay told the *Journal*, "but we like to think what we do has a positive influence on Utah's quality of life."

One church/state case under Pedler's direction challenged the LDS church directly and eventually reached the U.S. Supreme Court. Pedler gained the help of two attorneys, fresh from a few years' practice in New York, who would impact the organization significantly.

In the spring of 1983 David Watkiss, Jr., and Elizabeth (Terry) Dunning filed *Amos v. LDS Church*, challenging the requirement of employees of church-owned businesses to hold a temple recommend—a certificate allowing entrance into LDS temple rites. Recommends were granted only to those who tithed, attended all church meetings, abstained from alcohol, tobacco, tea, and coffee, and professed loyalty to church leaders. Complaints came from people in several businesses who had lost their jobs.

From the outset Dunning counted herself lucky to be chewing on such a meaty case so early in her career. Previously she had pursued a New York City sex discrimination case, becoming familiar with Title VII which protected race, sex, religion, and national origin. When the ACLU reported protests from workers in non-profit, church-owned industries, Dunning offered to research the matter. Already a Christian television station in the East had lost on Title VII. But they were a for-profit operation, and the Utah case involved non-profit entities. The complaints came from a truck driver for the Mormon goodwill shop, Deseret Industries; a janitor at the Deseret Gym; and six Beehive Mills employees who sewed underclothing worn by devout Mormons.

Church attorneys argued that the employees were engaged in religious activities and thus the businesses were protected by Title VII's religious exemption. The church moved to have the lawsuit dismissed, but federal judge David K. Winder refused. Dunning and Watkiss won a year's worth of discovery. They then moved for summary judgment.

Winder dismissed the claims of the former Deseret Industries truck driver, ruling that an intimate relationship existed between the activities of Deseret Industries and the religious tenets of the church. But in January 1984 Winder ordered the Corporation of the Presiding Bishop to rehire the Deseret Gym janitor with back pay and benefits. He found "nothing in the running of Deseret [Gym] that suggests that it was intended to spread or teach the religious beliefs and doctrine and practices of sacred ritual of the Mormon Church. . . . "

The Beehive Clothing Mills employees prevailed, as well. Their attorneys gleaned "some nice language," Dunning recalled, from U.S. district judge Bruce Jenkins. Dunning and Watkiss were now regarded by their friends in the East as "famous First Amendment lawyers" who had claimed a major triumph for the ACLU.

Dunning reminisced about the seemingly improbable outcome: "We were told, 'You will never get discovery against the LDS church. You'll be thrown out of court.' But," she continued, "we did get discovery, and we won in Utah. That showed that people's rights can be protected even against very powerful institutions."

Immediately, however, the LDS church, joined by the U.S. Justice Department, appealed to the Supreme Court under a procedure that bypassed the Tenth Circuit Court of Appeals. At that point, Dunning recalled, there was "a little shoving" in New York among national ACLU attorneys who wanted the case. "I'm a New Yorker, born and bred," Dunning said, "but I lived in Utah. I reminded them that they didn't have a client they were representing."

Ultimately, in March 1986, Watkiss argued the case before the Supreme Court. His performance was favorably noted in *The American Lawyer*. By that time the law firm of Watkiss and Campbell had contributed well over a quarter million dollars in billable hours put in by the volunteer attorneys.

"The thing that gives the ACLU tremendous power and value," Dunning said, "is the expression of real people's intense concern about their constitutional rights." Even as they awaited the decision of the Supreme Court, the ACLU lawyers felt that the atmosphere in Utah was changing. "In 1983 [before the Amos case], people were willing to brush off the ACLU and its lawsuits. That has forever changed," Dunning said later. "People get mad at the ACLU, but it's not written off as an insignificant voice."

Regional director Dorothy Davidson agreed. "The issues were always there." The challenge lay in strengthening the affiliate to the point of effective advocacy. She added, "Some said that the Bill of Rights didn't apply in Utah."

As the national ACLU restructured its organization, it decided to help professionalize the affiliates. Davidson visited Utah and analyzed its impact and needs. In some respects the Utah ACLU was still invisible, she found. She checked with the court reporter at a local newspaper to see if he called the ACLU for comment. No, he didn't. She asked the police chief if he knew the name of the executive director—no, he didn't.

Yet Davidson also noticed that, given a forum, Pedler's comments were picked up on the evening news. "She was articulate in outlining the principles of the ACLU." With a board member, Davidson drew up recommendations. If achieved, the affiliate would get a development grant from National that would allow significant growth.

Pedler outlined the affiliate's challenge in the 1984 awards dinner program. "This year new financial policies promulgated at the national level went into effect," she explained. "The purpose of these policies is to assist 'small' affiliates, such as ours, to self-sufficiency. The problem is, there's no escape-clause; we either achieve self-sufficiency or we go under."

The affiliate needed to raise $20,000 in membership income, event revenue, and foundation donations to qualify for the first of four annual grants beginning at $12,500 and reduced by 25 percent each year. "If we fail to raise as much as we did this year for two consecutive years," she added, "we lose not only our grant, but our share of membership income, which has been averaging around $11,000 per year."

If the affiliate succeeded, Pedler explained, it would then move into a second phase and have to raise at least $40,000 annually. "At the end of phase two we are strictly on our own," she wrote. "We will have the kind of organization the local population is willing to support."

In his banquet address, board president Ross Anderson celebrated the affiliate's victories. "We have successfully challenged state laws requiring parental notification and consent for minors seeking contraceptive services and counseling," he said. In addition, "We have recently obtained reinstatement of an employee of the University of Utah Medical Center who was fired because he expressed his intention to appear on a televised interview about problems faced by gay members of his religion." Anderson also noted, "We have successfully challenged ordinances which sought to censor the programs we can view over cable television, and we are currently challenging a similar statute enacted by the Utah Legislature."

As Anderson's comments indicated, censorship had resurfaced. Like the employment issues just litigated, the cable television dispute carried strong overtones of constitutionally-proscribed separation between church and state. Who should decide morality, and to what lengths could or should the government go to enforce which films could be viewed by its citizens?

The clash began with the 1983 Cable Television Programming Decency Act which prohibited the distribution of "indecent material" over cable television. Governor Scott M. Matheson vetoed the bill, stating it was probably unconstitutional, but the legislature overrode his veto and the cable television bill became law. Utah broadened the definition of obscenity to include any depiction or description of a sexual act, or the exposure of breasts, buttocks, or genitals "which the average person applying contemporary community standards for cable television" would find offensive.

Cooperating ACLU attorneys Patricia Metzger and Steven H. Blum filed a class action lawsuit against Attorney General David L. Wilkinson. Elsewhere in the nation similar cases had been filed, and the Utah attorneys monitored their progress. In 1984 the U.S. Supreme Court ruled on *Capital Cities Cable, Inc. v. Crisp* after accepting *amicus* briefs from the Federal Communications Commission, Morality in the Media, Inc., and Citizens for Positive Community Values. On August 10, 1984, the court heard oral arguments.

In the meantime Congress passed the Cable Community Policy Act of 1984, which became the first regulatory act governing cable television nationwide and achieved the recognition of the high court. The act maintained that regulating content was the responsibility of the Federal Communications Commission and that the states could not infringe upon that power.

After considering the actions of both Congress and the Supreme Court, U.S. district senior judge Aldon J. Anderson wrote of the Utah lawsuit: "Following Supreme Court precedent, today's ruling delineates an area in which private individuals, particularly parents, must assume an important responsibility for maintaining a decent society." Individual responsibility seemed the best way, Anderson wrote, of protecting First and Fourteenth Amendment freedoms. He ordered: "Based on the foregoing analysis, the court concludes that the Utah Cable Television Programming Decency Act is unconstitutionally overbroad and vague, and void on its face."

The issue raised hackles within the community in a way that would not be repeated until the abortion issue surfaced in the 1990s. "The cable TV bill was a loser and everyone knew it," Terry Dunning commented, yet it had evolved into a church/state issue "with the church trying to keep wickedness out. It was a frivolous issue, but the institution insisted that they be hit over the head with a Tenth Circuit Court decision."

In 1985 the *Tribune* reported another kind of controversy on the front page of the local section: "ACLU, City May Lock Horns Over Loitering Law." The article began: "A proposed Salt Lake City loitering law may be a 'we-don't-like-your-face ordinance' to discriminate against punk rockers and break dancers downtown, says the local ACLU office."

Shirley Pedler objected to the law under consideration by the Salt Lake City Council because it "doesn't define well enough what is prohibited" and could "be used arbitrarily to discriminate against unorthodox lifestyles." The article quoted an unidentified police officer who pinpointed the aggravation: "What they really need is a law that says you can't wear your hair up in a point and dyed purple. . . . "

Pedler sided with youth in another free speech controversy, this one sparked by University of Utah students who protested the university's economic ties with the apartheid South African government. The students erected several shanties on campus. When the administration ordered them dismantled, the ACLU stepped in. As in the case of war protestors, they defended the students' right to free speech. University of Utah president Chase Peterson argued that the shanties were an "attractive nuisance" and an expense for university security to protect.

In an *amicus curiae* brief the ACLU argued that "students should feel free to present and be exposed to diverse ideas on a college campus. Intellectual and academic freedom means very little if the extent, substance, and means of expression are arbitrarily limited." The brief found the university's "capricious" and "cavalier" ruling such "a sweeping and unjustified effort to stifle expression, it cannot be sanctioned under any constitutional analysis."

The students wrote to thank Pedler for her support. Once they had made their point, however, the shanties and the rest of the protest disappeared.

At age thirty-nine, with her master's degree in philosophy completed except for her thesis, Pedler decided it was time to move on, telling the *Tribune* that her "level of outrage" was waning and that "a good level of outrage is a qualification for this job." So in 1986 she moved to New Orleans to head the Louisiana affiliate. There many issues were literally black and white and sometimes violent. For instance, the board president's home had recently been bombed. Pedler would later view her tenure in Louisiana as an out-of-the-frying-pan-into-the-fire experience. "I thought I was pretty street smart coming out of Utah, but Louisiana was tougher any way you look at it." However, she did gain a staff attorney, a fund raiser, and a lobbyist in her new position.

She left Utah feeling proud of the victories the ACLU had achieved. Some were still reaching final conclusion, such as the *Amos* case that awaited word from the U.S. Supreme Court, but others had established legal precedent and made a lasting impact.

"The ACLU frequently fights its battles out of court," Pedler's "exit interview" with the *Tribune* explained. "Sometimes all it takes is a carefully worded letter." Pedler cited her discovery that, in Cache County, people who applied for public assistance had to state their religion and give a contact person in their church. "We simply wrote a letter and the practice was quietly dropped. . . . That usually takes care of it. It's not the kind of thing that gets in the paper but it's as effective as filing a lawsuit."

As Pedler prepared to leave, ACLU members pulled together to maintain the work load. Board member Jeff Montague recruited his wife, Nina Mitchell, an attorney in the state attorney general's office, to fill in as interim director.

Pedler's parting words for Utahns were sobering: "I wish everyone could have this job for two weeks. If Utahns could only hear and see what went on in this community, they'd realize there is no such thing as liberty and justice for all." Still she encountered "grudging respect" for the ACLU. She had learned that "the struggle for civil rights is a struggle for people's hearts and minds. The laws will change later."

Unknown to Pedler, the community's "grudging respect" for the ACLU was demonstrated after a notorious incident in October 1985 when a pipe bomb exploded on the sixth floor of the Judge Building, three levels above the ACLU office. A young businessman lay dead, and an unprecedented murder and forgery investigation was launched that would rock every power structure in the state. That morning, the investigators gathering nails, pipe shards, and human remains needed a temporary command post. They considered an office on the third floor—then read the sign on the door—"American Civil Liberties Union of Utah"—and decided to establish headquarters somewhere else.

4.
Welcome to Utah

Attorney Brian Barnard borrowed from Mormon parlance in quipping that Robyn Ellen Blumner "served a mission" as executive director. Not only was the period of time she spent in the Beehive State similar to LDS proselyting missions, but she carried a sense of purpose, as well. A New York City Jew, she came to the Mormon Zion intending to improve civil liberties among resistant natives. As she would confide to friends, "I never moved my bed to Utah."

Blumner's tenure as executive director of the Utah affiliate would become a significant juncture between the long and eventful period under Shirley Pedler and a dynamic era lying just ahead. Blumner refueled the organization's waning energy with her own enthusiasm, bolstered fund raising and membership efforts, impressed her contacts and audiences alike, and promoted both negotiation and litigation by the affiliate.

Flying west from Manhattan, Blumner knew she was entering a rugged outback in civil rights territory. She made an "ignoble arrival," in her words, touching down on the July day when the ACLU lost the *Amos v. LDS Church* case in a unanimous U.S. Supreme Court decision. The court ruled that employees could be required to keep a current temple recommend in church-owned, non-profit businesses. For-profit businesses—the *Deseret News* or the ZCMI department store, for instance—were not included in the exemption.

The *Salt Lake Tribune* lost no time in contacting the new executive director for a profile. Printed in mid-July, the article pronounced Blumner undaunted by the Supreme Court's "resounding defeat" of the ACLU. Blumner conceded the loss's significance. "I was hoping to be ushered in on the wings of victory and it didn't quite occur that way," she told the newspaper.

However, she explained, she did not interpret this as a sign that her new position would be irrelevant. "Where I find the battle is in the volume," she said. "The complaints come into the office by the dozen."

Blumner expressed surprise at the media's interest in her arrival. One of her first mornings in the state, she heard from inside her shower an announcement on a local news broadcast that she had arrived. Hailing from Manhattan, she hadn't expected even to be quoted in a newspaper, let alone anticipated that her advent would be newsworthy. When the reporter turned up, she decided that interest must be manifest "for all New York Jews who came to Utah."

Not every welcome was pleasant. She received a letter at the Judge Building office, reading, in effect, "Welcome to Utah, you worthless bitch." The letter proceeded to comment on her ethnicity and background, suggesting that Utah would not provide her a safe haven.

Blumner knew the ACLU would not wear the same fit in Utah as in New York. Indeed, she had applied for and accepted the directorship in the Utah affiliate much as an ambitious missionary might accept an assignment to "Cannibal Isle." Despite the hecklers, however, Utah generally would be impressed with this young attorney, and the affiliate would regard her warmly.

A press release preceding her arrival listed her accomplishments. She was assistant director of labor relations for the Staten Island Rapid Transit Operating Authority in Brooklyn, held a bachelor's degree in industrial relations from Cornell University and a law degree from New York University. What the description did not say specifically was that Robyn Blumner, then approaching twenty-five, was a prodigy.

Born in Queens and reared on Long Island by school teachers and union members, Robyn had grown up politically aware. Her mother was a registered Democrat and her father an independent who sometimes voted Republican. "My parents were always current, and you had to be extremely quick-witted to survive the evening meal."

By age eleven, Robyn was tucking leaflets under windshield wipers to promote Senator George McGovern's presidential candidacy. In high school she organized the Young Democrats of Glen Cove and graduated a year ahead of her class. By then she had decided that labor-management relations was akin to politics. "As in politics, there were two distinct sides, a goal to be obtained, and, often times, if you were working on the union side, you'd feel you were fighting for justice and due process."

In 1961 she became an intern for congressional Representative Elizabeth Holtzman. She worked on labor management with an eye toward becoming an arbitrator since she had "always enjoyed the process of negotiation."

At that point Blumner enrolled at Cornell University, knowing that its diploma would prove a valuable credential. "I couldn't afford to pay for an Ivy League education," she recalled, but learned that the State of New York partially subsidized labor relations students. She graduated with honors in 1982.

In pursuing a law degree, she discovered that she had adopted her grandmother's abandoned quest. Although her grandmother graduated from law school, she had not been able to take the bar exam without serving a legal apprenticeship. "No one would hire a woman in those days, and so she became a mother. It came as a total shock to me, upon application to law school, to learn that my grandmother had a law degree."

While studying law, Blumner worked most of the time for the American Federation of State, County, and Municipal Employees and for the Staten Island RTA. She graduated and passed the civil law exam in 1985 and began negotiating contracts with thirteen labor organizations. Said Blumner, "This was an exciting place to be, and a very exciting place for a young woman to be." At age twenty-three, she pulled in a salary of around $50,000.

"It didn't take very long for me to become disenchanted, though," she recalled. "It was a position that I felt required me to constantly lie.... You can call it puffery, you can call it bending the truth, you can call it colorful language, but often you were lying, and I despised that aspect of the job."

FRIENDLY FIRE

Ironically, considering her success, Blumner found her attention increasingly distracted by her volunteer work for the ACLU's Reproductive Freedom Project, where she found the energy "overwhelming, even after hours." She worked evenings with people "who were writing bits and pieces that would end up in arguments before the Supreme Court," while her days on the job were filled with "arguing over a stupid work rule on a railroad."

Soon she found the Reproductive Freedom Project "infringing on my day." Her transit colleagues didn't notice, but Blumner realized the attraction that civil liberties work held for her. She resolved to enter the paid ACLU ranks.

"When I first got the notice about the Utah position, I laughed. It was a lark, but I sent in my resume to Utah, which I could barely point to on a map. . . . I had never been there, and I only knew in the most general sense what the Mormon religion was, and the reputation that the state of Utah had."

Her attitude was typical in the Big Apple. "I think anyone from New York would consider Utah the outback, along with Mississippi, Alabama, Alaska, North Dakota, all of those. You know that when you take a job in Utah, you'll be isolated. You'll be within the 'Peace Corps' training aspect of the ACLU. You're going to be—what is the term we learned in history?—'civilizing the natives.'"

She had decided that the Utah affiliate didn't take her application seriously when she received a call from the affiliate's board president Gerald Nichols. In very positive terms he invited her to Salt Lake City for an interview.

"I was so confident before I even flew out to Utah, that I called the newspaper and advertised my apartment." For a New Yorker, this was extreme. Yet the thought of heading the Utah affiliate "was so absurd, I knew I'd end up doing it."

Quickly upon her arrival in Utah, Blumner sensed that the job interview was not exactly an audition—it felt more like a draft. Regional director Dorothy Davidson picked her up at the Salt Lake International Airport and "immediately began to prompt me for the interview." Ultimately, Blumner found herself in a room full of people—the board of directors.

Undaunted, Blumner fielded questions, realizing "that I would get the job; there was no question." Board members competed to wine and dine her.

"The day after I got back, Gerry Nichols called and offered me the job." On principle, Blumner negotiated a bit then accepted. Yet she remained incredulous. "For the longest time, I couldn't even refer to Utah without laughing, and saying, 'I'm going to fucking Utah.' I couldn't believe I'd taken that step."

In mid-May John Powell, national ACLU legal director, visited Salt Lake City to speak at the affiliate's annual banquet. He wove his remarks around the danger of thinking that change won't come, or will come slowly, if at all. Then Gerald Nichols arose to announce that Robyn E. Blumner would become the new executive director. Even if the Utah affiliate didn't fully realize it at the time, change was on its way.

Meanwhile, back on Long Island, Blumner, almost twenty-five, had been offered the assistant directorship of labor relations for the Long Island Railroad. The post would mean supervising around 30,000 employees. Her salary would rise to near $60,000. Instead she chose to attend a national ACLU conference in Philadelphia, then came west to Utah with the support of a 650-member organization. Her beginning salary was $22,000.

"You can't live on money," she would explain. "What good is a string of pearls if you don't enjoy your day?"

Almost as soon as she arrived and settled into an apartment on First Avenue, Blumner was quoted in the *Tribune* on issues ranging from release-time seminary, the lighting on the St. George temple with city revenue, to *Amos v. the LDS Church*. The fact that all of these issues involved the Mormon church was not lost on Blumner, who later commented, "Church/state issues permeated every day in Utah."

In the article she mentioned the Senate confirmation hearings of Supreme Court nominee Judge Robert H. Bork and then addressed prison conditions, especially medical care. "I have a number of complaints from prisoners who appear to be in severe pain daily, and who are denied medical attention," Blumner said.

Noting that the ACLU filed about ten to twelve lawsuits a year, the article continued, "Blumner said she would like to see more litigation, and bolstering the corps of volunteer lawyers is high on her priority list." However, the next paragraph picked up on the negotiator in her, as she added, "We attempt to solve people's problems without lawsuits. Lawsuits are expensive; phone calls are not."

The upbeat article closed: "Blumner even sees advantages to the fact that she is new to the state. 'As an outsider coming in to the community, I am going to have a very open mind and will certainly bring a new perspective to the organization.'"

Blumner's show of confidence, as she settled into the job, belied an inward trepidation. Later she would describe her adjustment as "very scary." She knew no one, really, and had no on-the-spot mentor, although office manager Steve Francis and attorney Michael Janesch helped out for a time.

As she gained her footing, Blumner advertised for an assistant. One job interview produced a minister's wife, who brought in clippings she had written for a weekly newspaper in another state. "With quiet almost modest answers, she responded to the interview questions and sheepishly showed me the clippings," Blumner recalled. As Blumner scanned the articles and noted the political activism listed on the resume, she realized that this community worker understood and could communicate complex issues. What she could not know was that Michele Parish sat before her a potential wolf in sheep's garb.

"I hired her, and she was the best thing I ever did for the ACLU of Utah," Blumner said. On July 17 the new assistant began work, and a vital mentorship began. In effect, Parish received a day-to-day apprenticeship unavailable to Utah's other directors.

Initially Parish managed the office and worked with the volunteers, gradually becoming Blumner's right hand. As she listened to Blumner vocalize her rationale of each issue and decision, Parish began to participate in the discussion. She soon substituted for her boss in several settings.

Before accepting the directorship, Blumner had negotiated a vacation in the East, and so she left in August. First she handed police officers a couple of especially virulent death threats, although she said she didn't feel physically afraid. "If you can feel invulnerable in New York City, you can feel invulnerable after receiving a few death threats in Utah."

The threats came as a reaction to her opposition to capital punishment, highlighted by the approaching execution of Dale Pierre Selby, convicted for three torture-murders in Ogden eleven years earlier.

With the help of Elizabeth Dunning, who headed the legal panel, Parish organized and addressed a candlelight vigil the night of the execution. The affiliate protested Selby's execution as a matter of principle. Since Gilmore's execution in 1977, seventy inmates had been executed nationwide. Unlike Gilmore, Selby vigorously appealed his sentence.

The following year Blumner would deal with a different twist in a death penalty issue, when Arthur Gary Bishop would be executed for the sex murders of five young boys. Since Bishop asked for execution, apparently without coercion, Blumner split with National and local precedent in deciding that the Utah affiliate would honor his wish.

Throughout the fall of 1987 Blumner turned her attention toward building membership and funding. The affiliate was committed to the development program laid out during Pedler's tenure and determined to become self-sufficient. Blumner signed a "Dear Friend" letter with board president Gerald Nichols, suggesting that donors celebrate the bicentennial anniversary of the Constitution by supporting the ACLU.

Another plea went out on October 21, this one from attorney and longtime ally Ross Anderson. He wrote that the "ACLU of Utah, under new and excellent leadership, is preparing to tackle a number of large and looming issues." He identified these as the "deplorable conditions" at the Utah State Prison, police brutality, and a bill that would eliminate the power to commute a death sentence.While accurately forecasting the affiliate's agenda, Anderson overlooked the perennially favorite topic: censorship.

Late that fall Blumner commented on a free speech issue after avowed racist Dwight McCarthy decided to replace his Counter-Marxist Hour with a racist format on KZZI-Radio. Blumner was quoted by United Press International, saying, "I would probably disagree with everything the Aryan Nation has to say, but it is a liberty for them to say it."

In September the *Salt Lake Tribune* featured Blumner on the nomination of Robert H. Bork to the U.S. Supreme Court. Blumner noted that Bork would limit free speech to political speech. "He would limit that category further by excluding from protection speech which advocates civil disobedience, which would subject to censorship the works of such writers as Thoreau, Ghandi, and Martin Luther King Jr. . . . ," she said. The article continued: "The ACLU also objects to Bork's assertion that the Constitution doesn't guarantee a right to privacy, according to Blumner, because that opens the door to governmental regulation of contraceptives, abortion and parental rights."

Utah state attorney general David L. Wilkinson answered this blast against Bork, writing in the *Tribune*'s Sunday "Common Carrier" column. Earlier Blumner had taken a swipe at a favored Wilkinson project, the ill-fated cable television bill. Now Wilkinson was eager to respond. He was identified in the *Tribune* as a former BYU graduate and Rhodes Scholar at Oxford University, with a law degree from the University of California at Berkeley. He had served as assistant attorney general and Salt Lake County's chief deputy attorney before his election.

Below the headline, "Who Is the Real Threat?" Wilkinson began: "I can think of only one better thing about Judge Robert H. Bork than the lift he has given to political cartoonists," which he said was his "extraordinarily high qualifications."

Wilkinson disputed Bork's widely alleged racial prejudice by linking him with Mormon apostle Dallin H. Oaks, well known to Utahns as a former state supreme court justice and a former president of Brigham Young University. Oaks and Bork, Wilkinson wrote, had been "fledgling lawyers with one of Chicago's largest law firms, Kirkland and Ellis," when the pair intervened to "adjust" the firm's ban on hiring Jews. Mentioning that Bork's first wife, "who died after a long bout with cancer, was Jewish," Wilkinson then left the issue of prejudice to attack the ACLU's disregard of issues sacred to Utahns.

He began with freedom of religion. "For some years now, as I presume the new director is aware, the Utah ACLU has waged a campaign to rid Utah high school graduation ceremonies of prayer." This, Wilkinson claimed, despite the "existence of state and federal cases specifically upholding the constitutionality of prayer at public graduation ceremonies." He cited a 1984 Supreme Court decision that "affirmatively mandates accommodation, not merely tolerance, of all religions." The ACLU, he continued, opposes prayer "despite the voluntary choice of an overwhelming majority of Utah's graduating seniors to include such prayer at their graduation ceremonies."

Since Bork supported school prayer, Wilkinson asked "whether it is really Judge Bork or the ACLU which poses a threat to the individual religious freedoms enjoyed by the citizens of Utah." Wilkinson also sided with Bork in opposing the "so-called 'right of privacy'" regarding reproductive rights.

Two weeks later, on October 18, the *Tribune* published Blumner's response under the headline, "Let's Meet the Real Judge Robert H. Bork." The *Tribune* listed Blumner's legal degrees and background, then noted that "the views expressed in the article reflect the positions of ACLU of Utah."

Blumner discounted Wilkinson's law firm story but deftly omitted any reference to Apostle Oaks. She wrote, "Wilkinson extols the virtues of Judge Bork by relating to us a touching anecdote which portrays Bork as a fledgling lawyer championing the rights of Jewish applicants at his anti-Semitic law firm." She continued, "This somehow proves to Wilkinson that Bork is not prejudiced. I suggest that rather than take a single isolated incident . . . , let us look to the record he himself has developed over a period of years as reflected in his writings and speeches."

Blumner listed Bork's criticism of the one-person/one-vote concept, statements favoring poll taxes and literacy tests for voters, his allowance of contracts that preclude real estate sales to African Americans, disregard for the rights of illegitimate children, disallowance of obscene language for political purposes, encouragement of government involvement in birth control decisions by married couples, and support of sterilization for habitual criminals. Regarding school prayer, Blumner said, "Indeed, the salient feature of Judge Bork's constitutional ideology is that he believes the power of judicial review should generally be exercised to facilitate the ability of the majority to impose its moral views on the minority."

Citing the founders' reasons for creating the Bill of Rights, she wrote: "Wilkinson points to the fact that a majority of Utah's high school students approve of prayer at their graduation ceremonies to support his contention that a challenge to that practice is a challenge to freedom of religion." However, she wrote, "freedom of religion is not a matter that can be decided by the majority. It is one of those freedoms reserved to each individual's conscience."

She then slugged her way through the privacy issue to this summary: "Judge Bork throughout the hearings systematically retracted, recanted and equivocated, obfuscated, abjured, and foreswore virtually every constitutional position he had previously taken in print and in public," before the Senate Judiciary Committee voted 9-5 to reject him. She concluded: "Although he attributed his previous dalliance in backward thinking to the need to write provocatively in order to remain publishable, he failed to produce a single published word on his equally provocative metamorphosis of thought whereby he came to this new-found enlightenment."

The new executive director lacked the legal and political experience accrued by the state's attorney general. But her response squarely articulated the ACLU's position. Young she was, but she clearly entered verbal battles fully armed.

Meanwhile, on the national level, the advisors to U.S. presidential hopeful George Bush "discovered that the ACLU's name evoked strong negative reactions among voters," Samuel Walker wrote in *In Defense of American Liberties*. "They thus devised an aggressive strategy of labeling his opponent [Michael] Dukakis a *liberal*, attacking his veto of a flag salute bill, accusing him of letting dangerous criminals out on weekend furloughs—and of being an ACLU member." According to Walker, the "connections were clear: the liberal Dukakis lacked patriotism, was soft on crime, and belonged to an organization that endorsed child pornography. Both Dukakis and the ACLU, Bush implied, were out of the 'mainstream.'"

At first the vice-president's charge—perhaps rousing a chuckle at its phrasing as "a card-carrying member of the ACLU"—brought "a rush of publicity and membership applications." However, the attack continued, and so shortly before the election "the ACLU responded with its own media blitz."

Executive director Ira Glasser chose his audience strategically in speaking to the National Press Club. Glasser joked "that if Bush lost the election the ACLU might appoint him director of memberships." The talk was broadcast live over National Public Radio and itself generated several thousand ACLU membership applications within the next few days.

All of this had the effect in Utah of focusing the spotlight more intently on Blumner. "Before I came to Utah, I thought I wouldn't ever do any of the media," she admitted. "I didn't want to do television, didn't want to do radio, didn't want to be in the newspaper. All that, someone else could do; I had no interest in it. I soon realized that responsibility was not possible to avoid, and ultimately I enjoyed it—it was probably one of the great parts of the job, even a compensation beyond all others."

Her schedule involved two evenings per week speaking at meetings or on radio and television. In October she opposed Bork at a press conference, countered LDS Special Affairs director Richard Lindsey on KSL Radio's "Public Pulse," and appeared twice on University of Utah television channel KUED.

As she met and spoke with Utahns, she decided "the most damaging condition to live under as a young person in Utah was to continue in your college career within the state. You had to get out and see the rest of the country." Young Utahns might return and settle, she reasoned, but with an enlightened perspective. Accordingly, when she spoke at high schools, Blumner invited any student who wanted to apply to a university outside Utah to ask her to help with their applications. Six or seven students took her up on her offer.

As predicted early in Blumner's directorship, prisoners' issues pressed their way to the forefront of ACLU concerns and public awareness. For years cooperating attorneys such as Brian Barnard and Kathryn Collard had investigated and litigated to improve conditions at the Salt Lake County Jail. Late in 1987, ACLU lawsuits against the facility encountered a surprising but logical sympathizer. Democrat David Yocom was elected county attorney, replacing Republican Ted Cannon who was beleaguered by legal and political problems.

Pledging to return professionalism to the county attorney's office, Yocom said he "tried not to be too adversarial regarding prisoner issues." A former prosecutor, he had defended inmates during his years in private practice. A new mental health facility had solved one serious problem, yet jail space was still tight and beds scarce.

Yocom began his administration a few months early due to Cannon's problems. When he toured the jail, he found people sleeping on mattresses on the floor in unsanitary conditions. "I had to step over mattresses and bodies in the women's section. It was so overcrowded, there weren't enough bathrooms." Yocom would reflect, "By anybody's standards, we were violating these people's rights."

Unlike the penitentiary, the jail held people who had not been proven guilty but were awaiting trial. Salt Lake County, with 42 percent of the state's population, dealt with 60 percent of its crime. The county tried releasing people held on misdemeanors, the new Oxbow facility was built in South Salt Lake City, and still the overcrowding persisted.

Meanwhile complaints about the Utah State Penitentiary in south Salt Lake County continued to flow into the ACLU office. Prisoners elicited little sympathy with the public, but the medical problems seemed not only urgent but unconscionably neglected.

True to her word, Blumner tried in 1987 and 1988 to negotiate with the Utah State Department of Corrections and its forceful executive director, Gary DeLand. Formerly an administrator at the Salt Lake County Jail, DeLand had tightened up security at the penitentiary. Before DeLand took over, Yocom would recall, the prison had suffered a couple of homicides a year and many assaults on guards. "Con bosses ran the institution," Yocom said, describing "bands of roving animals, every one with a shank in his boot."

Blumner maintained a cordial relationship both with DeLand and inspector general Lynn Lund. Nevertheless, "horror stories" continued to float into the affiliate. While maintaining administrative communication, the ACLU contacted attorneys and began amassing evidence for a complaint regarding the lack of medical care. When Blumner brought this material to a meeting at the attorney general's office, though, DeLand was incensed. He recalled this incident as the only time "Robyn and I really got crossways."

From the outset, and certainly in hindsight, DeLand liked Blumner. He took her to lunch, where she was "rather humorless—afraid I was trying to co-opt her, which is probably true." Still, DeLand said, he found her upbeat and practical. "She'd call up and say, 'Here's what we're hearing, now what can we do?' She was a pleasure to have in the office, and I wrote a kind article about her in the department newspaper."

The fact that DeLand could be charming was not lost on the ACLU leaders. It did not allay their concerns. "My concern with the prison was really basic," Blumner recalled. "There were medical care problems at the prison. Inmates were not receiving adequate or minimal care. That was the issue we were taking up when we were there. The negotiator in me attempted to work out an amicable solution to the problem. . . . "

DeLand said that he aided Blumner in seeing prisoner files so that she could check their tales against the facts. She admitted to him, he said, that the inmates' stories did not always check out. DeLand offered this hypothetical: "He said he saw a doctor once, but he saw him twelve times." Despite this optimistic example, DeLand recalled that Blumner told him the problems were "systemic."

Some of the incidents later included in the complaint conjured up the deprivations of a dungeon. Joseph Ward, for instance, had been injured while on a work release program and returned to prison after receiving treatment. However, in prison he was not given antibiotics, although "he complained repeatedly of pain, discomfort, and odor emanating from his injured foot." For nearly two weeks "Ward was forced to watch his foot die," the complaint claimed, until his leg was amputated above the knee due to gangrene and infection.

Another inmate, Timothy K. Duncan, was struck in the eye with a two-by-four, but his injury was overlooked for three days. He ended up blind in that eye.

According to the complaint, Theodore Kent broke his ankle falling down a flight of stairs after he refused to pay other inmates for protection. "Repeatedly, over the next two and a half months, Kent requested that he be able to see a doctor and have an x-ray taken of his ankle and be treated." Ten weeks after the injury he was admitted to the infirmary. His broken ankle had healed improperly, leaving him permanently disabled.

A heart attack felled John W. Dunning, Jr., in December 1985. The doctor said he needed immediate heart surgery, but the prison budget didn't allow for it. He suffered angina and other heart attacks for another six months.

While stories such as these haunted the affiliate office, the issue of overcrowding could not escape their attention, either. Despite the already cramped quarters, the state legislature recently established mandatory sentences for certain sex offenders, the Board of Pardons continued to detain inmates longer than the national average, and DeLand saw to it that parolees were hauled back for what the ACLU saw as minor violations.

Thus with around 1,600 inmates packed into the penitentiary, its three part-time doctors whose combined hours amounted to ten per week could not begin to serve the facility's needs. Medications that were supposed to be dispensed at 7:00 a.m. and 4:00 p.m. were frequently not distributed until evening. Sometimes inmates handed them out. Emergencies were redefined by delays, and physical exams were moved to the bottom of the list. These limitations violated federal standards.

But to the uninformed public, DeLand's hard-nosed approach was preferred over the ACLU's perceived desire to coddle prisoners. *Tribune* cartoonist Pat Bagley reflected this in his sketch of a bearded consultant inspecting the prison and asking in dismay, "What? No sensitivity seminars?"

Like the prisons, the Judge Building office was also filling up and becoming cramped. Blumner decided to move headquarters to about 400 East and 900 South streets, near Liberty Park. There, office space abounded, but the roof leaked and the building's temperature was unpredictable. So finally Blumner packed up again and moved to office 419 in the Boston Building, 9 Exchange Place, a half block south of the Judge Building and on the corner of Main Street. Resettled, office work could continue smoothly again, as a variety of new challenges filled the schedule.

While the 1988 state legislature convened, AIDS and AIDS testing were in the news. Michele Parish was assigned AIDS issues and lobbied against a bill allowing emergency medical technicians to require patients to take an AIDS test. The ACLU provided information to the state attorney general's office and requested that the governor veto the bill. Eventually issues were resolved without legislation.

Later that year Parish would speak out when Bureau of Vital Statistics director Harry Gibbons suggested that prostitutes with AIDS be quarantined, and when a Third District Court judge required that people be tested for AIDS following arrests for disorderly conduct. Parish gradually gained confidence, but she shook with fright at her first presentation.

Throughout 1988 the telephone continued to ring. The affiliate adopted the cause of two men who alleged harassment by the Drug Enforcement Agency and the Airport Narcotics Unit after they were detained for carrying a large amount of cash. A search showed no sign of illegal drugs. One, Dennis Barney, a masonry contractor from Salt Lake City, was defended by ACLU cooperating attorney Loni DeLand, a brother of the corrections chief. DeLand told the media his client had traveled to Denver to buy a motorcycle but did not make the purchase. The bearded, long-haired motorcycle club member was returning home to Utah when he was searched.

"No charges were filed and no arrest was made, yet . . . Barney was informed that in order to recover the money he would have to prove that it was clean," Blumner wrote, adding that "Barney left the airport that day with a receipt. It is utterly outrageous to think that carrying cash is indicative of unlawful conduct and subjects the carrier to forfeiture if discovered," she continued. "Consider for a moment the implications for Utah's tourist trade when the first skier from California has all his cash confiscated at the airport. The message won't take long to get out: 'Don't bring money to Utah.'"

Seven years later the Barney case would be settled after a review by the Utah Attorney General's Office. At that time, the *Tribune* reported, the federal government's war on drugs still prompted Drug Enforcement Administration agents to stop and search travelers for cash.

In another case the ACLU and the Utah Legal Clinic, with attorneys C. Dane Nolan and Brian Barnard, filed suit against the elite downtown Alta Club. The lawsuit stated that since the Alta Club served beer and acted as a state liquor store, it could not refuse to admit women as members without violating the Utah Civil Rights Act. For decades the Alta Club had welcomed its all-male membership through the front door on South Temple, while the occasional female visitor was ushered in through a side door. Megan Marie Peters visited the Alta Club in November 1985 and requested membership. Eventually the lawsuit prevailed, setting a precedent statewide.

Meanwhile issues concerning religion continued to arise. Said Blumner later, "There were constantly church/state issues that came up. There wasn't always litigation around them, but this was thematic of my career. The theocracy was such that the church and government acted in concert, and at times it was difficult to tell which was which."

"Most glaring," she recalled, were prayers offered in city council and county commission meetings. The prayers were "always Mormon," with public officials and department heads "pulling people out of offices to lead prayer." Some staffers regarded this as an orthodoxy test, which could reflect on their job security.

Although thought to be a revered tradition, attorney Brian Barnard found that this practice had evolved recently. Research showed that from 1911 to 1979 prayers were rare in city commission meetings; but in 1980, when the city switched to the council-mayor system, the prayers began. At that point the Society of Separationists, led by Chris Allen and Richard Andrews, protested and engaged Barnard as counsel. Now they were ready to take up the battle again and decided to sue.

When Barnard reported this to the ACLU board, the affiliate prepared an *amicus curiae*. "The media picked up the ACLU's involvement," Barnard mused, "and in the news it became the ACLU and the SOS without any explanation."

The city council voluntarily suspended prayers while it studied the matter. Encouraged, Blumner quietly sent city attorney Roger Cutler's memorandum to the Salt Lake County Commission, suggesting that the county suspend prayers as well. The commissioners decided to go on the evening news and denounce the ACLU.

Prayers at public meetings was business as usual in most Utahns' minds. Upon becoming aware that the "always Mormon" format offended or oppressed those outside the LDS fold, government officials offered to invite ministers of other faiths to participate. As a *Deseret News* headline announced: "Salt Lake County Backs Prayers and Diversity."

In an effort to continue the prayers, the city drew up rules: they must be nondenominational, must not mention deity, and must not proselyte. Barnard pointed out that the state constitution made it clear that government was not supposed to support religion. Now the government was not only telling people to pray, but how to pray. But the issue faded from newspapers and television broadcasts as the lawsuit pended, only to resurrect later with enough energy to prompt a constitutional crisis.

Although Blumner was aware of prayers in the schools, just as Shirley Pedler had been, no one who contacted the ACLU yet wanted to go public. However, other religious conflicts came in. In one instance Blumner received calls from a woman getting a divorce. The judge happened to be her LDS stake president and sent the couple home from the courtroom to pray, apparently forgetting, Blumner concluded, "what role he was in."

Another call came from the parent of the only non-Mormon child in a southern Utah public school. Her son was asked in class why he worshipped "the devil" (by virtue of his being non-LDS).

Utahns were aware of the LDS influence but compared it to the predominance of Catholicism in Boston, or Jewish influence in some areas of New York City, or Baptist influence in the South. Blumner did not see it that way. "Of the places I've lived where there's a majority religion, none come anywhere close to what happens in Utah," she said. "The reason is isolation. Utah is not highly populated, not diverse, and the surrounding region is relatively barren. So the pressure to conform, and the church's free hand to impose itself into government goes unchecked. [The influence] is significantly more substantial than in New York in Jewish areas, or Boston in the most Catholic areas."

As a result, Blumner said of the ACLU, "We were the lone dissent in Utah. There was no other organization, private or public, whose function it was to ensure that church and state stayed separate." An example, she reported, was the controversy over prayer. "No other organization, private or public, really stood with the ACLU."

Patriarchy pervaded in Utah beyond the LDS church. By March, news of *Reynolds v. Reynolds* appeared in the newspapers and on television. This involved a Salt Lake County father's suit for custody of his two children, one still in the uterus of his estranged wife who was seeking an abortion. The ACLU supported the woman's right to choice, and in May Reynolds became national news, discussed in a *Newsweek* article on reproductive rights and restrictions.

Michael Jon Reynolds and Jennifer Franks Reynolds had been married for less than two years. Jennifer was pregnant when divorce proceedings began, a pregnancy which was nearing the end of the first trimester. When Michael filed for divorce on March 22, 1988, a restraining order was issued to prevent Jennifer from terminating her pregnancy. The father stated "that he desired custody of the parties' living child and of the unborn child, and that he would absolve his wife of all responsibility . . . , including care and expenses. [She] argued that she had an absolute right to abortion."

Although Michael Reynolds asked the court to "balance the rights and interests of the parties as in other domestic relations matters," Judge David Young dissolved the restraining order and refused to extend it for another day while the husband obtained an interlocutory appeal.

When the hearing ended, Michael Reynolds and his attorney appealed to another judge for interlocutory appeal and a temporary restraining order. It was signed five minutes before 1:00 p.m. The order was served on a Salt Lake clinic about one half hour later. However, the abortion had already been performed.

In another instance dealing with marital and personal rights, on November 9, 1988, the *Tribune* reported that the ACLU was appealing a Vernal district judge's ruling that a divorced graduate student must keep her married name since it was the same as her child's. If the woman remarried, the judge ruled, then her name could be changed to that of her current husband.

In spring 1988 the Utah affiliate celebrated its thirtieth anniversary with an annual dinner and "Liberty Ball" featuring dancing to the band Condo Hostages. On Saturday, April 30, at the University Park Hotel, the now annual Renie Cohen Memorial Award was presented to Senator Frances Farley, a former board member who "consistently sponsored most of the progressive legislation to be introduced" in "an aggressively conservative Republican legislature," according to the program.

Dr. Howard Ball, the keynote speaker, entitled his remarks, "Crosses in Dixie/ Swastikas in Illinois: Reflections on an ACLU Crisis by a Participant." Ball, dean of the College of Social and Behavioral Sciences at the University of Utah, was described as a long-time civil rights activist and ACLU member.

The topic was appropriate, for free speech and censorship issues rose repeatedly in 1988 regarding the licensing of adult sexually-oriented businesses. Blumner warned the Salt Lake County Commission that a proposed ordinance would not pass constitutional muster. In July Blumner spoke in support of the AIDS Foundation's intent to distribute educational literature and condoms at the Neighborhood Fair in Liberty Park. Although Blumner would write an articulate open letter clarifying how such a practice was protected under the First Amendment, most Utahns were unimpressed.

A response, published in the *Deseret News* a few days before the holiday, asked: "What kind of a mind does Robyn Blumner have to say that the AIDS Foundation has a right to distribute condoms with the educational brochures at the neighborhood fair at Liberty Park on Pioneer Day?" The writer continued, "Personally, I have had enough of the many crazy decisions the ACLU tries to foist on us."

Through the year, meetings continued with the Department of Corrections and the attorney general's office over medical conditions at the penitentiary. Complaints also continued to come in. Finally both sides agreed to ask Bonnie Norman, the consultant who had inspected the facility in February 1987, to make another on-site evaluation. This time Norman, a registered nurse and part-time consultant for the National Institute of Corrections, would focus on medical facilities and procedures.

On July 20, 1988, the Department of Corrections and the ACLU drafted a joint press release announcing Norman's five-day visit, beginning August 1. "Norman is expected to identify deficiencies, if any, and make substantive recommendations," the press release stated. It noted that after her earlier inspection she had recommended a significant increase in medical personnel staffing levels. Since that time some new staff had been hired.

The press release continued: "The parties have agreed that Norman's recommendations which can be implemented within the confines of the 1988 budget will be implemented promptly." However, it added, "items which require additional appropriations will be implemented only with appropriate department and legislative action."

The public heard nothing about the inspection's outcome until reporters became aware in October that a seven-page report had been prepared. By order of the Department of Corrections, the report was kept secret. Assistant attorney general Stuart Hinckley explained in a *Deseret News* article, "As their legal counsel, I would tell them to keep it confidential because the reason this document was produced was a threatened lawsuit."

DeLand provided Blumner with a copy of the report after securing her promise that she would not share it with the media—a promise that miffed reporters. Blumner explained that she could only discuss the report in general terms, telling the *Deseret News*, "I thought it was a relatively positive report that put the department in a rather good light." She added that the half dozen calls per month the ACLU received about inadequate medical care had dropped to one call every other month. The article continued: "She attributed the change to the number of nurses and medical technicians which has been boosted by one-third." Nevertheless, Blumner told the newspaper that "the report suggested that a full-time doctor should be hired to replace the three part-time doctors currently providing medical care."

Overall, the so-called "bad press" appeared to take a toll on the morale of prison staff, reported Christopher Smart at the *Tribune*. On October 26 Smart wrote that the acting medical director and four staffers had quit. "Marked improvements in the delivery of medical care at the Utah State Prison may have hit a snag when at least five medical employees resigned, possibly from a flap over the medical audit report."

The article continued: "Televised accounts concerning the report and stark cases of abuse may have proved too much for the staffers." He added that both DeLand and Blumner had described the television reports as unfair. "Those cases, they say, are old cases which occurred before the present administration took over."

The article pinpointed a particular news report in which Deland said the tape was edited to make him appear as though he agreed with the ACLU on the way in which an inmate lost a foot to gangrene. "It makes it sound like I agree with Robyn Blumner, that I'm letting people's feet fall off out here," DeLand complained to Smart. He suggested that the medical walk-out was due to better work opportunities outside the corrections system.

From DeLand's perspective, Norman's report confirmed that the penitentiary was essentially meeting constitutional requirements. He assigned the present medical director to write a manual delineating proper treatments and procedures. DeLand said the director was unable to do so because he was too burdened with work, a reason, in Deland's opinion, "which was partly true, partly not." Over the medical director's protest, DeLand sent his deputy director to run the medical unit. As DeLand would tell it, his deputy said, "'I don't know anything about medical,' and I said it didn't matter, they needed a manager."

When DeLand shuffled administrators into a task force, he described it to Blumner as a powerful combination. She said, "Fine, if you do what you say, we'll leave you alone." He never could quite understand why things changed.

The ACLU believed the reason was obvious. Without medical treatment plans and quality control, the prison could not expect to meet constitutional standards. Blumner would recall that at first DeLand "made some mild overtures toward negotiations." Over time, despite her efforts at arbitration, Blumner doubted that prison conditions would significantly improve. In meetings she noticed how the attorney general's office attempted to move DeLand closer to the ACLU position in order to forestall a lawsuit. This reinforced her own impressions that problems persisted at Point of the Mountain.

Such issues were clearly beginning to outlast Blumner's patience. "We were like gnats, always in their face," she said of people in power. "They'd swat at us and we'd go away, and then come back. We were always an annoyance."

Prisoners' rights represented a prime example: "The prison project was not completed by the time I left. By the waning months of my tenure in Utah, it appeared that a negotiated settlement was highly unlikely." Blumner explained, "We hit a dead end in the implementation, the most important part. As far as I could see, it didn't happen."

That sluggishness seemed to represent resistance to change that Utah, itself, symbolized. "The ACLU can't really change anything," she said. "We just hold things at bay until change comes from within." Quietly, Blumner was job hunting.

"I virtually started looking for something as soon as I arrived . . . ," she said later. "I knew Utah would be a temporary stopover, that it was a training ground in effect, that I would never be able to truly make a life in the state of Utah, that I would seek my fortune elsewhere. I thought I would be there a little longer; I thought I'd be there two years. But when Florida became available, I applied." She missed the green coast and wanted to live in a more populated state.

"I'm a New York Jew from an Ivy League school, who felt 100 percent licensed to operate in Utah because I had no ties to the state," she explained. "I went there intending to go after the issues because I knew my position was temporary. In Utah we could work through the courts and the legislature, but we couldn't do anything affirmative or pro-active."

Although Blumner directed the affiliate for only one and one-half years, certain advances were made. Utah still depended on National but was now flexing the muscle of improved finances. "My board was thrilled with what had occurred. We had raised money; we had memberships; we had won respect, grudgingly; we were winning if not in court, at least on the telephone and behind the scenes a lot of times," Blumner recalled.

Nor was the board entirely surprised with her decision to leave. A new board member, Boyer Jarvis, would reflect that Blumner "had far too much ability and ambition to stay in Utah very long." He further observed: "Robyn had a remarkable ability to advocate and push the issues of the ACLU without antagonizing people."

Dorothy Davidson observed that Blumner built on the membership base that had been laid by Shirley Pedler. In addition, as Utah's population continued to shift toward the Wasatch Front, a more urban and liberal citizenship was developing. As Blumner left in early 1989, the Utah affiliate was, in fact, nearing the kind of issue-driven jet stream that the national ACLU had soared along on in the 1960s. Three high-profile lawsuits, each with tremendous energy, were about to rise from the plethora of complaints to seize the public's attention.

Blumner felt she left the affiliate prepared to cope with whatever the future held, and she had no doubts who her successor should be. "Michele was the natural choice to follow me. She had all the talents necessary to be an executive director."

The board of directors was more cautious. Parish lacked Blumner's law background and work experience. Jarvis later commented: "There were some misgivings. It was clear that Michele was no Robyn; in fact they were very different." However, Parish was appointed acting director with a chance to prove herself before a final decision was made.

Blumner left just before some issues peaked, but her farewells were said in the wake of personal accomplishment. "I left on a high," she said. "I did not wait until they asked me to leave. I did not wait until the honeymoon period was over."

On January 15, 1989, the *Tribune* reported that Blumner had "a heightened understanding of the culture, leaving 250 more card-carrying ACLU members in the state" than when she had arrived. It quoted Blumner saying that "Utah is a very special place. The thing that makes it so special is that there are more unsung heroes per capita here than probably any other state in the nation." She said she had been surprised by the complexity of the society, yet still found an overwhelming leveling influence. "I have never before lived in a place where one's religion so affected one's social choices," she said. "One's religion here seems to dictate the choice of friends, associates, activities and even business contacts. I find that disquieting," she concluded.

Blumner was praised by Skyline High School administrators who had taken advantage of her youth and articulateness. "She has been a great role model for the girls in the sense of motivating them to set goals early, to aim high and work hard to realize those lofty aims," the *Tribune* quoted Vice Principal Betty Yanowitz.

Blumner was praised by assistant attorney general Paul Tinker, chief deputy to former attorney general David Wilkinson. "I thought Robyn did a good job as ACLU director," he told the newspaper. "I'm not one to agree with every ACLU position, but we found some we could agree on, and even on those we didn't agree, we were able to make progress. Robyn was good because she sincerely wanted to find a solution to the problems she found that we could all live with. She listened to our position when it differed from hers. She didn't have a chip on her shoulder, which is the case with some other ACLU officials I've dealt with before."

"An affiliate is built in incremental steps," Davidson would comment later. "Each director made a substantial contribution in strengthening the ACLU presence in Utah."

When Blumner arrived in Florida, her presence did not attract the same attention as in Utah. However, before long she was embroiled in a high-profile case involving the Santerian religion, a case that would be argued and won before the Supreme Court. By 1992 Blumner was serving on the executive committee of the national ACLU.

On November 18, 1990, the *Tribune* ran a feature on Blumner, datelined West Palm Beach, Florida. The article began with an incident that likely would not have been well-received in Utah:

> It was yet another debate on the censorship circuit and Robyn Blumner . . . decided to have some fun with her anti-pornography antagonist.
>
> Before beginning a slide show of nude portraits, Blumner warned that some people might want to leave lest they become "irresistibly overcome by the need to commit a sexual assault."
>
> She turned to her [opponent]: "John?"
>
> John Tanner—the Volusia County, Florida prosecutor, born-again obscenity crusader, and Ted Bundy prayer partner—raised his middle finger to suggest that Blumner commit an anatomically impossible act.
>
> "I started verbally prodding him, which is my style, and he flips me the bird," said Blumner, twenty-nine . . .
>
> Since the New York native and attorney arrived in Miami in February 1989, the civil liberties group and its telegenic executive director have become increasingly visible in the wake of high profile cases. . . .
>
> Supporters credit her with re-energizing the ACLU's flagging Florida operation by capitalizing on renewed interest . . . [in the] right-wing rollback on civil liberties.
>
> Her willingness to defend all comers—from chicken-sacrificing Santeria followers to gay prisoners forced to wear pink tags—has put authorities on notice that even casual violations of constitutional rights will not be tolerated. . . .

Near the article's end came Robyn Blumner's pronouncement on Utah. Regarding the land of her first directorship, she said: "Utah is the bland leading the bland."

5.
To Pray or Not to Pray

Michele Parish would come to see her directorship as a fulfillment of both prayer and prophecy. Ironically many Utahns regarded her as the antithesis of prayer and certainly of prophetic religion. That contrast, and other ironies, inspired local cartoonists to illustrate the prevailing conundrum—the war over public prayer plus Michele Parish.

The prayer Parish saw fulfilled in Utah was uttered in all sincerity by herself and the Reverend Wesley Parish-Pixler. She and this United Methodist minister had hyphenated their surnames when they married in 1975. She then "followed him around" for more than a decade from one parish to the next. Anticipating a move from Colorado to Utah, the couple prayed that Michele would find a job that would involve "more than being a minister's wife" and allow her to become "her own person."

A few years earlier at a leadership seminar, one speaker had informed the trainees that, typically, a woman experiences three levels of power in becoming effective. At first she is known by relationship, in Parish's case as a minister's wife and a mother. At the second stage she is known by what she does (public relations director for her church, columnist for the weekly newspaper, and a librarian). At the third stage, the speaker said, "You know you're wielding some power because you're referred to as 'that bitch.'" Parish would reach the third stage as she led the Utah affiliate, becoming its most conspicuous executive director.

Born February 7, 1950, in Muscatine, Iowa, Michele combined her love of people, politics, and literature in a bachelor's degree in English from the University of Iowa in 1973. Two years later she commenced graduate studies in pastoral counseling and theology at the Southern California School of Theology. Then she married a minister and "stretched the borders" of her wifely role.

While leading the Utah affiliate, Parish would think often of her confirmation verse: "Do justice and love mercy, . . . walk humbly with your God." For that occasion she and her husband had commissioned an anthem to include a scripture from the Book of Philippians in the New Testament: "if there is anything virtuous, lovely, or of good report, seek after those things." The verse she chose is quoted in the Articles of Faith of the LDS church.

Given Parish's religious orientation, she thought when she moved to Utah that she understood Mormons' commitment to religious issues as they appeared in the public forum, even though she did not share their beliefs. Much of the populace who knew Parish primarily through sound bites on the evening news would not agree.

Freedom of religion entwined with another prime conflict during Parish's tenure—prison conditions, a major concern while Parish had served as associate director under Robyn Blumner. Parish and DeLand, however, would quickly develop an enmity that became public, one that first bloomed over a question of prayer. The courtroom resolution brought a cherished victory to Parish. DeLand later would consider the lawsuit one of two mistakes he made during his years heading corrections.

The prayer question involved Native American inmates at the Utah State Penitentiary who wanted a sweat lodge to allow them to practice native rites. The lodge consisted of a flexible willow frame that, during ceremonies, would be covered with canvas and heated with coals baked in a fire outside the lodge. Symbolizing the dark, confining womb and ultimate rebirth, the sweat lodge represented a spiritual purge of pride and negativity and a physical purge of toxins.

Sweat lodges, which dotted the Native American landscape, were becoming accepted in prisons nationwide. Used by tribal members on reservations and even in cities, their rigor—almost torment—struck a deep and traditional chord. Now inmates and their families on the outside wanted that cleansing available within the prison.

When the sweat lodge issue arose, DeLand said later, he felt that he already had been more than fair to Native American inmates. Conversations with attorney Gary Montana and Travis Parashonts, state executive director of the Division of Indian Affairs, had led him to soften the policy of requiring collar-length hair, DeLand said. The penitentiary would exempt Native Americans "with a legitimate need to keep long hair," at his directive.

But next, as DeLand told it, Montana was demanding a sweat lodge, medicine bags, and so on, "and the sense seemed to be, 'do it or I'll sue,'" DeLand said. "The best way to get me routed toward court is to do that. I liked defending lawsuits. It's a lab exercise for me. I teach this stuff, and going to court is how I test it."

The sweat lodge cause later passed to another attorney, Danny Quintana, who once had worked for DeLand and his brother Loni. "When he deposed me," Gary DeLand recalled, "I told him, 'Danny, you're going to lose this one and lose it big,' and Danny said, 'Well, Gary, I guess that's what courts are for.'"

Quintana took the lawsuit to the ACLU, and the affiliate filed an *amicus* brief written by cooperating attorney Michael O'Brien. As a result, on February 8, 1989, only days after Robyn Blumner flew east, acting executive director Michele Parish issued a press release arguing that, based on the freedom of religion, the prison should make appropriate worship facilities available to Native Americans just as it did to LDS, Catholic, Protestant, and other inmates. This would not apply to maximum security prisoners.

Throughout March, Department of Corrections officials heard from the ACLU indirectly, as the clergy of various religions lobbied for the sweat lodge. The Very Reverend William F. Maxwell wrote Governor Norm Bangerter on behalf of the Central Salt Lake City Council of Churches, urging him to influence corrections officials. The Catholic Diocese and the Congregation Kol Ami added their voices.

Meanwhile, prison officials suggested a greenhouse where prisoners could sweat but still be observed through the glass. While physical stress might be produced in a greenhouse, the impact of the dark, introspective environment would be lost. The offer was rejected.

DeLand wanted the sweat lodge lawsuit defended vigorously. The discovery process should include questioning inmates regarding their beliefs and whether they had used sweat lodges before coming to prison, he thought. He wanted evidence presented that an inmate had been raped in a sweat lodge in another state, that another inmate had hid in one and escaped. Worries over precedent drove his resistance, he later claimed, for if corrections lost the lawsuit, religious groups might start demanding synagogues, temples, who knew what? He was disappointed when the state's lawyer failed to prepare the kind of case he envisioned.

DeLand was not anti-Native American, he would say: "I love the Old West and reading Indian history." He said that corrections already allowed smoke and drum ceremonies in the prison chapel, despite complaints, and that he thought the ceremonies had "a certain amount of charm."

In contrast, the ACLU's entry into the sweat lodge issue brought an initiation for Parish in several ways. The lawsuit was the first of several significant ACLU cases that would be heard by Judge Thomas Greene in federal court, and it represented the first lawsuit brought against the Department of Corrections under Parish's leadership. Most important to Parish, and most private, was her invitation from Quintana to attend a sweat lodge ceremony on the Uintah-Ouray Reservation in northeastern Utah shortly before the court hearing.

Clad in swimming suits, Parish and the other participants crawled into the sweat lodge. Amid the heat, songs, steam, sage, and cedar, they prayed for the success of the lawsuit. Of the experience, Parish said, "It was so moving, so religious, and was such a privilege to be invited to participate."

The afterglow continued as Judge Greene struck down the state attorney's arguments and objections. Parish recalled how one argument—that an inmate could sneak a shank into the sweat lodge—brought sudden laughter to the courtroom. Those who had endured the almost intolerable heat knew that no metal could be hidden on the body. When Greene read his previously written decision in favor of the sweat lodge, the rumble of native drums rose in the courtroom. Parish left the hearing elated. "It was a great day for me because the case involved both religion and civil liberties—and we won."

DeLand wanted to appeal, but the governor dissuaded him. "He wanted to know how badly I wanted to fight this," DeLand said. "He said, 'I'll back you, but . . . ' and that was all I needed to hear." The governor, DeLand understood, dealt with the tribes on water rights and other critical issues. Bangerter later said the state's loss on the sweat lodge issue had not been major and not worth appealing since it was divisive.

In retrospect, DeLand mused that had Quintana approached him differently, he might have allowed the sweat lodge without a court fight. Instead he "let ego get in the way—but then that's my stiff-necked approach to life." He added, "Danny whipped my ass, but I still like him."

DeLand's recollection that earlier he had softened the prison's hair length policy was curious, since this was never apparent to the public. In fact, on August 1, 1989, the ACLU filed a complaint in U.S. district court alleging that prison policy prohibiting male Native Americans from wearing long hair as a tenent of their religion violated the First and Fourth amendments. Nor could Parish resist a bit of gloating in the press release issued at that time: "This case follows on the heels of the ACLU's success in forcing the Department of Corrections . . . to permit Native Americans access to sweat lodges for religious services. . . . " The note of jubilation proved premature, for in September the affiliate asked the court to dismiss the claim regarding hair length, while still insisting on the principle.

The Department of Corrections itself began considering making exemptions for long hair in February 1994, years after DeLand's tenure. Pam Elliot, a corrections administrator overseeing prison policy, checked the records and said the short hair requirement was maintained before and throughout DeLand's years at the helm. If the line had ever softened for "legitimate causes," no policy change was recorded. In fact, the ACLU's inability to press the issue with corrections in 1989 allowed the department its own bit of gloating via the media.

Interestingly, the attention drawn to religious freedom at the prison brought relief to Jewish inmates and even a moment's harmony between parties. On October 25, 1989, the Department of Corrections, the ACLU, and the Congregation Kol Ami released a statement that Jewish inmates would now be able to "attend weekly religious services in the prison's Wasatch Chapel as a result of an out-of-court agreement reached this week. . . . " The services would be "led by lay volunteers from the synagogue late Friday afternoons, and prayer books, yarmulkes, and prayer shawls provided by the synagogue will be stored by the Department of Corrections for use in the services." This united approach to religion represented another kind of victory for the affiliate and meant a concession on DeLand's part. Unfortunately, this first sign of accord would be the last for some time.

Early in 1989, while tackling religious issues at the penitentiary, the ACLU also defended the civil rights of the state's most powerful religious denomination—the LDS church. Intending to promote tourism, the 1989 state legislature deliberated a bill to allow liquor in limousines and on "fun buses," which shepherded revelers to Nevada's nearby casinos. The bill, which Governor Bangerter supported, would simplify life for tourists by easing Utah's complex liquor restrictions. However, making liquor accessible had never been a priority among Mormon lawmakers. The fun bus bill ran out of gas after the LDS church lobbied against it.

Typically, the Salt Lake City newspapers split on their coverage of the bill. On February 25, 1989, the *Tribune* headlined the story, "Liquor Bill Died After LDS Officials Phoned Senators." Three days later the *Deseret News* headline modified the stale news under, "LDS Officials Say Legislators Were Contacted for Clarification."

Cartoonist Calvin Grondahl's interpretation appeared in Ogden's *Standard-Examiner*. The cartoon depicted the gold-plated Angel Moroni statue atop the Salt Lake temple spire blowing his horn toward a dog perched on top of the Capitol. From the horn came the words, "Vote no on the fun bus." The caption read, "His master's voice."

The LDS influence waxed strong on Capitol Hill since most legislators were Mormon, male, and thus often priesthood bearers and lay clergy. However, a direct contact from the hierarchy to the priesthood ranks, even in a setting of secular power, commanded such deference that the implications seemed newsworthy. The church was seldom so direct. Routinely the church's wishes were second-guessed and filtered through lawmakers' own opinions.

On March 1 Parish and the Utah affiliate issued a press release stating that officials of the LDS church can lobby just as anyone else can. Parish followed up with a letter to Richard Lindsey, managing director of the LDS Special Affairs Committee, the body in charge of the church's political interests. Although the press release was consonant with the ACLU's commitment to free speech, the ironies were apparent in the affiliate defending the resident titan. Parish framed Grondahl's cartoon and tacked it on her office wall, where it would soon gain company.

The following month, April 1989, the new acting director tackled another LDS-related religious issue. In this one, the historical implications set the affiliate at odds not only with the contemporary Mormon church, but with the national ACLU.

Two months into Parish's tenure, the Utah ACLU filed an *amicus curiae* brief in the Utah Supreme Court on behalf of a polygamist couple, Vaughn and Sharene Fischer. They sought to adopt six children, the offspring of Vaughn Fischer's third wife, who had died of cancer. The Fischers maintained that before her death the mother had asked her husband and his legal wife to adopt the children. However, the mother's sisters, horrified by polygamy, had contested the adoption. The Fifth District Court ruled in their favor based on the illegality of polygamy.

Parish wrote in a press release that the ACLU had a history of insisting, based on privacy, that non-traditional lifestyles and family arrangements "should not automatically disqualify adults from adopting children if the adoption can be demonstrated to be in the best interests of the child. . . . " In this case, she continued, involving "a polygamist family, where the practice is based on sincerely held religious beliefs, First Amendment issues of freedom of religion enter in, as well."

The affiliate encouraged the court to conclude that polygamy alone should not determine the adoption decision. "In the event that the court chooses to base . . . [its] ruling solely on the grounds that polygamy is against the law, we challenge the constitutionality of such a law, as a violation of [the] First Amendment guarantee of freedom of religion." Parish related the current lawsuit to its roots in nineteenth-century Mormon history, when Supreme Court rulings outlawed polygamy, resulting in "relentless persecution of Mormon families. Unfortunately, there was no American Civil Liberties Union at that time to stand up against this religious persecution."

No sooner, however, had Parish attempted to remedy in a small way a century-old injustice, but a spate of concerned telephone calls from other affiliate directors informed her that donors were upset by her challenge to National policy. True, the policy stated that religious belief in plural marriage was protected by the Bill of Rights. However, due to criminal statutes, the practice of polygamy was not defended by the ACLU.

Belatedly Parish reviewed the policy, deciding it allowed the freedom to "talk about it as long as you don't do it." She declared, "Most religious people will tell you it is impossible to have free exercise of religion if you are not allowed to 'practice what you preach.'" Conceding that the Utah affiliate clearly, if unknowingly, had contradicted National policy, Parish then proposed that National conform to the Utah position. The Utah policy stated "that the right to advocate and practice plural marriage is constitutionally protected."

She explained its underlying assumption that personal relationships between consenting adults were protected by the Constitution and that freedom of religion and freedom of expression were fundamental rights. "Criminal and civil laws prohibiting the advocacy or practice of plural marriage are constitutionally defective." Eventually she won the point.

In a profound irony the ACLU's intervention, which might have seemed a literal godsend to nineteenth-century Mormons, set the affiliate directly at odds with the modern LDS church which avoided any reminder of polygamy. While the state occasionally brought civil sanctions against polygamists, since the 1950s it had abandoned criminal prosecutions. The LDS church, however, viewed the practice or advocacy of plural marriage as excommunicable.

The affiliate's reasoning was anathema to current LDS policy, as well, which opposed adoptive rights of non-traditional families including homosexuals and single parents. The church frequently emphasized its support of the traditional, patriarchal, nuclear family, discouraged divorce, and excommunicated homosexuals.

The Utah Supreme Court declined to rule on the religious question but essentially upheld the ACLU's argument that the best interests of the child should prevail and that the practice of polygamy should not singly prohibit adoption. The case was remanded to the lower court, whereupon the Fischers obtained custody and the aunts and grandparents received visitation rights.

Amid these controversies, Michele found Wes, her husband, courted by the local powers in a way not proffered to the Parish-Pixler who ran the ACLU. He was invited to pray in Salt Lake City Council meetings and invited to attend the LDS church's general conference. Impressed by this ecumenical spirit, the reverend could not understand why his wife viewed such overtures with suspicion. "Our house often seemed like a sitcom except it was too unbelievable," Michele sighed.

Thus far Parish's tenure had been lively and productive, and in September the board of directors voted to make her executive director. Her beginning salary of $28,000 as acting director would eventually rise to $38,000 as her experience increased and donations flowed into the affiliate's treasury. In announcing Parish's appointment, both Salt Lake newspapers noted the current prison and church/state issues that Parish was handling.

When she addressed the forty-sixth annual ministerial luncheon, Parish chose as her topic "Separation of Church and State in Utah: Fact or Fiction?" Within her speech she clearly outlined the differences between the Utah ACLU and the LDS church.

According to a *Tribune* report, Parish "spoke openly of the role the Church of Jesus Christ of Latter-day Saints plays in affecting public policy, telling the clergy the ACLU has opposed some things the church has done, but defended others." Currently, Parish explained, "The ACLU is challenging the constitutionality of a law which gives state powers to BYU campus police, because church employees should not be empowered to be state police. . . . " It continued: "The ACLU is opposed to prayers in government meetings or at schools and opposes the use of public funds for religious displays. It also opposed giving graduation credits for seminary classes." The article noted her support of the LDS church to speak "on political issues, such as alcohol . . . use in limousines and buses. . . . "

Former board president Michael Rudick and executive directors Shirley Pedler and Robyn Blumner had addressed similar themes in the past. Yet Parish's comments provoked listeners and readers, perhaps due to her logical but blunt approach. "In answer to a question from the audience, [she] suggested that if people did not like the influence of the LDS church on the legislature, they should elect officials who do not listen to the church."

Deseret News staffer Dennis Lythgoe—formerly a historian from the Boston area—found his interest piqued. Rather naively, he said later, he wrote a feature on Parish. Editors found fault with the first submission, which seemed too favorable. Pressured to "balance the story," Lythgoe sought comment from Parish's opponents—Gary DeLand, his new sidekick Scott McAlister, and LDS church representatives.

LDS public relations director Bruce Olsen confirmed that regarding the liquor/limousine bill, the affiliate "did indeed speak out in favor of the church." But, Lythogoe wrote, while press spokesman Jerry Cahill "hesitates to call the ACLU the church's enemy, he says the church 'is not excited' about some issues the ACLU has promoted."

Lythgoe continued: "Most notably, Cahill remembers the effort to defeat the released-time program for seminary students, an issue decided in the church's favor in 1981." Cahill viewed the church triumphant since released time for religious studies had continued. He did not mention that graduation credit for classes was denied and ACLU attorneys had been awarded substantial fees. Cahill objected to the ACLU's insistence on secular holiday displays in public settings instead of Christmas nativities or religious music.

Parish found religious displays objectionable if the government paid for them. As for seminary, she said: "Everybody's schedule seems to revolve around released time for that one church."

With that statement from Parish, Lythgoe captured a profound contrast in perspective. Parish's puzzlement might be expressed by many an "outsider"—but few Utahns, Mormon or not, would refer to Mormonism as "that one church" or openly question the activities and traditions that revolved around it.

Her years as a minister's wife had prepared Parish for the spotlight of her post. As she began to be recognized in public, she compared it to living in a small town when "people would say to me, 'Oh, I'm glad you pull up the curtains on your windows. The last minister's wife didn't.' Or, 'You left your air conditioner on all night last night.'"

TO PRAY OR NOT TO PRAY

Forging into the fray on issues that had long jangled local nerves and tempers brought more than casual comments. Parish found a solid and quick-witted ally in civil rights attorney Brian Barnard, who liked Michele's activism. "Brian's attitude seemed to be, 'Oh, good, finally here's someone to play with.'" Both frequently worked late hours, and the telephone lines between their offices glowed as Barnard watched Parish "build up a tolerance for controversy." Because she lacked the law degree Robyn Blumner held, he felt Parish "had to talk louder and faster" to be heard.

Parish would wryly summarize her first year as, "Grow or die." She drew strength from a visionary experience at her first biennial ACLU conference. Her journal on June 15, 1989, noted: "During devotions this morning the Lord put into my right hand a sword of justice, and into my left hand the keys of knowledge, enabling and empowering me for this work which is before me." She then jotted notes on speakers and topics.

Despite the acceleration in her own sphere of activity, Parish participated in her husband's ministry at the Hilltop United Methodist Church. She served on both a board and a task force, helping to coordinate a capital campaign that raised $500,000 for a new chapel. But the praying that concerned her most wasn't occurring in church.

The prayer debate in Utah was complicated by the type of prayers common to LDS church members and thus frequently offered in public. Most LDS prayers were improvisational and might be given by anyone, even an unbaptized child. If the prayer did not refer specifically to church founders, leaders, or scriptures, Mormons considered it non-denominational and therefore appropriate to a secular group even by definition of the U.S. Supreme Court. By contrast, liturgical prayers fell in alien cadence upon Mormon ears.

On the other hand, non-Mormons hearing the standard "Our Father in Heaven," followed by improvisational language but habitual phrases, and closing with "in the name of Jesus Christ, Amen," considered these prayers Mormon. Offered in classrooms, meetings, before sports events or school plays, and at graduations, they seemed to define who was truly included and legitimate, both within the activity and before God.

In the late 1980s complainants stepped forward. Brian Barnard

99

represented two Brighton High School students in filing suit against Jordan School District, claiming that prayers at their graduation exercises were "blatantly denominational" and, therefore, unconstitutional. On September 26, 1989, district officials announced that they would rather discontinue commencement prayers than expend scarce resources on protracted legal battles.

Other districts, however, announced their intent to continue prayers. In January 1990 the ACLU urged attorney general Paul Van Dam to advise schools to follow Jordan District's lead, saying that although the ACLU was prepared to undertake litigation, "we encourage an informal resolution of the matter, provided that such a resolution squares with the requirements of the United States and the Utah State Constitutions."

On this issue, however, Utahns were ready to fight. The school prayer issue would generate more media coverage, letters to newspaper editors, and threats against the ACLU director than either of the concurrent battles over prison conditions and abortion.

Repeatedly, Parish explained to reporters that she did not oppose prayer but rather promoted the separation of church and state in order to protect religious freedom. Despite the cartoons showing a prayerful Parish petitioning God for success in preventing prayer in schools, the public response suggested that the distinction wasn't making an impression.

Several newspapers editorialized in the ACLU's favor. On April 8, 1990, the *Tribune*'s Sunday morning editorial headline read: "Prayers at Graduation Threaten Separation of Church and State." Suggesting that the Alpine School District's decision to continue graduation prayers was venturing "into a mine field," the editorial warned that caution was in order considering both the U.S. Supreme Court's 1962 court decision banning "organized prayer" in schools and the attorney general's refusal to defend school prayer.

"Rather than deny the existence of a god, the prayer ban acknowledges that everyone is entitled to his or her spiritual beliefs. Americans are essentially free to pray as individuals when and where they want, even in school," the editorial read, adding that when school officials "sanction praying, they run the risk of promoting one person's religious beliefs at the expense of another's. There simply is no prayer that encompasses the religious beliefs of all human beings." It offered this practical note: "For a district with more students than money to educate them, Alpine is risking too much for a misguided cause."

On June 6 faculty editor Nancy Williams editorialized in *The Cache Citizen* in Logan, home of the seminary battle, the experience of non-Mormon students. She suggested that Mormons are oblivious to the discomfort they create for others.

Governor Norm Bangerter, who would lend the state's support to school districts wishing to preserve school prayer, said later that Mormons ought to be sensitive to the feelings of others. But, he added, "There are a rare few people who really object to prayer in public places. Most are like me. I see things that make me dang mad, but I just bow my head and keep my mouth shut."

During 1990, as the disagreement mounted between the districts and the ACLU, tensions exploded within the Utah affiliate in uncanny symmetry. A prayer issue at the prison had polarized relations between Parish and DeLand; now the heat surrounding prison battles and school prayer would spark the tinder gathering under the affiliate's board of directors, which felt the heat of public displeasure.

John Morris, a faculty member at the University of Utah Law School and later a university administrator, joined the ACLU board of directors in 1988 and then chaired the legal panel. His counsel was often sought within the affiliate itself. "Michele was looking for someone to help her work through relationships within the board," he recalled. "She was a lightning rod for controversy, and that's the single most important thing Michele did for the structure of the ACLU. She had a rare ability to galvanize the membership."

Morris's ability to maintain a cool head and a discerning eye proved invaluable during what he called the "pyrotechnics" of Parish's tenure. In retrospect, he would provide an insider's thoughtful analysis. Parish's style, Morris noted, represented a dramatic departure "even from Robyn's time, and Robyn was no wallflower. Michele had a peculiar ability to get people to support or oppose her. She was not a consensus builder."

In a community that valued harmony and respected authority, Morris did not view this as a fault. "In our state, I believe it's important to have some groups that are not involved in building consensus." Sometimes, he said, Utahns "build consensus at the cost of everything else."

However, board president Gerald Nichols had selected for his replacement as board president the consummate consensus builder. University of Utah communications professor and administrator Boyer Jarvis had allowed Nichols to "twist his arm," becoming president shortly after Parish became executive director.

Though a new board member, Jarvis was well known. As Morris described him, he "is one of the truly great people in this community. He has put more of himself into liberal causes and done more than almost anyone else." He added, "He doesn't like confrontation." Jarvis's strategy, Morris explained, was to set parameters around the issues, then say, "'Let's be friends.' That is why he has access to so many parts of the community. And that was not Michele's style at all."

By the time Jarvis became president in January 1990, the Utah affiliate had filed a substantial medical lawsuit against corrections, a powerful state department, causing a strong reaction that quickly exerted pressure on the board. Jarvis supported the lawsuit and Parish publicly but let her know that he did not like her confrontational style. He also went out of his way to "make friends" with Gary DeLand.

"The first time I met Michele," Jarvis recalled later, "I went to a board retreat. . . . I perceived Michele as a sort of rambunctious person who was talking beyond her talents. . . . She was certainly dedicated, but I was not particularly impressed with Michele like I had been with Robyn and Shirley."

Within his few months' tenure as board president, Jarvis was disturbed by disagreements within the organization. One arose, he said, when affiliate secretary Mary Dickson protested that Parish edited the minutes of board meetings, which Dickson, a professional journalist, had taken, written up, and signed. Jarvis tried to get the two to work out their differences. Parish might at least contact Dickson if she felt information needed to be protected or conflicts kept quiet. But ultimately Dickson resigned.

Jarvis said, "I knew it wouldn't be easy for me, the way I am, to work with Michele," who, he said, "thrives on confrontation. I am not confrontive." Some people, Jarvis said, might even call him passive-aggressive. "When I come across something I don't agree with or support, instead of getting into a confrontation, I recede. I may disengage entirely or try to start working from another point. . . . "

To confront or to conciliate—the two styles inherent in the affiliate's history—now found expression concurrently in two personalities leading the affiliate—the board president and the executive director. An incident that might otherwise have seemed a classic case of much ado about nothing dramatically demonstrated the issues of power and its dynamics in Utah.

Style, in fact, was openly named the target—Michele Parish's versus Boyer Jarvis's—when the artillery erupted. But that was an easy façade, propped up before the less-discussed bulwarks of authority, deference, and tradition. Who would exercise influence, and how? Who would speak with whom? The emotional landscape of school prayer possessed at its core the more cosmic issue of who could importune God, when, and how. Finally, the feud-turned-family made good media copy.

Oddly enough, the tempest began in a friendly "teacup" shared by Michele Parish and LDS general authority John K. Carmack. The two had struck up a correspondence regarding public prayer. Carmack, a California attorney before he had entered high church leadership, enclosed with his letter of November 6, 1989, a copy of a speech by Apostle Dallin Oaks. Speaking in Boise, Idaho, Oaks had criticized the "religious censorship" of organizations that resisted prayer in schools, including the ACLU.

When Parish responded to Carmack's letter, she explained her views without mentioning Oaks's speech. In January 1990 Carmack replied, writing that he considered Parish's view "consistent and responsible," but emphasizing the "legal reasoning" in Oaks's Boise talk. Ultimately, Carmack asserted, the matter of prayer must be resolved by the U.S. Supreme Court.

Again Parish responded without mentioning Oaks. While an apostle's speech carried weight among Mormons, Parish didn't pay much attention until a version of it appeared in the *Wall Street Journal* and suddenly reached a far wider audience.

In his speech Oaks said: "Religion should have a place in the public life of our nation." Specifically, he wrote: "To honor this principle with prayers in the graduation exercises of high school students is to honor the religious plurality of our nation and the religious liberty it was founded to protect."

Immediately Parish "wrote a strong response" in a letter to the *Wall Street Journal* and sent a courtesy copy to the LDS public information office. She did so, she said later, as a matter of course. Her approach was consistent with ACLU goals and within her purview as executive director.

The letter itself was vintage Parish, grounded in fact but penned with more passion than diplomacy. She wrote:

> What Mormon religious leader Dallin Oaks blithely disregards in his recent . . . article on school prayer, is that if there is any state government which should avoid even the appearance of an establishment of religion, it is Utah, where the patterns and practices of theocracy die hard; the only state where all non-LDS persons—Christians, Jews, Unitarians, Muslims, atheists alike—are derisively known as "gentiles";
>
> Where public school students are subjected to formulaic LDS prayers, proselytizing, and often the teaching of academically discredited LDS versions of history and anthropology;
>
> Where school counselors reportedly pressure students to participate in "release time" daily religious indoctrination classes at LDS "seminary" buildings, always conveniently located adjacent to public school property;
>
> Where coaches require athletes to kneel in the locker rooms and on the playing field before and after games; where prayers before student theater productions, dance recitals, awards banquets, school assemblies, PTA, faculty meetings, and school board sessions are commonplace;
>
> Where parents, students, and teachers who object are told, "The majority rules."
>
> Newcomers from other parts of the country who never quite understood the Supreme Court's ban on prayer in school become ardent defenders of secular public education after moving to Utah, as they discover firsthand what religious minorities have always known: that

the free exercise of religion is in direct proportion to the separation of church and state.

The ACLU will continue to fight for freedom of religion in Utah until it becomes a reality.

Although the *Journal* did not print Parish's letter, Oaks quickly responded after his subordinates received their copy. Oaks did not contact Parish to complain. He sought out the board president.

Jarvis first heard of Parish's letter when he received a telephone call from Bill Evans, staff for the church's Special Affairs Committee. Did Boyer happen to know the name of the president of the local ACLU board of directors? Yes, Jarvis answered, and soon received an angry letter from Oaks, which enclosed a copy of the letter Parish had sent to the *Journal.*

Oaks wrote briefly, but with passion similar to Parish's, on church letterhead dated June 22, 1990: "Are the ACLU's legal arguments so weak that its executive director must exaggerate and distort the facts in an *ad hominem* attack upon my church and the public school counselors, coaches, and teachers of this state?"

Reading through the pages of correspondence, Jarvis was miffed that Parish had written to the *Journal* without his knowledge, especially a letter that he "agreed was intemperate and disrespectful—not disrespectful to an apostle but to anyone, to the mayor, or to Gary DeLand."

Immediately Jarvis wrote back to Oaks, sending a copy to Parish. He told the apostle that he had been unaware of Parish's *Journal* letter. He explained up front that he had no problem supporting the ACLU attorneys' intention to take the school prayer argument into the courts. "On the other hand," Jarvis continued, "I am chagrined by [Parish's] letter. . . . If I were in your shoes, I would feel insulted more by the blatantly provocative tone than by the meager content of her letter." This dismissive comment was followed by an affirmation of Parish's commitment to the Bill of Rights, "even though she seems to prefer to be challenging and confrontive in situations where I myself would strive for conciliation and compromise." In closing, Jarvis reminded Oaks that Parish had defended the church's right to lobby against the liquor-limousine bill.

After posting the letter, Jarvis went to the Boston Building office to see Parish. She was unhappy that he had responded to Oaks without her knowledge.

"I said, 'Boyer, you should have talked to me first,'" Parish recalled. "He said, 'I didn't because I was afraid you'd talk me out of it.'"

Jarvis told her he resented her writing to the *Journal* without his knowledge and took the opportunity to make other differences known. "In that conversation," Jarvis said, "we really kind of had at each other for a while." Jarvis said maybe he ought to resign, but Parish didn't want him to. She suggested weekly lunches to improve their communication. Jarvis recalled that as he left, Parish said, "Boyer, I have just one request—that you not talk to anyone in the media."

Jarvis, who had not the slightest intention of calling a reporter, agreed, assuming the promise went both ways. Parish meant it both ways but had already mentioned Oaks's complaint to a Channel 2 reporter, and an apostle's wrath directed at the ACLU quickly became a story. The day after Jarvis and Parish met, a small article ran in the *Tribune* under the byline of Dawn House, a friend of Michele's.

Opening his newspaper that morning, Jarvis said, "I knew it was all over. I had a serious conversation with myself about the best next step. I could call a meeting of the board and ask their support to fire Michele, or I could resign. I decided it was in the best interest of the ACLU not to have a big blow-up, and so I resigned."

Now Jarvis wrote to Parish: "The fact that you have publicly drawn me into your controversy with Dallin Oaks . . . makes it impossible for me to continue as president of the board of directors. . . . " He added, "Please be assured, however, that I will continue to be a dues-paying, card-carrying member of the ACLU."

Interestingly, not only had Jarvis written conciliatory words to Oaks, but now he sent a copy of his resignation letter to DeLand's deputy director, Nick Morgan, a personal friend. He wanted to let Morgan know, Jarvis later explained, that their talks about prison conditions would come to an end. According to DeLand, Jarvis also sent him a copy of his resignation letter.

In any case, Parish first heard from a reporter that not only had she added an enemy in the LDS hierarchy to her war with the corrections chief but that her own board president had quit in exasperation. Furthermore, church, state, and the ACLU board president seemed remarkably in touch with one another in deploring her actions.

Not surprisingly, Jarvis's resignation prompted a new ripple of media interest. Now both Oaks's speech and parts of Parish's unpublished letter saw print in Utah. Parish explained to the *Tribune*: "When the state is not able to separate itself from the people who run the church, it is a problem. And I said the truth. In Utah, there is a blurring of the line."

To that point in her explanation, many Utahns might agree. Yet her final statement flicked like a whip. "In Utah, there are people who don't believe in separation of church and state, who don't believe in the Bill of Rights."

Explaining his resignation, Jarvis told the *Tribune*: "I don't go out of my way to be offensive. I would not write a letter that way." Because his own style "differed completely" from Parish's, Jarvis said, he had decided to resign.

Later Jarvis distinguished between his conflict with Parish and feeling pressured by an LDS apostle. Had the issue not become public, Jarvis might well have smoothed relations with Oaks as he had with DeLand.

"Most people inferred that my decision to resign was because someone in the Mormon hierarchy was speaking to me; nothing could be further from the truth," Jarvis insisted. "I'm as willing to offend Dallin Oaks as anyone, maybe more so than Michele Parish would be." Nevertheless, just as Parish revealed naivete regarding the risks in issuing a public challenge to an apostle, Jarvis exposed his preference to avoid offending anyone.

Within the affiliate, the earth trembled. John Morris emerged, at Parish's request, as board chairman. Morris had replaced Jarvis, upon retirement, in his administrative position at the university. Now he telephoned Jarvis to explain that he would follow as board president, but he didn't want that to come between them. It didn't, he learned. Boyer wasn't interested in hurting the ACLU.

Morris then held a press conference in conjunction with Parish and took on the venerable feed-or-fight-them issue. "My personal background allows me to be confrontational without being uncomfortable," he said, as reported in the *Tribune*. "I have no interest in insulting Dallin Oaks or the LDS church, I want to make that clear. On the other hand, these are issues that tend to bring out sharp statements, and sometimes that's useful in a debate." Morris predicted that the ACLU might well bring litigation regarding both school prayer and prison issues, which he defined as its most pressing concerns.

Privately Morris observed the differences between two ACLU leaders he liked and admired. Boyer, he noted, couldn't understand why Michele needed clash. After the split, Michele mistrusted Mormon males, no matter how liberal. Try as he might, Morris could not get her to invite another to join the board. When the going got tough, she believed, they would not confront the opposition. What's more, her experience with Oaks, Jarvis, and DeLand left her convinced that any male authority held in common would adhere.

During the summer as the Utah affiliate readied its lawsuit, the school prayer question reached the U.S. Supreme Court via a Rhode Island ACLU case. After the U.S. First Circuit Court of Appeals ruled graduation prayers unconstitutional in *Lee v. Weisman*, the Rhode Island school district had appealed to the high court. If the Supreme Court denied the appeal, the unconstitutionality ruling would answer the question of school prayer for Utah and all states.

However, prayer advocates in Utah noted that the Rhode Island case related to prayers offered by clergy, while in Utah the prayers were given by students. Whether that difference would prove significant remained unclear, but the Utah ACLU readied a brief clarifying the dominance and orthodoxy of prayers given in Utah. Ultimately the *amicus* brief would be discouraged by the Rhode Island ACLU, which was concerned about appearing to pad the page limit allowed by the court.

The confusion regarding clergy versus students became apparent in mid-July when the *Deseret News* reported that a group called Families Alert was threatening its own lawsuit. The pro-prayer entity would sue school districts "that do not allow students their constitutional right to pray privately in schools as established by recent U.S. Supreme Court guidelines." Executive director Joy Beech, known for her crusades against cable television and pornography, told the newspaper that if students were not allowed to pray on their own in school, in contrast to "school-sponsored" prayers, then the group would sue.

The article quoted Parish saying, "Families Alert doesn't understand the prayer versus public school issue. The ACLU will announce its plans to seek legal action against districts in which teachers and administrators have coerced pupils to participate in prayer."

Again Parish tried to explain: "They can't organize themselves into prayer during school hours. If they want to do it after school and want to pray individually and privately, that's fine too. But when they're in school, they're supposed to be studying. . . . " She added, "Prayer is wonderful but you can't have the state endorsing religion. . . . "

Beech replied in the *Tribune* that she had a "two-inch file on the ACLU" as a left-wing group bent on opposing religious principles. "If you destroy religion and people's concept of religion, especially among youth, then we think that they are fighting right at the root of what we stand for."

The next day newspapers reported that the prayer issue might do more than tweak Utahns' religious sensibilities. Property taxes might be raised to enable school districts to cover court costs. The ACLU was considering suing the Alpine, Jordan, Granite, Emery, Logan, and North Summit school districts, which meant taxpayers would feel the ache in their pocketbooks. Nevertheless, the school districts were not going to retreat.

July 1990 ended with the ACLU's announcement that it would, in fact, sue Granite District in Salt Lake County and Alpine District in Utah County. The lawsuit named Granite High School for allowing prayers at graduation and among cast members and faculty prior to plays and Eisenhower Junior High for allowing graduation prayers. In Utah County, Lehi High School was named for prayers at graduation, school assemblies, and pep rallies, while Orem High School would be sued for prayers at graduation, baccalaureate, and choir rehearsals and performances. The civil complaint filed in U.S. district court alleged violations of the First and Fourteenth amendments of the Constitution and the Utah Constitution's guarantee of freedom of religion and separation of church and state.

The *Tribune* quoted Parish: "The Utah affiliate will spend as much money and will take the lawsuits as far as the districts and Governor Norm Bangerter want to go," she said. "All our efforts to resolve these problems out of court have been rejected and we feel we have no alternative but to submit our complaints to the courts for a final resolution."

Interestingly Elder Oaks's *Wall Street Journal* article rose again in this news report. His argument was used at Orem High School when a school counselor and other faculty members objected to graduation prayer. Apostle M. Russell Ballard also publicly supported prayer in school, the article said. A rather clear line was thus drawn with two LDS apostles on one side and the ACLU on the other.

Joining the LDS church on the pro-prayer side of the line, Bangerter and the State Office of Education quickly offered support to the school districts that were "under attack from the ACLU." On the other side, the Salt Lake City Central Council of Churches, which did not include the LDS church, protested that school prayers tended to manipulate students and their beliefs.

The *Tribune* editorialized regarding the state's entry into the prayer battle:

> Governor Norm Bangerter's needless entry into the graduation prayer lawsuits with a "defense fund" would squander state dollars and aggravate whatever religious hostility exists in Utah. There are more pragmatic—and less divisive—ways for the Utah majority to make its wishes known.
>
> The governor claims that state money in the form of a supplemental appropriation is needed to defend school districts from "attacks by the ACLU."
>
> In fact, the Utah chapter of the American Civil Liberties Union has tried for years to persuade districts to honor the constitutional prohibition against school prayer. Only after those districts repeatedly defied those requests—and the law—did the ACLU finally file suit against Alpine and Granite school districts Monday.

In 1994 a mellowed and retired Bangerter would describe the school prayer issue as "kind of a yawner," saying that he could live with or without prayer in school. Either way he'd taught his own children and didn't depend on the schools. "The ultra left and ultra right choose to make battles where most of us prefer to have a discussion," he explained. He demurred at calling the ACLU ultra-left except that—"some of the issues they choose in Utah seem that way." Nevertheless in 1990 he committed the financial resources and power of the state.

In Ogden the *Standard-Examiner* took another tack, wanting prayer defended but not by public funds. Claiming the lawsuit "launched an attack on the fundamental value systems of Utah," the editorial claimed:

> However enormous the legal costs, Utah must stand on principle and defend this challenge in the federal court system. It can be done without digging into the pockets of taxpayers.
>
> Since the ACLU filed the suit against Granite and Alpine school districts, there has been a swelling of support flowing from all directions. Offers of financial assistance as well as Utah attorneys stepping forward to offer services free or at minimal fees have been forthcoming.
>
> Utah has been propelled into the national spotlight with a lawsuit that wrongly leaves impressions of pervasive religious biases. What it amounts to simply stated is telling a student body president that it is constitutionally wrong to ask a graduating classmate to lead in a moment of reverence or saying that praying aloud does not have constitutional protection.

The school prayer fight was reported throughout the nation. For instance the *Chicago Tribune* datelined an article by Jim Robbins Salt Lake City, Utah:

> The long-simmering differences between Mormons and non-Mormons in Utah—where virtually every aspect of life is dominated by the Mormon church—have come to a full boil.
>
> Angry and bitter public debate was sparked when a lawsuit aimed at ending Mormon prayer in public schools was filed this summer by the Utah affiliate of the American Civil Liberties Union.
>
> "It's about time somebody polarized the community," said Michele Parish, executive director of the Utah ACLU. "It's been festering for years. It's time to get the poison out."
>
> Mormons claim, however, that they are the victims of the discrimination in their Utah homeland, which they refer to as Zion.

"There's an element of religious bigotry in the state directed against Mormons," said Bud Scruggs, Bangerter's chief of staff. "The ACLU is trying to capitalize on this. They're hostile to religion."

The article further advised readers that 70 percent of Utah's population was Mormon, with an even higher proportion comprising the government and power structure.

Locally the prayer fight was illustrated almost daily with cartoons, editorials, and letters to the editor. After retirement, Bangerter would dismiss the furor as primarily media-generated: "How many letters?—a few hundred? That's nothing."

One letter writer derided the sentiment to squander a tight state budget in social services and education, adding:

> Pray any time you want, to yourself, to your own God, but leave tax money which is given by all people of this diverse state alone. The Mormon Church most clearly has an agenda. It is not satisfied with running the state legislature, they want to run the schools and force non-Mormon children to listen to their prayers.

A Provo reader wrote: "It seems to me that the ACLU is trying to take away the freedoms our ancestors fought for and I myself fought for in World War II. . . . Why should we bow to the wishes of less than one percent of the people in this great state?"

Another reader answered the majority rule argument by reminiscing: "When I was in elementary school, classes were shut down during the weekday session of the LDS general conference, and the proceedings were broadcast throughout the school for the teachers' benefit."

The letter continued: "By the time I entered high school that practice, along with teacher prayers, had stopped. But every event, be it a basketball game, class play, pep rally or assembly, began with a student prayer." He was harassed for refusing to pray at a pep rally. The writer concluded: "Before anyone starts throwing labels at me, I am not an atheist. I am a devout Christian who believes in America. I should have the right to pray—or not to pray—as I wish. Utah is still part of the United States, isn't it?"

Cartoonist Calvin Grondahl encapsulated the issue by draping a caricature of Bangerter in a flag reading "School Prayer" alongside U.S. president George Bush, wrapped in the American flag. "Very becoming, Governor," Bush was saying, while Bangerter replied, "Thank you."

By 1990's end various diplomats, including University of Utah law professor Edwin B. Firmage and Democratic state representative Grant Protzman, encouraged the adoption of a moment of silence to resolve the divisive issue. Moments of silent prayer had already been ruled unconstitutional, but Protzman said his moment would provide quiet "without requiring anything."

In the *Standard-Examiner* Parish responded for the ACLU: "I hate to always be saying something negative, but I think this is really nothing more than an attempt to do an end run on the U.S. Constitution and slide prayer through the back door. . . . " Parish, the *Standard* added, "questioned whether the moment of silence would even be legal," adding, "but 'Whether or not something is legal doesn't really have anything to do with what passes in Utah,' she said." Her comment was not necessarily untrue, but it was again, by local standards, not nice.

As the battle raged, Brian Barnard celebrated the bicentennial of the Bill of Rights by giving the ACLU a $1,000 investment certificate. Having fired the first shot in the prayer battle by suing Jordan District, Barnard was quoted in the *Tribune*: "Given the need for eternal vigilance to protect civil rights, I'm sure the ACLU will be serving an important function two hundred years from now. . . . And I'm equally sure the Bill of Rights will still need protection."

Looking back over the years of Barnard's support, both public and private, Parish would comment, "If there's any hero in all this, it's Brian. He's worked with every executive director. Despite our friendly rivalry to see who could get the most press, he was always there for me."

Barnard's practical foresight was justified when, in May, the *Deseret News* reported that U.S. district judge Thomas Greene had denied a preliminary injunction prohibiting prayer at an Orem High School graduation. "The ruling means the judge was not convinced that the American Civil Liberties Union is likely to win its lawsuit against graduation prayers in Granite and Alpine school districts," the *News* reported. "Students at Granite and Olympus voted not to have prayer at their graduations. Granite High students have chosen instead to include a poem or thought in the ceremony. Olympus students opted for a moment of silence."

As the controversy simmered, Barnard continued battling on another front, this time representing the Society of Separationists. They had sued the Salt Lake City Council for opening meetings with prayer. The council responded with guidelines for prayers that encouraged diversity in those who offered them.

Prayer at city council meetings was ruled unconstitutional by Third District Court judge J. Dennis Frederick. Parish had sent more than 200 letters to government officials over this issue, urging them "to clean up the church/state stuff."

The *Deseret News* quoted Parish saying: "We can do this the easy way, or we can do it the hard way. I'm fully prepared for either way . . . But I expect there will be some officials who want to use taxpayers' money to fund their own religious point of view. They will end up in court." The *Tribune* reported that some city councils planned to continue praying. Woods Cross voluntarily discontinued prayers, and Parish commended city officials.

The strategy of prayer proponents in Utah began shifting. If prayers offered in schools and government meetings were unconstitutional, the thinking went, why not change the content of the state—or even the national—constitution? The *News* began to editorialize that "it should not be difficult to draft" an amendment, adding, "the simpler the language the better."

The language that needed to be amended appeared in Section Four of the state constitution:

> The State shall make no law respecting an establishment of religion or prohibiting the free exercise thereof. There shall be no union of Church or State, nor shall any church dominate the State or interfere with its functions. No public money or property shall be appropriated for or applied to any religious worship, exercise or instruction, or for the support of any ecclesiastical establishment. . . .

The latter sentence, in particular, was cited by Frederick in finding city council prayers in violation. Public time and, therefore, money were spent on arranging and offering prayers. After Frederick's decision a truce ensued while the Salt Lake City Council appealed to the Utah Supreme Court.

Now Bangerter encouraged legislators to seek a special session to resolve the issue. If the courts would not allow the practice, perhaps a legislative solution was in order, as suggested by the *News*.

Under the governor's supervision a group was organized to consider an amendment. Known as the Religious Liberties Amendment committee, its first four members were all Republican, all male, and all LDS. This caused a predictable stir, and Democrats and non-Mormons were added, eventually including clergy from most of the state's denominations.

Thus the groundwork was laid for continuing public prayer in Utah even as the U.S. Supreme Court issued its anxiously-awaited ruling on *Lee v. Weisman* in the summer of 1992. The high court determined that prayer at high school graduations violated the establishment clause of the First Amendment. This resounding ACLU victory halted prayers in Utah's schools except when an occasional student leapt to the podium, prayed, and then was applauded.

In Utah the larger issue was not yet decided, for both the high court or the legislature could act to re-open government meetings to prayer. In December 1992 the Utah Supreme Court heard arguments regarding the Salt Lake City Council lawsuit. City attorney Roger Cutler maintained that prayer had a secular purpose and should be allowed since it was not "necessarily a religious exercise."

Brian Barnard insisted that Utah should be tolerant of religion but intolerant of government-supported prayer. The *Deseret News* quoted ACLU attorney Kathryn Kendell that such prayers were "an impermissible endorsement of religion."

While the Utah Supreme Court deliberated, the drive to amend the constitution gathered energy. Astonished, the Utah ACLU realized that the public prayer battle might lie not in the past but in the future. The rhetoric changed quickly. Rather than threatening litigation, representatives of the ACLU and the Separationists began urging caution and due process. Why rush into anything as fundamental as a constitutional amendment? Why risk offending Utahns who were not Mormon at the least, or at worst hazard igniting a religious war? The question was before the Utah Supreme Court. Certainly any constitutional change should wait for that ruling, they suggested. The court's ruling, however, would not come swiftly.

The December 1992 issue of *Church & State*, published in Maryland by Americans United for Separation of Church and State, featured the Utah controversy in a cover story by Rob Boston entitled "Whither Zion." The article began:

> Chris Allen never intended to spark a constitutional crisis in Utah. The 46-year-old Park City resident simply wanted government officials to abide by the Utah Constitution's church-state separation provisions.
>
> "The language of the Utah Constitution was being violated all over the place," charges Allen, director of the Society of Separationists, a statewide church-state separation group affiliated with Texas-based atheist leader Madalyn Murray O'Hair.

After giving background on the lawsuit against the Salt Lake City Council, the article continued: "Their surprise courtroom victory earlier this year brought an unexpected backlash: efforts by the state legislators to rewrite the Utah Constitution. As a result, Utah is now locked in a heated debate that could bring big changes in religious liberty for residents of the Beehive State."

As usual, within that debate the ACLU would talk as loudly and fast as anyone.

Spencer L. Kimball, acting dean of the University of Utah Law School and eldest son of LDS church president Spencer W. Kimball, became the first ACLU representative in Utah in the mid-1950s. (Courtesy University of Utah Archives, Manuscripts Division, University of Utah Marriott Library.)

Adam "Mickey" Duncan, an active Mormon, succeeded Kimball as ACLU representative in Utah and, with the award of their first charter in 1958, became the Utah affiliate's first board president. (Courtesy Utah State Historical Society.)

The black face motif of the Coon-Chicken Inn illustrates the degree of racism and segregation accepted in the Salt Lake community. (Courtesy Utah State Historical Society.)

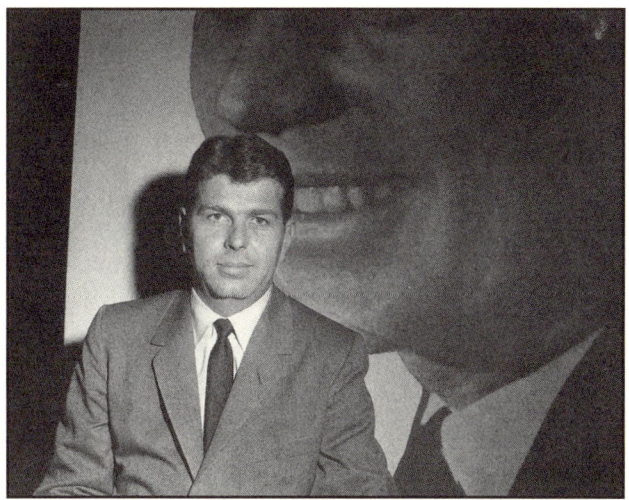

Steven Smoot, who followed Duncan as board president, began his involvement with the ACLU as an undergraduate concerned with Utah's "own little microcosm of McCarthyism," which led him to butt heads with ultraconservatives. (Courtesy Utah State Historical Society.)

Jim Joy, a doctoral student at the University of Utah, became involved with anti-pornography issues just days after taking over as the Utah affiliate's part-time executive director. Advocating economic pressure rather than censorship, Joy was linked to the likes of Roy Rogers. (Courtesy American Civil Liberties Union of Utah.)

Brian Barnard, who early on teamed up with the ACLU as a cooperating attorney on the *Deep Throat* obscenity case, joined with the ACLU on issues as diverse as school prayer and prisoners' rights. (Courtesy University of Utah Archives, Manuscripts Division, University of Utah Marriott Library.)

Robyn Blumner, a self-described New York Jew, approaching twenty-five when she became head of the Utah affiliate, took little time before engaging in church-state issues and prison affairs. (Courtesy University of Utah Archives, Manuscripts Division, University of Utah Marriott Library.)

Gary DeLand, forceful executive director of the Utah State Department of Corrections, began negotiating with the ACLU and Blumner over medical rights for prisoners. The relationship turned sour after Michele Parish assumed leadership of the Utah affiliate. (Courtesy *Deseret News*.)

Michele Parish took over direction of the ACLU of Utah in 1989. Her high-profile positions on prison conditions and public prayer kept her in the mind of political cartoonists and government officials alike. (Courtesy University of Utah Archives, Manuscripts Division, University of Utah Marriott Library.)

After receiving a major grant, the Utah affiliate was able to hire Kathryn Kendell as its first staff attorney. (Courtesy American Civil Liberties Union of Utah.)

Utah governor Norman Bangerter clashed with the ACLU in actively supporting graduation prayer and prison director Gary DeLand. (Courtesy Utah State Historical Society.)

The Utah ACLU affiliate has been the focus of local and national media attention over the years: school prayer was brought to a head when the Alpine and Granite school districts were sued; the response of Michele Parish to LDS apostle Dallin H. Oaks's *Wall Street Journal* article led to a falling out between Parish and ACLU board president Boyer Jarvis; double bunking at the prison was one of several issues Parish and the Utah affiliate took up with prison officials; a counter-attack by prison officials suggested that Parish precipitated a prison riot; Carol Gnade was heralded as "contemplative and careful" after Parish's volatile administration.

The Capitol Rotunda served for a Pro-Choice Coalition rally organized by the local ACLU. (Courtesy University of Utah Archives, Manuscripts Division, University of Utah Marriott Library.)

The ACLU-sponsored advertisement in the *New York Times* noting Utah's abortion law implied that abortion was punishable by death in Utah. Although it provoked a bitter backlash locally, the ad prompted a special session to amend the law.

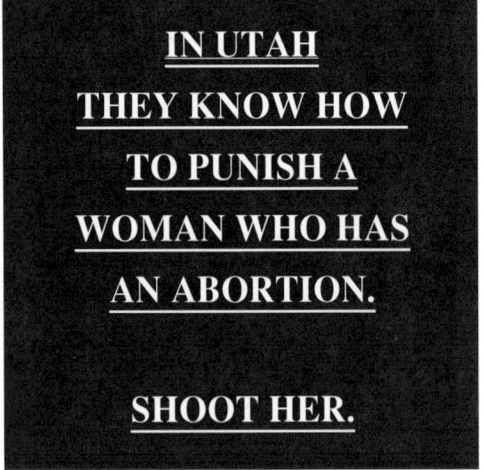

Carol Gnade, who originally signed on as the Utah affiliate's first development director, took over as executive director in 1993. (Courtesy American Civil Liberties Union of Utah.)

On several occasions reproductive rights protesters demonstrated on the grounds of the Utah State Capitol. (Courtesy University of Utah Archives, Manuscripts Division, University of Utah Marriott Library.)

Calvin Grondahl, editorial cartoonist for the Ogden *Standard-Examiner*, noted the influence of the LDS church on the "fun bus" bill, but the church found itself with strange bedfellows when the Utah affiliate supported the right of LDS officials to lobby as an act of free speech. (Courtesy Calvin Grondahl.)

U.S. president George Bush and Utah governor Norman Bangerter wrapping themselves in the "issues." (Courtesy Calvin Grondahl.)

The ACLU *Reporter* reprinted *Salt Lake Tribune* cartoonist Pat Bagley's "Anti-*Roe v. Wade* Super Patriot Missile" cartoon. (Courtesy Pat Bagley.)

Before she departed, Calvin Grondahl sent Michele Parish a final cartoon which appeared in the *Standard-Examiner*. (Courtesy Calvin Grondahl.)

Utahns and the ACLU have not always seen eye to eye. (Courtesy Pat Bagley.)

6.
Guns Blazing

"The prison issue was a dead-bang winner for us," said John Morris, who served as board president during several years of the ACLU lawsuit. "They were clearly in violation."

That statement rang with a clarity seldom heard during the long struggle to improve medical conditions at the Utah State Penitentiary. At times it seemed the primary lawsuit might well have read *Michele Parish v. Gary DeLand*, the exchanges were so heated between the affiliate and the Department of Corrections.

Two other principals played visible if supporting roles in the made-for-media conflict. Governor Norm Bangerter firmly backed his department head, whom he later described as "flamboyant," then becoming "testy," and then, after a barrage of lawsuits and investigations, as a man for whom it was "just time to leave." Investigative reporter Christopher Smart used Parish and prison sources to outstrip the rest of the media in his dogged pursuit of DeLand and his administration.

In the end the winners and losers became clear, though neither side conceded. The lawsuits reached settlement, the penitentiary received its first mental health unit, and taxpayers paid the ACLU cooperating attorneys hundreds of thousands of dollars in court-awarded fees. By that time neither Parish nor DeLand, Bangerter nor Smart, appeared preeminently in the public eye. Each still had plenty to say.

Bangerter probably represented the typical Utahn. The next-to-youngest of ten children, he grew up on a farm in Granger in southwest

Salt Lake County. Like the county itself, he moved from a rural to urban emphasis as a builder and eventually as a major developer in the south valley. He served as an LDS bishop and was a stake president when first elected to the House of Representatives in 1974. A moderate Republican, Bangerter became a powerful leader, unanimously re-elected Speaker of the House. When elected governor in 1984, his administration aligned easily with U.S. president Ronald Reagan's administration, both of which were supported by the majority of Utahns.

As he began his administration, Bangerter concluded that, under Democratic governors, state corrections had become "totally oriented toward rehabilitation. Some were even talking about removing sidearms from certain law enforcement officers. . . . The prison wasn't a very secure, safe place." A smattering of escapes during recent years heightened the public sense of insecurity. "The first reason you have a prison, in my view, is for the health and safety of the public," Bangerter said.

In searching for a new chief of corrections, Bangerter consulted with DeLand, a self-made expert within the corrections community. Bright, arrogant, and aggressive, as a deputy sheriff DeLand had transformed a three-week jail assignment into an administrative position. Among other law enforcers, he was considered tough but fair, a by-the-book administrator, which seemed logical considering that DeLand had written "the book"—first an operations manual for the jail, then another for the corrections department.

DeLand had discovered that corrections law—invented for all practical purposes in 1970 when the concept of prisoner rights emerged—was an unharvested but fruitful field. He read the few years of case law and began teaching classes, then consulting. By 1979 he earned twice as much, by his own account, in his spare time as he did tending jail for the county, so he resigned.

When approached by Bangerter, DeLand said he did not want to head the state's corrections system. Still, he cannily proffered his own attributes as a recommended profile of the new administrator. As DeLand recalled one conversation: "Bangerter asked, 'Can you stop the escapes at the prison?' I said, 'In my sleep . . . but I don't want your damn job.'" However, DeLand let Bangerter persuade him, cautioning the governor that he might be controversial and would "probably be carried out on my shield." Bangerter was convinced that he had found his man.

Later DeLand described his initiation. He summoned the Lifeflight helicopter several times to save ailing prisoners. The day after Christmas he described the breadth of prison corruption to Bangerter who authorized an investigation involving the Salt Lake County Attorney's office, the Utah Attorney General's office, and the Federal Bureau of Investigation in order to wrest control away from powerful inmates.

Under DeLand, the philosophy of rehabilitation withered while improved security thrived. Therapy to change prisoners' beliefs and values and thereby their behavior had proven useless nationwide, DeLand maintained. He conceded an economic factor in improving prisoners' skills, given the fact that virtually every inmate would be released. "Do we need education programs and work programs?" he asked rhetorically—"Yes, and hell yes." He did not define these as rehabilitation, so the programs continued.

Security was DeLand's hallmark, even after order reigned. The prison population increased, a second prison was built in the town of Gunnison in Central Utah, and DeLand developed an enviable SWAT team. Corrections enjoyed the reputation of a tightly-run and powerful state department, solidly backed by a Republican administration.

Despite the energy DeLand brought to corrections, no "book" existed when it came to providing medical care to inmates, as consultant Bonnie Norman discovered. She found no operations manual, no volume listing approved procedures, no quality assurance standards. Such a lapse, DeLand had to concede, could lead to problems because no uniformity of treatment was ensured—not that problems occurred, he would add.

In fact, he would insist even after the long legal battles and negotiations that inmates received better medical care than citizens on the street, especially citizens without insurance. "You can't get a doctor's appointment as fast as an inmate can see a doctor," he claimed.

Bangerter's priorities were clear and economic. "Say you don't have premier medical coverage at the prison at the level the courts say prisoners should have. Look in the kindergarten classes in the state. Some kids have no health care at all. A segment of society has the impression that prisoners live in luxury. I've been there, and they don't. At the same time, they may have services available to them that some citizens who haven't hurt anyone do not, especially children. You have to find a balance when you're moving dollars around," he explained.

Later DeLand professed surprise when he found himself nearing the end of the governor's first term. He was still chief of corrections, though he admitted that "someone with my style and the stiff-necked, aggressive approach I have to life couldn't work long in state government."

In 1988 Bangerter, who had been forced to raise taxes during his first term, won re-election despite an uphill campaign and a three-party election. The night Bangerter triumphed by a two-point margin over former Salt Lake City mayor Ted Wilson was, DeLand said, seductive. "I'd told the governor I'd stay through his first term. But then he came back from thirty-eight points down in the polls. I was at the Little America hotel watching the election returns come in, and he was beating Ted, my old friend. In a situation like that you get so excited you do dumb things, and I agreed to four more years." Of Bangerter, DeLand added, "I dearly love the man."

Entering Bangerter's second administration, DeLand led corrections with the confidence only political and bureaucratic success could bring. But this would change.

Prison officials had performed a long slow dance with the ACLU locally and nationally. DeLand remembered discussing jail conditions with both Jim Joy and Shirley Pedler, and later would laud them as reasonable people. He said, "When I heard Jim Joy was leaving for Denver, I almost cried." DeLand also said he once asked Shirley Pedler why the ACLU didn't sue over a particular problem, and she said they didn't have the resources.

Once Michele Parish was executive director, DeLand would lament losing Robyn Blumner to the Florida affiliate. "She was bright, tough, aggressive, and would kick your ass in a heartbeat, but she was fair and knew what was going on around her. She accomplished more without anybody knowing what she did than anyone else before or since."

DeLand's praise for Parish's predecessors did not extend to Parish herself, during whose term DeLand and the Utah State Penitentiary endured bruising criticism and grudging reform. As Blumner flew east,

Parish, as acting executive director, attempted to resolve the medical issues without a lawsuit. For starters, she took Blumner's chair on the evaluation board for medical services but served with waning optimism.

Heretofore Blumner and Parish had worked primarily with Inspector General Lynn Lund, who was also the prison ombudsman. But Lund since had left corrections, becoming executive director of the State Government Trust. Early in 1989 DeLand recruited a friend, Scott McAlister, assistant director of corrections in Oregon, to replace Lund.

"McAlister was the best litigator I'd ever seen," DeLand said, "enormously arrogant, which was okay with me as long as he won in court." Somehow McAlister bypassed the standard security check and quickly assumed a triple post: inspector general, prison ombudsman, and assistant attorney general. He became the eyes and ears of the prison system—DeLand's DeLand.

Later the corrections chief ruefully recalled that both McAlister *and* McAlister's supervisor had thanked him for getting the new inspector general away from Oregon. Hiring him, DeLand would say, constituted his major mistake, and fighting the sweat lodge his minor one. But this remorse came much later. For the time being, McAlister's hands-on authority was virtually absolute.

When Michele Parish heard that Lund had been replaced, she decided she should establish a relationship with his successor. She heard that McAlister had slugged through some "major go-rounds" with the Oregon ACLU and decided to try early to find common ground.

In February 1989, only weeks after Blumner left, Parish drove to the Department of Corrections offices in Murray, south of Salt Lake City, and, as she would recall the appointment, chatted with McAlister's assistant for about twenty minutes before he appeared. Parish began by saying that she thought they had some things in common. For instance, they both wanted a well-run prison and wanted it run in a constitutional manner.

McAlister would have none of that. He announced that they had nothing in common. The ACLU knew nothing about prisons. He had learned that in Oregon. Prisoners had no constitutional right to rehabilitation, he emphasized. In fact, the penitentiary would not provide medical care if it had any choice. (DeLand later said he thought his

121

assisant had been misunderstood regarding the latter comment.)

Parish was not particularly surprised by McAlister's opinions, but his disregard for diplomacy caught her somewhat off guard. He seemed to be "laying out what I could expect in working with them," accompanied by "a lot of chest thumping." She inferred that he considered himself brilliant and herself and the ACLU inept by definition. "The meeting was very confrontive on his part, and that's about as cordial as the relationship ever got."

Parish did not mention these impressions to McAlister's boss when, on February 28, she wrote to DeLand commenting on the Norman report and expressing reservations regarding a certain medical company's proposal. The proposal seemed evasive and sloppy in naming specific services and costs, and it estimated low figures for special services and hospitalizations. Nevertheless, she expressed hope that as acting director she could "continue the cooperative endeavors initiated by yourself and Robyn Blumner."

When the evaluation board did not recommend the medical company's proposal, the reform process became bogged down. Much had been discussed, not much had happened at the inmate level, and so, on the last day of March, Parish nudged again, writing DeLand for the "present plans and progress in implementing the recommendations made by Norman." She listed questions about medical contracting and accreditation, then closed with, "We appreciate the cooperation you have shown the ACLU and hope that we can continue to work together to improve the conditions at the penitentiary."

For some time the complaints the ACLU received from inmates and their families had been augmented by concerns expressed by corrections employees and guards. The fact that employees would complain alarmed the affiliate and was especially galling to corrections chiefs. As the year progressed, Parish said later, their calls from prison staff carried the message that no improvement seemed imminent: "You'd better go ahead and file the lawsuit."

By now DeLand's control of virtually all aspects of the penitentiary was accomplished. For instance, investigation of alleged crimes fell within the jurisdiction of Salt Lake County. Yet as DeLand stiffened the training of his own investigators and developed SWAT teams, county deputies and investigators found the penitentiary doors closed in their faces. One minor instance illustrated DeLand's "by-the-book" approach even among fellow law enforcers. Subpoenas issued by the Salt Lake County Attorney's Office were returned undistributed because they had been printed on photocopy paper, considered contraband.

On a more visible level the penitentiary's SWAT team was a new, effective, but somewhat startling entity, one that civil libertarians viewed as dangerous, especially when investigators or the team operated outside prison grounds. It became known to most Utahns when one officer was killed during the multi-agency siege of an armed family compound in Marion, east of Salt Lake City.

The larger question was not whether the funds that poured into prison security superseded the demand, but whether they prohibited a decent dental, medical, and mental health program and also limited education and counseling. The attitudes articulated by McAlister, DeLand, and other officials suggested as much, certainly to the ACLU.

DeLand would maintain that medical costs rose 1,200 percent during his tenure, including contracts and equipment. "When I came there, the main treatment table had water dripping on it. You had to brush away the paint chips. I fixed that."

True, he admitted, documents showed that he returned money every year to the state from the medical column of the budget; but "that was as close as we could get to the budgeting," he defended, "and we were damn sure going to err on the side of caution." A general budget overrun of one-half million dollars during his first year made him conservative, he said, especially during an era of budget cuts.

DeLand responded briefly to Parish's overtures. In one letter he indicated that she would be allowed to visit the prison without guards monitoring her conversations. He may have viewed this as generous since the sweat lodge issue was coming to a head. In mid-May she wrote again to DeLand requesting budget information and a list of current staffing patterns.

From the outset, Parish had strong feelings about prison conditions. As assistant director she had screened the complaints and horror stories, and as executive director she continued to check many personally. "They were all seriously harassed," she said of the inmates who joined the lawsuit. "These were brave people who went ahead." Along with intern Marlayn Cragun, Parish would interview inmates and frequently intervene in individual plights. "Sometimes I felt like I was living in the prison," Parish recalled. "We interviewed probably hundreds of people and wrote letters."

A sense of close proximity affected Parish in another respect. As chance would have it, her family bought a home in Sandy, bordering on Draper, near the penitentiary. Her daughters attended a gifted program in a Draper school, and many of their classmates' parents worked at the prison. As tensions rose, the girls began hearing comments on the playground and in school halls. The family moved to the Avenues area of Salt Lake City.

Given her religious orientation, Parish actually "felt the churches should be doing what we were doing with the prison. They should be demanding medical care and humane conditions since it's directly within their purview." Quietly she pushed the LDS and Protestant churches in that direction with some success.

The correspondence and committee meetings involving the Utah affiliate and the Department of Corrections erupted finally into a court drama on June 6, 1989, when the ACLU "challenged the Department of Corrections' planned move of 248 inmates in the Wasatch Facility at the Utah State Prison from single-cells into undersized double-bunked cells." The affiliate requested a temporary restraining order "until it can be determined if the size and conditions of the cells meet constitutional standards."

The cells in question, the press release stated, ranged from forty to seventy square feet, or between twenty and thirty-five square feet per inmate. "Into this cramped space, the size of most people's bathrooms, are squeezed two inmates, a bunk bed, a toilet, and what few belongings prisoners are allowed to possess." The press release signed off with this tidbit: "We have also received many complaints that prison officials have coerced inmates into signing consent forms for this move under threat of being written up for a major infraction, refusing a direct order."

DeLand fired back in the June 1989 corrections *Rap Sheet* newsletter, directing a sarcastic and detailed message at Parish, saying she "has let her lack of legal expertise lead the ACLU into a battle it cannot win."

He defended the double bunking, saying that modifications resulted in recreation space, a new staff control room, and improved lighting, ventilation, doors, and new paint. DeLand's comparative praise of Parish's predecessors, "non-lawyers like Robyn Blumner and Shirley Pedler," overlooked Blumner's law degree.

As DeLand recalled: "We started double bunking in eighty-square-foot cells that had a toilet in each room." This was the honor tier, he said, and comparatively posh. When the corrections officials "got hit with a restraining order," he defiantly double bunked a block of smaller cells, prompting a reprimand from federal magistrate Ronald Boyce.

"Hell, yes, I was tweaking him, but not just to be vexatious," DeLand said. These smaller cells had only "four shower heads on the whole damn floor" and the "recreation area" was simply a hall between cells. DeLand brought in an out-of-state friend, "another non-lawyer who makes a fortune teaching lawyers."

The magistrate, DeLand claimed, ended up ruling against the first project and allowing the second. DeLand trumpeted this irony during a debate with Boyce at the University of Utah Law School, declaring, "Running corrections by restraining order has to stop." In that forum he referred to himself as "a South Idaho country boy who never spent a day in law school."

The lawsuit involved in the overcrowding issue, *Baker v. Humphries*, combined two cases, one filed by the ACLU and one by Brian Barnard. The eventual 1992 settlement would be claimed as a victory by all—the ACLU, Barnard, and corrections. It allowed some double-bunking where prisoners spent time in areas outside their cells and prohibited double bunking in other areas.

"The conditions of confinement for inmates will have dramatically improved from when we filed the lawsuit," Parish told the *Tribune*. Both sides were probably right in claiming victory, and this a win-win resolution. Prison conditions improved somewhat, and the state saved money at the same time.

In any case, DeLand claimed he only lost eight cells to the lawsuit. His overall reaction revealed the pride in his legal expertise—"I charge lawyers their fees to teach them their business," he claimed.

This preoccupation with law degrees interested Barnard, who considered DeLand a frustrated non-attorney. The two went back to 1979, when Barnard filed an overcrowding suit against the Salt Lake County Jail. In consequent encounters, Barnard said, DeLand punched his knowledge of case law into virtually every conversation.

DeLand's aggressiveness was equated in Barnard's mind with the oppression within the prison. The civil liberties attorney shook his head over the prison employees who came to his office to consult about mistreatment they felt they suffered on the job. Barnard would bite his tongue to keep from asking them what they expected, considering the tales he heard from inmates.

Allegations of abuse at Point of the Mountain took numerous forms. One of the more documented involved a call on July 21 to the affiliate office from inmates who feared for the safety of inmate Kyle Harding. A guard had discovered Harding in a sex act with security captain Albert Walles. McAlister's investigation found "no evidence of forcible sexual abuse," and he allegedly warned the inmate to keep quiet. McAlister then allowed Walles to resign "for personal and health reasons."

By this time *Tribune* reporter Christopher Smart had "sift[ed] through hundreds of inmates to find reliable sources," one of whom told him that Harding's experience was not an isolated case. When Smart spoke with Harding, he was told that the young man had been assaulted many times. Smart sat down with McAlister and listened to his taped interviews. Smart concluded that the case was disregarded because the inmate was thought to be gay. Thus the encounter did not, in McAlister's view, constitute a non-consensual violation.

Believing he had uncovered both criminal conduct and an administrative cover-up, and knowing that crimes cannot be alleged in print without legal charges, Smart consulted county attorney David Yocom. Yocom had his own bind, he told Smart. He could not send investigators to the prison unless the complaint came to his office. Smart found a way for Harding to speak directly to county investigator Richard Forbes, and Yocom ordered an investigation. Smart wrote the story.

Later DeLand shrugged off the incident. McAlister had told him they had a problem, but it was investigated. Since Harding said nothing had happened, and Walles said his health wasn't good and he would retire early, and the officer who caught them didn't see much according to McAlister, DeLand figured the incident was resolved.

Ultimately the county filed criminal charges against Walles, and the Third District Court accepted a guilty plea. Not only did the conviction of a former corrections captain involve considerable "bad press" for the prison, but Smart later heard how incensed DeLand was to discover the reporter's role in getting the county involved.

Meanwhile ACLU cooperating attorney Ross Anderson negotiated Harding's removal to a halfway house or a county jail. Then, at the end of August, the Utah ACLU filed a class action lawsuit in Third District Court "on behalf of Kyle Harding and all other inmates in the Utah State Prison System who have been or are in danger of being assaulted by other inmates or prison personnel."

The lawsuit requested damages for Harding for assault and battery, "intentional and reckless infliction of emotional distress, and violation of United States and the Utah State constitutional protection against cruel and unusual punishment as evidenced in unsafe conditions of confinement." Thus the incident that corrections thought was not worth pursuing ended with a criminal conviction and a privately settled civil lawsuit.

"If it hadn't been for Chris Smart and Rocky Anderson," Yocom would say later, "we never would have discovered McAlister's cover-up of criminal activity." True, DeLand preferred in-house investigations, Yocom said, "but if that meant suppressing crime within the prison walls, that was of great concern to me."

DeLand, not surprisingly, resented the coverage overall. "Unnamed sources," DeLand would sneer. "Unnamed sources are nice because you can make up what you want to and fill in the holes."

"Making up" the news was not considered responsible journalism within the profession. Publishers became rightfully edgy when reporters used unnamed sources to shine a light into corners that would otherwise remain hidden. Smart protected the names of certain sources in the prison and began to gauge his effectiveness as a reporter by the ability of other journalists to follow his coverage. The age of pack reporting, however, involved inherent risks for both the reporter and the publication venturing too far in advance of the rest. As the heat rose under the Department of Corrections, the rumor circulated that the energy in the

Tribune's coverage stemmed from Smart's personal vendetta against DeLand.

Smart had come to the newspaper from a Park City weekly and took over the prison beat from social issues writer Carol Sisco. He did so, he said, without any strong opinions about corrections, initially giving DeLand the news space to respond to an article in another newspaper about deficient medical care. However, Smart's empty slate quickly developed a firm line down the middle.

While getting his bearings, Smart covered two luncheons that proved memorable. The Footprinters meeting of law enforcers heard a prison official explain that under DeLand's leadership rehabilitation was out. "We're going to put these guys behind bars until they're too old to commit crimes," a pleased audience heard.

At a Quantus Club luncheon, Smart heard Michele Parish tell a resistant audience that prisoners had certain inalienable rights, and that if the state was going to incarcerate them, it became responsible to see those rights protected. As he listened, Smart perceived two attitudes that were not only distinctly drawn but diametrically opposed.

The way DeLand remembered it, he originally liked Chris Smart and told prison officials to "feed him stuff, give him a break." But a misunderstanding over how and when Smart would run a story quickly eroded DeLand's enthusiasm. He liked to know what to expect.

By the time the prison sponsored a media tour to deflect pressure, the relationship was tense. As Smart remembered the event, DeLand kept "giving me the hairy eyeball" during the press conference. At the end Smart said, "Gary, why don't we clear the air." The other reporters filed out, and DeLand "yelled at me for a while," which was the beginning, Smart said, of DeLand "trying to bully me."

DeLand's memory differed. Smart, he said, "got cute" during the press conference, and DeLand dressed him down in front of his peers. DeLand claimed that the accompanying *Tribune* photographer, whose name DeLand could not recall, telephoned to say that Smart had sworn to get even. After that, DeLand said, "he came at me with a vengeance."

Both recalled a shouting session at the *Tribune* offices when DeLand and his aides came in. Editors fielded the complaints but backed their reporter in what DeLand would describe as "a very poor meeting."

Before long Smart would make the governor mad, too. At the end of a press conference at which Bangerter defended DeLand, Smart handed him a pathetic letter from an inmate, a letter Smart had opened on his way to the state capitol. Bangerter brushed it away, saying he got a lot of them, Smart recalled; but the reporter left it in his hand and walked off. Bangerter, who made his reply to Smart's back, considered the encounter an insult.

"Chris Smart was rude and out of line," Bangerter said, "and I called his editor and told him I wanted him to know he was rude. I got an apology." Bangerter would lay a good portion of DeLand's troubles at Smart's door, calling his coverage "unbalanced. He took what the prisoners said as law."

As the news coverage increased, the pressure on the Utah ACLU heightened, as well. Parish received criticism for playing to the media. From her perspective, the incidents reported were few in proportion to the incidents the affiliate encountered.

One received no publicity at all. The day after the sexual harassment lawsuit was filed, Parish wrote to Salt Lake County sheriff Pete Hayward, thanking him for his help in returning an AWOL inmate to prison. Fearing peer violence, the inmate had left a work detail, then didn't know what to do next. He called his mother and his wife, who called the ACLU. When Department of Corrections investigators found Parish's telephone number with the inmate's family, their visible outrage threw the family into a panic.

"DeLand was frantic to get him back," Parish recalled. "His family worried that prison security would shoot him." Unable to find an attorney eager to intervene, Parish finally called the sheriff. Now she thanked him for sending two deputies to meet the surrendering inmate at a Circle K convenience store in Sandy.

Although county attorney David Yocom confronted DeLand regarding the Harding case, as top county administrator he too tussled with the ACLU from time to time. The Salt Lake County Jail housed inmates convicted of misdemeanors, felonies, and—most crucial for civil libertarians—defendants awaiting trial. The jail population soared beyond its limits during the summer of 1989, and at September's end the Utah affiliate sued to drop the population to a previously negotiated limit. A class action suit was filed by Barnard, claiming jail conditions violated prisoners' Eighth and Fourteenth Amendment rights.

Dealing with Yocom regarding the jail, however, was different from dealing with DeLand. No ideological differences fueled the fight. Yocom juggled numbers within various categories of security between the downtown jail and the South Salt Lake facility which only accepted misdemeanants. Additionally, the county was suing the State of Utah for the costs of state prisoners sent to the jail rather than to prison.

In January 1991 Salt Lake County agreed to pay $12,000 to jail prisoners who claimed their rights had been violated. Parish praised Salt Lake County to the *Tribune:* "When we first got involved in this, conditions were very bad at the jail. When you overcrowd a space, it's unsafe for guards and unsafe for inmates." She added, "We've made a lot of progress in the last year. I think the county is to be commended for its sensible approach to this problem."

Yocom declined Parish's suggestion of a joint news conference. Nevertheless, he added, "I got along great with Michele, never a cross word."

Gradually penal officials across Utah were learning that a lawsuit could rattle dollars from lawmakers' pockets without politicians having to appear as if they liked prisoners. The ACLU could take that rap.

For instance, the Ogden *Standard-Examiner* reported a threatened ACLU investigation of overcrowding in the Weber County Jail, north of Salt Lake County. "Sheriff George Fisher said he's been expecting to hear from the ACLU, but he hopes the jail can work out the congestion problem without a court order." These negotiations would continue into 1993, with the help of the courts, although a lawsuit was not filed. An editorial cartoon showed Parish on a firing range taking aim at the Weber Jail after downing the Salt Lake County Jail and the Utah State Penitentiary.

In September 1989, when *Deseret News* columnist Dennis Lythgoe explored the ACLU, prison issues loomed large. Just as he had solicited comments from LDS spokesmen regarding religious issues, Lythgoe also called DeLand and McAlister to fulfill his editors' requests that he "balance the story," an effort that resulted in far fewer column inches given to Parish's comments than to her detractors'.

While church spokesmen were mild in their criticism, prison officials went after Parish with guns blazing. They blasted the ACLU's efforts to exempt long hair for traditional Native American inmates and to limit double bunking. In what would become a familiar theme, DeLand compared Parish unfavorably to her predecessors, claiming she had a "combative style":

> DeLand says some tension between corrections and the ACLU is healthy, but that tension has become extreme. He remembers having major arguments with previous directors, all of whom were strong personalities, but then negotiating differences without resorting to litigation.
>
> DeLand thinks this balance has been destroyed under Parish [due to] too much litigation and "gratuitous name calling." Both DeLand and Scott McAlister, inspector general, maintain that Parish takes her complaints to the press first, without first trying to solve problems. McAlister prefers strong communication, followed by a joint press conference, as an open, desirable way for them to work.

In response, Lythgoe wrote, "Parish thinks McAlister 'is not the easiest person to get along with.' She says that because corrections officials are 'unwilling to work with her,' the only way to deal with them is with attorneys."

However, he added, "McAlister believes Parish as a non-attorney previously inexperienced in ACLU procedures, suffers from ignorance. Those pursuing these cases for the ACLU, he says, 'don't know what the hell they're doing.'"

DeLand would later explain that McAlister went out of his way "to ruffle Michele's feathers." Although McAlister came across as belligerent, DeLand felt that Parish's stridency would assist corrections in the courtroom because judges tended to prefer discreet behavior.

Parish would have agreed only in part. She felt she could be outspoken because she was not an attorney. "Attorneys on the case can't raise hell," she explained.

Despite McAlister's blasts, the first dent was about to appear in his own armor. On August 18, 1989, a small Associated Press story about

McAlister was headlined in the *Deseret News*: "Utah official is questioned in Oregon slaying but isn't suspect." McAlister's former boss, Michael Francke, executive director of the Oregon Department of Corrections, had been murdered. Six months later the crime was still unsolved. The article began: "The inspector general for the Utah Department of Corrections was among people questioned in the unsolved slaying last January of the Oregon Corrections director, but he is not a suspect, officials said."

McAlister told the reporter the questioning did not "bother me at all." He added that he took a polygraph examination in order to satisfy members of Francke's family, whom McAlister believed had pressured investigators to question him since McAlister had been at odds with Francke. The article noted that McAlister left Oregon five days before Francke was killed outside his office. "Some news reports in Oregon have suggested the killing stemmed from corruption in the Oregon corrections department," the article reported, adding that it was a suspicion the district attorney denied. Eventually a former inmate was convicted, but, in hindsight, the story seemed a harbinger that not all of McAlister's ties to Oregon corrections could withstand scrutiny.

During the second half of 1989, as the battles shifted to prison officials opening inmates' mail from their attorneys and subsequent harassment, Parish poised a behind-the-scenes assault against McAlister. On October 11, 1989, attorney general R. Paul Van Dam received a hand-delivered letter from Parish regarding "an apparent conflict of interest between the intended role of the office of inspector general for the Utah Department of Corrections and the position of special assistant attorney general," both held by McAlister. "Because of this concern, the ACLU requests that your office clarify the responsibilities . . . of the inspector general."

The letter alleged that McAlister's combined role deprived inmates of an administrative grievance procedure even as independent investigations of prison policies and practices had vanished. "Thus, the only forum for inmates' challenges to prison practices is the courts. This consequence is inconsistent with the express role of the office of inspector general. . . ."

Though a non-attorney, Parish's points were given due consideration. Before the month's end the attorney general's office ruled that the two positions must be filled by separate officials—one as inspector general and the other as director of operations. In effect, McAlister had just lost a good share of turf.

By the end of November the battle reached the state's Republican legislature. Smart reported that Senator Kay S. Cornaby, co-chair of the appropriations committee over corrections, "has formally requested that the auditor general conduct a 'performance audit' of the Department of Corrections. The action," Smart wrote, "follows repeated calls by the American Civil Liberties Union for a full review of the Department of Corrections by the auditor general."

DeLand was quickly coming to regard Cornaby, a political conservative, as an enemy, probably due to "a clash of egos," DeLand said. He claimed that he and the governor had earlier discussed an audit by a "blue ribbon committee," which presumably would validate corrections. But now the timing would suggest an erosion of Bangerter's support for DeLand. Realizing they "had been beat to their own punch," DeLand said, Bangerter backed off.

Next Parish tried to open another front, when, on December 8, 1989, she sent presiding judge Scott Daniels of the Third District Court a memo requesting a grand jury investigation of the prison and the Salt Lake County Jail. Thirteen judges, however, decided against a grand jury probe as too time-consuming and costly.

A week later Parish testified before the House Judiciary Committee as an expert witness regarding the denial of access to the courts for prisoners. Her statement cited the monitoring of attorney-client communications, tampering with mail, confiscating legal materials, denying legal assistance, denying legal resources, and other allegations. In addition, she informed the committee head that the affiliate was about to file its class action lawsuit demanding improved medical, dental, and psychiatric care.

If the year's onslaught against the Department of Corrections represented artillery fire, the Utah ACLU now brought in its tanks. Parish's first year as executive director ended by filing the lawsuit on December 18, 1989. Cooperating attorneys Cullen Battle and Kathleen Switzer of Fabian & Clendenin led the front, joined by attorneys from the Legal

Center for the Handicapped. The class action suit alleged "that the deficient level of medical and mental health care provided by the institution constitutes cruel and unusual punishment prohibited by the Bill of Rights.

"Our named plaintiff in the suit is Sandra Henry," the lawsuit continued, naming an inmate with AIDS, "who has been repeatedly denied access to medical treatment. . . . But this suit is not just about her case . . . [but] on behalf of all Utah State Prison inmates, who are entitled to receive adequate, competent medical care. . . ." The ACLU provided historical background and asked the court to enter a permanent injunction to remedy the deficiencies in medical and mental health care "or to cease incarcerating inmates at the prison."

Battle shouldered the medical lawsuit out of lawyerly idealism, the sense that one should tackle a civil liberties case from time to time. When he realized the massive investigative detail and legal research involved, he willingly shared the load with Switzer, a new attorney eager to engross herself in a complex and significant case. "The medical conditions we ran into would shock the average conscience if people knew about them," Switzer said.

Both lawyers found Sandra Henry to be a suitable plaintiff. "We needed one person to go forward as the sole representative of the entire class," Battle explained. Some inmates with verified accounts of mistreatment wanted only to serve their time quietly and be released. Others seemed more interested in money or manipulating issues. But Henry made an impression. An HIV-positive inmate in poor health, she was being denied ACTH, the main treatment for AIDS at the time.

Once the lawsuit was filed, Henry achieved immediate notoriety within the penitentiary. "Everyone at the prison knew who Sandra Henry was—she took a big risk," Battle said. "At the time, she had no way of knowing she would get anything out of it but grief. She said, 'I have a fatal illness and nothing to lose. I want to make a contribution.'"

As if conflicts between the ACLU and corrections had not made the year 1989 sufficiently eventful, the year ended with a pair of implosions as Smart left the prison beat and McAlister exited corrections. The latter was a blast that would travel underground until it burst into the media shortly after the new decade began. McAlister's disgrace would be one story that Smart would not break.

The *Tribune* incident began, from Smart's perspective, as he considered a short stack of letters from inmates. Although the correspondents were housed in different cell blocks, they each alleged sexual abuse during strip searches. Even with corrections now in a defensive stance, Smart sensed his editors were growing weary. Nevertheless, he checked out the information and won an editor's support.

The article hit print, Smart recalled, just as one inmate, "David Jolivett, went crazy and had his own mini-riot." Corrections guards videotaped Jolivett's behavior in the day room, edited it down to a few frightening seconds, and turned it over to the television media. The timing wasn't good at the *Tribune*.

"Not only had I just written an article mentioning genitalia," thereby offending higher-ups, Smart would recall, but now his editors watched on television as an inmate railed and threatened prison officials. With his objectivity in question, Smart was taken off prison stories.

DeLand's tactic in publicizing the Jolivett incident not only shot down his media nemesis but took aim at Parish, as well. With the medical lawsuit filed, Parish had visited the prison and spoken with Jolivett and other inmates. Later that day, while screaming his fears and threats, Jolivett claimed that Parish told him his life was in danger. DeLand concluded that Parish had instigated what the electronic media billed a prison riot.

DeLand sent a transcript of the incident to the Utah ACLU's incoming board president, Boyer Jarvis, suggesting that the ACLU investigate itself just as corrections was obliged to do. On page four of the transcript, just before surrendering, Jolivett had said: "You have been hurting me every day since I've been in here. Physically and mentally. And I don't care."

The prison guard responded, "Well, I care about you, Dave."

The typed transcript indicated that Jolivett then said, "I'm gonna murder tonight," but an annotation in pen reworded it to say, "you're gonna be part of a murder tonight." Jolivett continued: "Do you know I had a meeting with the ACLU today. They told me you guys were trying to murder me. You are. You're gonna come in here and murder me."

Nothing, Michele Parish stressed later, nothing she had told Jolivett could be construed to suggest that his life was in danger.

DeLand's letter to Jarvis followed a mutual television appearance. Substituting for Parish, who had the flu, Jarvis had complimented DeLand, off-camera, for performing a difficult job well. On-camera Jarvis lobbied for additional funds so that corrections could respond to ACLU concerns. Disarmed by his opponent's affability, DeLand had agreed after the program to meet privately with him to discuss corrections issues.

Jarvis filled in for Parish only reluctantly. He said: "I'll go, but you have to remember I'm not going to perform the way you would perform. With that understanding, I will reluctantly show up."

Although Boyer enjoyed overcoming the correction chief's initial "belligerence," he found Michele "absolutely devastated" by his performance. "She felt that I had let her down, and I had double-crossed her. That was a major point in the development of our adversarial relationship."

Now DeLand wrote: "Following our joint appearance on KSL-TV's 'Focus' program, I expressed to members of my staff renewed hope and confidence in improved relations with the ACLU, and an end to the hostile, inflammatory rhetoric" from Parish. But, DeLand continued, "the events of the past week seem to indicate my optimism was premature."

As DeLand described the recent incident, "two inmates in the Utah State Prison's maximum security unit began assaulting the Uinta II day room area, breaking glass, destroying a television, an emergency exit sign, a wall-mounted telephone and a mail-drop box." The incident lasted two hours, Deland said, until the SWAT team "restored order in one minute and forty-five seconds using non-lethal take-down methods."

DeLand requested that Jarvis "investigate the actions and conduct" of Parish regarding "the role she may have played in triggering the disturbance" and her "unfounded, inaccurate claims concerning the event in interviews" with the media.

On January 9 Jarvis wrote back, indicating the board's support of Parish and dismissing DeLand's suggestion that she had triggered the incident. Jarvis suggested a meeting between DeLand, Nicholas Morgan

(DeLand's deputy and Jarvis's friend), Jarvis, and Parish at the ACLU office. This meeting did not occur. However, Jarvis later paid DeLand a personal visit to explain the board's position.

Even in retrospect DeLand clung to his view that Parish had provoked the violence. "She didn't say riot, but she said something relative to Jolivett's safety and what we might do. Then he took it a step further than he intended it to be taken." For a time DeLand refused to allow Parish at the prison without monitoring, but eventually he withdrew that restriction.

Recalling the incident, Jarvis said later, "We supported Michele fully, and she deserved to be supported. Those guys were trying to blame Michele for problems they weren't dealing with successfully. They were looking for a scapegoat, and Michele's behavior gave them ammunition."

Jarvis saw the legal pressure the ACLU was placing on corrections as separate from the cordial dialogue he wanted between administrators. "My recollection is there was no inclination on the part of the board to let up pressure on the lawsuit. I tried to mitigate the fireworks and stick with the issue." After the board's supportive vote, he told Parish he was going to meet with DeLand despite her disapproval. From that point on, Jarvis, DeLand, and sometimes Morgan would discuss "how to deal with miscreants and treat them humanely."

Despite these discussions, Jarvis was not trying to influence the lawsuit, he said; rather, "to let them know that I, at least, and other board members didn't think they were ogres, didn't want to embarrass them, but I was unwilling to muzzle our executive director." He added, "I was trying to get them to quit bear-baiting Michele!" Later Jarvis expressed puzzlement at the idea that he had traversed a proverbial minefield.

"Boyer thought of himself as a CEO and me as a secretary," Parish sighed. She interpreted Jarvis's inclination to fraternize with the legal adversary as well-intentioned but not harmless. Both at the time and later her view of herself as an activist determined her approach. "If you're going to play power politics with people in power, what are you going to play with? The people in power don't give you concessions to be nice, or even because it's the right thing to do. Because we were willing to be in their face and file lawsuits, we got things done."

On January 21, 1990, with Smart off the prison beat, *Tribune* staffer Paul Rolly examined Parish's latest dunk into hot water. He sketched her "front-line stand" with corrections officials on overcrowding, medical, and legal access issues, and DeLand's accusation that she had incited a riot by telling Jolivett his life was in danger.

Not only did Parish deny ever making such a suggestion, Rolly wrote, but "the prison has since recanted the claim, and the ACLU Board has taken the position that . . . DeLand is attempting to discredit" its executive director.

"My stands on behalf of inmates at the prison do not mean I like criminals," the article quoted Parish. "My client is the Bill of Rights. That's what ACLU is all about, and if we don't ensure constitutional protections for the fringes of our society, then they eventually won't mean much for the rest of us."

For a year Parish seldom visited the prison unless a major issue required it. Her board advised now, "You are in too much danger down there. At least get an attorney to go with you." For some time most business with inmates would be transacted by mail, even though the affiliate knew the mail was monitored. Any specific abuses that came to the affiliate's attention could be referred to lawyers.

The second implosion involved Scott McAlister. Even as DeLand flailed at Parish, he was losing his point man. The public was informed that McAlister had accomplished his goals and was therefore resigning his less-than-one-year tenure.

On December 29, 1989, the *Tribune* editorialized regarding McAlister's departure, exuding confidence in the paper's coverage and sounding a measured call for reform. The editorial suggested that ACLU lawsuits and other criticisms of the prison might well be placed at McAlister's door and noted that the attorney general had bisected McAlister's position. It also mentioned what the prison called "unfounded" charges of sexual harassment.

In fact, those sexual harassment allegations had Smart seething as he watched McAlister make a graceful exit. Smart knew that two women had obtained an attorney and were going public with their complaints. Unable to follow the story himself, Smart passed the information to a television reporter.

DeLand was experiencing a rough December. Later he said that he had reprimanded McAlister about relocating to his own office a corrections secretary he was dating and had investigated other rumors of hanky panky involving McAlister. While DeLand never believed coercion was involved in McAlister's relations, he also knew the law. As a supervisor, McAlister had power over the women's employment—that power formed the crux of sexual harassment.

Three days before Christmas, flanked by two administrators, DeLand called McAlister to his office. Immediately, DeLand said, one administrator insisted that DeLand leave the discussion to them. DeLand demurred, he said, but his associate persisted, saying that McAlister had been warned before. DeLand, who had been experiencing chest pains, went in for medical tests. By the time he returned, McAlister had been fired but wanted to see his friend.

DeLand met with him, he said, and assured McAlister he did not personally believe he was guilty of harassment. "I won't fight it," McAlister said, according to DeLand, "if you'll let me quit." On those terms, McAlister's resignation became public.

Then two weeks later KTVX-TV broke the story of McAlister's alleged sexual abuse of women employees. John Harrington reported live as FBI agents searched McAlister's home for evidence. Harrington telephoned Smart and invited him to the U.S. Attorney's Office for more on-camera coverage, but Smart was still stinging from his treatment at the newspaper. "No, you guys do it," he said. "I'm going to watch."

While the McAlister story caught and flared in one media outlet after another, the *Tribune* remained uncharacteristically silent. Finally, Smart recalled, an editor asked, "You want to get us something on this?"

"Yeah, sure," Smart replied. He was back on the prison beat.

On the "second-worst day of my life," DeLand said, noting that the first had been when two family members were killed, he walked into the Capitol for a budget hearing. The place was packed with reporters, cameras, and television lights—as DeLand described it, "the most news people I ever saw—if you threw a grenade, you could end a lot of people's troubles."

The reporters questioned him about the lewd films the FBI had found in McAlister's possession. Oddly enough, DeLand mused later, on the day he "ran the gauntlet" at the Capitol, Smart stayed the longest and showed the most sympathy.

On February 2, 1990, Smart reported that the FBI had seized forty-five videotapes, some of which involved children, after receiving information from a corrections employee. "The movies may have been evidence in a pornography case in Oregon, according to a federal search warrant," Smart reported, adding that transporting child pornography across state lines for exhibition was a felony.

County attorney David Yocom said he was offered the case by U.S. attorney Dee Benson, who felt the federal penalty was too harsh for the situation. Thus McAlister was arraigned in circuit court on a second-degree felony charge of exploitation of a minor. He was bound over to Third District Court. In due course a plea bargain was arranged, probation awarded, and McAlister left the state.

Ultimately four sexual harassment civil lawsuits were filed against McAlister and another prison administrator, each naming DeLand as corrections chief and demanding state funds in damages. Typically, DeLand wanted to fight. But the attorney general's office did not. In one instance DeLand insisted that the state hire private attorneys for him.

His lawyer told him "how bloody it would get, and that if I couldn't take it, I'd better settle." DeLand answered, "I already judge whether to read the newspaper by whether my wife's crying or not." One lawsuit alone was settled with a payment of $95,000 in taxpayer dollars and several other settlements followed.

Somewhere around that time, DeLand went to see Bangerter, who was considering running for a third term. "I said, 'Maybe I'm a problem for you. If you want, I'll resign. I'm not doing what I promised I could do for you, and did do in the first few years.'" Early on, DeLand said, Bangerter's press secretary had expressed amazement at the positive press coverage corrections had received.

Now, DeLand claimed, "The governor said, 'Gary, every time you have a battle with Chris Smart or the ACLU, my mail goes up enormously and it runs two hundred to one in your favor.'" Nevertheless both the governor and the corrections chief would begin their separate plans to leave public service.

Throughout 1990 the ACLU kept the pressure on, protesting overcrowding of inmates and the parole policies that promoted it. However, some quiet changes were happening behind the scenes. On June 15, 1990, Parish wrote to Lynn Lund at the State Government Trust to document four points of agreement regarding mental health care within the criminal justice system.

Also in 1990 Parish lobbied the legislature for funding for the Department of Corrections to improve medical care, relieve overcrowding, and boost education and rehabilitation programs. She hoped this effort showed her clash with prison officials represented a true reform effort and not simply a battle of personalities.

The cast of characters was changing on all sides. In June 1990 Jarvis resigned as board president after a final tiff with Parish, and John Morris became board president. "John has a great ability to untangle things," Parish would say later, "and he did it a number of times. He ran interference for me."

By year's end Gary DeLand announced he intended to resign in a year or so. "I knew what it was costing me," he said later. "It was hard on my wife, and my sons had grown up during those seven years. I thought of the things I used to be able to do—take a month off, or take my wife with me [consulting], and then stay an extra week if we wanted to."

As Bangerter, who had decided not to run for a third term, would explain: "Over time, DeLand became more testy, and it was just time to leave, the same as it was time for me to leave." DeLand, Bangerter maintained, had done a good job. A friend of DeLand's, Lane McCotter, was being eased into prison administration. Few knowledgeable observers doubted that McCotter, plucked from the Texas corrections system, would become the Department of Corrections' next executive director.

Nevertheless, Parish thought it worth trying to influence the selection of DeLand's replacement. On March 19, 1991, she wrote to Bangerter's chief of staff, Bud Scruggs, to "follow up on our discussion of possible nominees. . . ." Parish suggested several and referred Scruggs to Al Bronstein, heading the ACLU's National Prison Project. She closed with, "Personally, I hope the ACLU can develop a working relationship with corrections, so that problems can be resolved amicably as they arise without having to resort to the courts at the expense of Utah taxpayers." She added, "I regret that with Scott McAlister and Gary DeLand this relationship has not been so characterized."

The next day Scruggs wrote back, thanking Parish for her suggestions and saying, "I need to get to work on this right away since I have no idea how long Gary DeLand plans to stay and do not want to see us rushed into a decision on this one."

A month later Dennis Lythgoe wrote an upbeat feature on Lane McCotter for the *Deseret News* with a traditional headline, "Utah really is 'right place' for prison official's family." The article pointed out that McCotter, DeLand's expected successor, moved to Utah from Texas for personal reasons. The McCotters' oldest son had been killed in an accident in Puerto Rico while serving an LDS mission, and the family had decided to bury him in Utah where they wanted to retire. "So they buried him in Midway and then bought a home intended for their retirement, without realizing that they would be back sooner...." Wrote Lythgoe: "He said he enjoys working with DeLand, has great respect for him, and hopes DeLand will be persuaded to stay on longer—at least through Governor Norm Bangerter's final term in office and even beyond."

In reality, DeLand already had one foot out the door and McCotter one foot in. After resigning, DeLand continued his consulting business, writing jail standards, prison standards, and testifying in numerous lawsuits for penitentiaries and jails. He and his wife would relocate to St. George in southwestern Utah and build a house near Snow Canyon.

At his retirement roast, DeLand received an inflatable doll named Michele. Although during his tenure his language turned blue when discussing his nemesis at the ACLU, over time his memory would trigger more ire for Chris Smart. Parish "ran her mouth before she got her brain in gear" and was combative, he said. "It became a personality thing," he said dismissively, "a sideshow."

No one watching corrections was surprised when McCotter became one of Bangerter's last appointments before retirement, or when the new governor, Republican Mike Leavitt, confirmed McCotter's post.

New faces appeared in the editorial offices of the *Salt Lake Tribune*, as well, even as corrections continued to protest Smart's coverage. The articles appeared less frequently and were buried inside, in Smart's opinion, rather than given front-page coverage. Smart asked to be taken off the prison beat again and by fall 1992 was covering city-county government. Occasionally he heard from prison sources and once in a while wrote an article since he had no official replacement.

As the 1992 election approached, Smart listened to an inmate's telephoned complaint that they had been ordered to destroy prison property. Currently Smart was covering the attorney general race and a referendum on whether a light rail should be built through Salt Lake County. He asked some questions, jotted notes, and hung up. He never found time to check out the information, let alone write a story.

In late October a thick, cross-referenced transcript was hand-delivered to the *Tribune* editor. It contained excerpts from years of Smart's telephone conversations with inmates. (All inmate conversations were taped, DeLand said, but Smart's had been "red-flagged.") Underlined were Smart's offhand comments about DeLand, other prison officials, and even editors who would not always print his stories. Reporters would recognize Smart's comments as typical "schmooze" that builds rapport, resists manipulation by sources, and explains printed results. On most beats, perhaps, the language would be more refined.

Still, a series of demoralizing meetings followed, Smart said, and he decided to finish his election stories and then quit. Yocom ordered an investigation into the prison wiretapping, but no wrongdoing was found. In the flurry of press following Smart's departure, the *Tribune* denied having been intimidated by the Department of Corrections, and the newspaper alternately praised and criticized Smart's coverage. "One day I was a 'courageous reporter' and the next day I was a bum," Smart summarized.

McCotter defended corrections' actions to the Associated Press, claiming that Smart had been a security risk. Biased coverage, McCotter claimed, might reduce appropriations to corrections by the next legislature. That could reduce the number of prison guards. When Parish heard this, she hooted. But when she was quoted, she discreetly denounced McCotter's reasoning as "Nixonian logic."

During 1991 and 1992 Parish enjoyed the satisfaction of a hard-won triumph as stipulations were hammered out regarding prison medical care. The fall 1992 ACLU *Reporter* announced: "ACLU Wins Five Year Battle: Prison to Build Mental Hospital." It reported that the Department of Corrections had agreed to build a forensic psychiatric hospital as well as to "institute critical improvements in the treatment of mentally ill inmates, who constitute approximately 15 percent of the inmate population." Medical and dental stipulations would follow in the next few months.

The article recognized the attorneys responsible for the victory including Cullen Battle, Kathleen Switzer, and Robert Heineman of Fabian & Clendenin; Alexa Freeman and Mark Lopez from the ACLU's National Prison Project; and Mary Rudolph and Lisa Marcy from the Center for Persons with Disabilities.

Perhaps Parish, more than anyone, understood the measure of that victory. She knew firsthand from inmates and their families, from the blast of pressure from the state, and sometimes from within the affiliate how high the stakes had been. If the Utah ACLU had not been willing to take on the combined power of DeLand and the State of Utah on behalf of those least empowered, she said, no one else would have stopped the abuses.

Yet even as the stipulated agreements were grudgingly welded into legal documents, DeLand fired a final volley. "It's the ACLU's job to file suit against the prison," he said, "it's what they sued me over that I don't like. Robyn Blumner and I had made a deal, a gentlemen's agreement on medical care, and I was keeping it."

Accordingly, the state attorney general's office filed an appeal protesting payment of the ACLU lawyers. DeLand claimed that the prison had been in line with, or ahead of, its "master plan" in reforming medical conditions, and that the former ACLU executive director had confirmed its progress. Thus the lawsuits were mean-spirited and frivolous, DeLand claimed; what's more, they had not accomplished a thing.

7.
The Scarlet Issue

The gap between the State of Utah and the ACLU on civil liberties matters widened to a polar position on reproductive rights. The Utah ACLU stood firmly with the national organization on this vanguard issue; automony within one's own body crystallized the essence of civil liberty as the concept of privacy developed as an implicit constitutional guarantee. The state aligned itself with LDS church policy, which had liberalized in recent decades only to the extent of weighing the mother's life, health, or victimization in dire and documented instances against bringing a pregnancy to term. Each entity reached far into its own ethos when it came to the legality of abortion, with neither inclined to compromise very much.

Of course the Catholic church presented a strong anti-abortion stance across the United States, but in Utah that burden fell most heavily to Mormonism. The official view was that abortion represented a "like unto" sin associated with the Old Testament's commandment, "Thou shalt not kill." Even if a pregnancy endangered a mother's life or health, or resulted from rape or incest, a woman needed priesthood authorization to abort. The counseling might include her spouse, parents, or doctor. Disobedience jeopardized church membership.

Given the strength and commonality of this philosophy among Utah's citizenry, perhaps it was not surprising that while abortion politics disrupted some cities, the Beehive State remained quiet. Demonstrations on both sides blossomed outside the annual meeting of the legislature, but broader protests were discouraged by the power structure as divisive, distasteful, and unnecessary.

In the early 1990s the mostly Anglo, male, Mormon legislature prepared to lead the battle against legal abortion. No one doubted that any restriction would be challenged by the Utah ACLU under *Roe v. Wade*, which only gave the contemplated law a far wider impact. If successfully defended, a law passed on Capitol Hill could affect the nation.

The law that was enacted in 1991 echoed LDS church policy, passing the secular decision to terminate pregnancy from priesthood leader to doctor. Again, regardless of circumstance, the pregnant woman could not decide on her own. Thus the law essentially constituted a ban, although it allowed for certain exceptions that were unpopular among die-hard pro-lifers.

Significantly, though coincidentally, the abortion issue sizzled to a boil during the same years that the school prayer issue erupted in its own cloud of steam. Throughout, the affiliate sued for prisoner rights and pressed a host of less publicized concerns which, in the public mind, mingled to give an overall impression. From the traditional ACLU perspective, the affiliate's causes were classic defenses of those with minimal power—prisoners, minority religions, unbelievers, and marginalized women. The opposite view held that the ACLU coddled those most dangerous to society and decried all that was holy, including the beginnings of human life.

A wrinkle that lay buried in the gray matter of Mormon culture and invariably filtered into issues of life and death was the nineteenth-century concept of "blood atonement." Though historians demurred as to its actual practice, the doctrine that held sway in sermons and folklore claimed that major sins such as murder and adultery could be atoned only by shedding a sinner's blood. Whether blood atonement was practiced commonly, rarely, or never in the nineteenth century, it remained conceptually present in temple rites and still affected people's thinking around the death penalty. For instance, while the ACLU battled to prevent Gilmore's and Selby's executions, within at least two other high-profile multiple murder cases in the 1980s relatives expressed preference for execution. This, they thought, would redeem their wayward relatives in the afterlife.

With abortion considered like unto murder, the concept of blood atonement cast an indefinite but pervasive shadow. Likely it would never be mentioned during a secular discussion of abortion, yet among a people feeling so strongly the appropriate penalty for murder, it could not be discounted. Mormons argued the abortion question along the rational track taken by most pro-life groups, but below that track lay somewhat different ground.

Given all these factors, the Utah ACLU operated in an inflamed climate. For some Utahns the very acronym was a buzzword for the hiss of the anti-Christ, and the ranks against the ACLU tightened, waving the abortion ban like a banner. For others "ACLU" represented more than ever the champion of individual rights in an overwhelmingly homogeneous state. Accordingly, members and dollars flowed toward the affiliate in an unprecedented wave. As with prayer, prison, and other hot issues, the abortion question became a rallying point.

Michele Parish boosted the number of affiliate members donating more than $1,000 per year from a single generous donor to more than thirty. One tactic involved encouraging sympathetic lawyers to take others to lunch and ask for the donation. When issues heated up, Parish became "mildly notorious" as a lunch partner who would exchange stimulating discussion for a donation. "I was always looking for ways to raise money," she said, explaining that this was how interested bystanders "got to play" in the political arena.

A poll in the *Salt Lake Tribune* on January 30, 1990, illustrated the polarity the ACLU provoked among the general public. Nineteen percent approved of the ACLU stand on capital punishment, its challenge to prison conditions, or its effort to clarify the legality of prayer in schools. Forty percent disapproved. Interestingly, a total of 42 percent either abstained, were undecided, or were unaware of one or more issues—perhaps the majority that Governor Bangerter observed as considering such discussions "yawners." Nevertheless, the poll showed that among those who cared, easily twice as many condemned the ACLU as supported it. The abortion question was not included, but nothing suggested that the results would differ.

As executive director, Parish spoke for reproductive rights as forthrightly as she did on other issues and found a responsive audience among those aligned with women's issues. In 1990 Parish received the Woman of Courageous Action Award from the Utah National Organization for Women. The NOW newsletter cited "her unswerving dedication to the principles of the Bill of Rights, her fight with prison administrators, her battle against prayer in the public schools, . . . and her willingness to speak out on the abortion issue." A year later Parish received the Susa Young Gates award from the Utah Women's Political Caucus. She also became secretary of the national ACLU's International Human Rights Task Force and began dreaming of organizing an ACLU affiliate within the Soviet Union, which was then undergoing social change. As the issues bore her into battle, Parish's horizons widened and her sense of what might be accomplished increased.

During cross-affiliate chats with Robyn Blumner, Parish would recall her mentor's surprise: "Robyn would say, 'God, I can't believe you're the same woman!—this quiet little minister's wife who came in with a huge unfinished novel and a handful of clippings.'" In reality, throughout 1990 Parish found it more and more difficult to remain a minister's wife. Fencing with skilled and determined foes in one ideological arena after another and claimed by an incessantly ringing telephone, her attention was compelled by each day's challenges. Her work became so absorbing that family and church, which once dominated her life, now seemed far less urgent. Tensions developed as her priorities changed.

"You need a certain level of hysteria to be happy," she would recall her husband saying. Parish considered that hyperbolic. Yet she admitted that if she ever became bored, she would probably "get into trouble." Her husband's reaction to her NOW award carried a sting: "You're not a woman of courageous action. You're just a neurotic, driven woman." In retrospect she would "feel more compassion" for that response, realizing the gap that had widened between her public and personal worlds. But before year's end, Parish would conclude that her prayer to be more than "just a minister's wife" in Utah had been answered in the most painful way she could imagine—with a divorce. Yet her ACLU directorship seemed to culminate her political activism during college and all the years she spent caring for people and developing a spiritual life. "This job was a real fulfillment of all those parts of my life." They removed the hyphen between the last names Parish and Pixler, and their daughters divided each week between Michele's home in Salt Lake City and Wesley's new home and congregation in Ogden.

While struggling with the dissolution of her marriage, Parish threw herself into ACLU battles. In her odd moments, she consulted with small ACLU affiliates on fund raising and administration. Early in 1991 she visited the University of Utah and organized a student chapter, with Marlayn Cragun as representative and staff associate. All in all, she did not appear likely to become bored soon. If nothing else, the abortion battle would see to that.

Right to privacy was a concept that did not emerge all at once but gathered force during the long conflict over a Connecticut birth control law which U.S. Supreme Court justice John Marshall Harlan argued was "an intolerable and unjustifiable invasion of privacy in the conduct of the most intimate concerns of an individual's personal life." Quoting Harlan, author Samuel Walker wrote, "Privacy was no longer a question of search and seizure but a civil liberties issue that directly touched the lives of millions of middle- and upper-middle-class Americans."

The idea gained strength in 1965 when "an activist civil libertarian majority," as Walker called it, ran the highest court. "In *Griswold*, Justice William O. Douglas found a constitutional right of privacy in what he termed the 'penumbras' and 'emanations' of the Bill of Rights. . . ." These subtleties, Douglas wrote, were apparent in the First Amendment freedom of association, the Third Amendment prohibition of quartering soldiers, the Fourth Amendment protection against unreasonable searches and seizures, the Fifth Amendment protection against self-incrimination, and finally the Ninth Amendment declaration that people retained rights not specified in the Constitution.

This sweeping assertion surprised legal scholars who hastened to understand its full impact. Certainly *Griswold* confirmed the public's rapidly rising expectation of privacy, but it also laid the foundation for a constitutional attack on existing criminal abortion laws. A backlash was certain, although it took a little time to develop. "Penumbras" and "emanations" seemed shaky to some legal scholars. When the newly affirmed concept of privacy underwrote a movement as controversial as reproductive rights, the backlash became fierce enough to polarize Americans from the mid-1970s on.

ACLU involvement preceded the action by almost a decade. It adopted the issue in 1967 and refined its stance in 1968, supporting a woman's right to an abortion "prior to the viability of a fetus." The stage was set for the historic and controversial Supreme Court decision.

Walker wrote: "*Roe v. Wade* swept aside existing criminal abortion laws, with Justice Harry Blackmun holding that the right to privacy included a woman's right to an abortion." Blackmun did not uphold an absolute right but differentiated by a pregnancy's trimesters with the state's interest increasing as the pregnancy advanced. "Sorting his way through the complex moral and medical considerations, Blackmun rejected the anti-abortion argument that the fetus was a person entitled to protection of the Fourteenth Amendment."

As the high court stood firm through the 1970s, Utah's senator Orrin Hatch introduced a constitutional amendment in 1983 stating that "a right to abortion is not secured by this Constitution." It lost by only one vote in the senate. A year earlier the senate had tabled a similar human life statute, again by one vote.

Although the right-to-life movement became increasingly vocal, most Americans favored keeping abortion legal. One in five favored the extremes—an unlimited right or no right. The remaining 60 percent wanted abortion legal in consultation with a physician and restricted by the stage of the pregnancy.

After Congress failed to pass an anti-abortion amendment, "the right-to-life movement began to unravel in an acrimonious feud between hard-liners who wanted to ban all abortions and pragmatists who were willing to accept an exception for rape and incest victims," Walker wrote. Ultimately the power to decide remained with the Supreme Court. For almost two decades following *Roe v. Wade*, the court upheld it against attempts to breach the bulwark. However, the composition of the court changed, and during the 1980s the justices began to retreat. At that point, the ACLU, among others, switched tactics, fighting not to gain ground but to hold the line.

THE SCARLET ISSUE

By the early 1990s states were allowed to express a preference for pregnancy and to restrict access to abortions, although they could not prohibit them entirely. Bit by bit, state regulations tightened access. Pennsylvania required informed consent—mandatory counseling and advisement of other options, then tried to impose a twenty-four-hour waiting period and spousal consent, but those were struck down.

As the fortress door inched open, forces pushing against it took heart and pushed harder. The Utah legislature hoped to provide the hardest shove of all, one with enough muscle to knock it down.

When the legislature convened in 1990, Governor Norm Bangerter would say later, the body expressed the hard-liners' eagerness for an absolute ban, which the more moderate governor considered indefensible. From Walker's point of view, Bangerter was a pragmatist in a pro-life camp, insisting that sensitive aspects of the issue be considered. A transcript prepared for the ACLU and Planned Parenthood by affiliate intern Sharon Smith caught the governor's words in his State of the State address:

> The depth of our desire to protect the unborn must be tempered by two important considerations: first, we must be sensitive to those limited circumstances, and I emphasize the word "limited," in which women ought to have abortion available as an option. In cases where there is a grave threat to the life and health of the mother, or when the fetus suffers from profound and irreversible disabilities, or in cases of rape or incest, termination of the pregnancy may be appropriate. . . . The decision as to whether or not to have an abortion is the most difficult a woman in counsel with her loved ones and her doctor will ever make. . . . One of the founding principles of our republic is that we do not punish those who in good faith and in good conscience make the very best decision they can. We need to honor this principle as we attempt to legislate the activity of those who struggle to make morally correct decisions that protect the sanctity and dignity of life, both of the born and the unborn.

Another consideration was that since *Roe v. Wade* was decided in 1973, legislatures had not controlled the issue, Bangerter continued:

FRIENDLY FIRE

> In 1989 the *Webster* decision signaled the beginning of a process that I personally hope will eventually lead to the reversal of *Roe v. Wade*. . . . There is, however, no indication that the Court is willing to accept the kind of wholesale restriction of abortion most of us would like to see. Let me spell it out very carefully. If we pass a bill that is ruled unconstitutional we will not have saved the life of one child. Not one. Does this mean we can only pursue a measure that is guaranteed approval by the Court? Of course it doesn't. We must be willing to take some risk . . . but we must not waste our time or resources on dramatic gestures that have no real chance of success.

Bangerter wanted the legislators to "do their homework." That meant hearings throughout the state to learn what the general citizenship wanted. This process provided a legislative history to show judges or justices the intent behind the law.

Doctors who wished to participate in the hearings and later became ACLU plaintiffs perceived the hearings as one-sided, tipped dramatically toward the anti-abortion position. Jeff Oritt, an attorney well versed in reproductive rights, agreed to champion the cause for ACLU-Utah and, in the spring of 1990, invited colleague Howard Lundgren aboard. Along with Planned Parenthood, they considered a lawsuit, knowing that the national ACLU would shoulder most of the burden. As legislation was postponed until the following year, Lundgren said, "all actors were put on notice that something would happen in 1991."

Even as both sides assembled their ammunition, the *Salt Lake Tribune* reported in June 1990 that two other states were lobbying volleys against the Supreme Court. In a six-to-three vote, the court upheld an Ohio law requiring notification of one parent when unmarried girls sought abortions. With a five-four vote, the high court split even closer, striking down a Minnesota law requiring notification of both parents. By another five-four vote, however, the justices upheld a portion of the Minnesota law requiring approval of both parents or a judge.

The newspaper reported that Utah was split as well: "A Utah pro-life group said the decisions clear the way for the state to enact tougher parental notification laws. But the [ACLU] sees the rulings as eroding women's rights. . . ." In Utah doctors were required to notify parents or a guardian "if possible" of a minor's abortion. Rosa Goodnight, president of Right to Life of Utah, told the *Tribune* her group wanted both parents to be notified, with no exceptions.

The ACLU regarded the judicial trend as chilling, so Parish announced that she would not challenge the current parental notification law and risk the high court's decision. "I sympathize with parents wanting to be involved in their daughter's decision, but teens who don't want to notify their parents usually have a good reason," she said, citing incest as one example.

Bangerter did not relish an abortion war in Utah; later he would vigorously and unsuccessfully resist congressional hearings in the state. "I would have preferred that the battle be fought somewhere else because in our community these issues end up becoming so divisive." However, lawmakers surged through their "homework" hearings and emerged in January 1991 with another total ban. The governor was not pleased. "I told them, 'I don't agree with this, and it will never pass muster with the Supreme Court.'"

In his 1991 State of the State address, the governor announced that if the legislature sent him the bill they'd drawn up, he'd veto it. After the speech, "the pro-choicers thought I'd done away with it," Bangerter related. "But I'd outlined what was acceptable to me, and that's what they passed." The exceptions specified reported rape or incest and medical causes—precisely those allowed by the LDS church.

Bangerter said he had not known the exact LDS position on abortion, and that church leaders never tried to influence him on the subject. Nor did they lend support when he resisted a total ban. A pro-life stance was ingrained within the community consciousness, and LDS policy fell with slight variation from the lips of most candidates for public office, to enter the public's ears sounding familiar and reasonable.

The Criminal Abortion Statute slid through the 1991 legislature on January 21 and landed under the governor's pen with such speed that it shocked the ACLU and other pro-choice advocates. As Lundgren recalled: "Then this bill came to the floor, and in a matter of hours had passed, and in a matter of days had been signed. That bill was entirely contrary to what we thought [Bangerter] would do."

Democratic attorney general Paul Van Dam told the legislators he did not believe their bill was defensible in court. But not even that slowed the impetus. As a result, the complaint that Oritt and Lundgren had readied for district court and recently set aside suddenly gained immediacy and focus.

Bangerter would call the Criminal Abortion Statute "my bill." Personally, he said, he conceded the mother's dominant right to decide, "but there comes a time when the fetus needs someone to consider its lesser right. The mother has the right, but needs another opinion to support her interest when at the expense of the baby."

The new law neither allowed abortion unconditionally with a doctor's consultation during the first trimester, as did *Roe v. Wade*, nor banned it completely after the first trimester, as many pro-lifers advocated. Even *Roe v. Wade* favored pregnancy over abortion as fetal development advanced.

Bangerter viewed it as a "pro-choice bill, if you read it." He explained, "We just required a doctor to say there is a good reason—a deformed fetus, rape or incest, or health of the mother. Then you don't have a little girl making a decision in a vacuum. At least a doctor is backing her up." Bangerter felt that willing doctors would not be hard to find. "We give doctors a lot of sway in our society," he said. "You turn on LDS general conference and someone says the church president isn't there because his doctor said he shouldn't come."

Civil libertarians could scarcely grasp this reasoning when it was explained to them. No reason other than a woman's choice was needed during pre-viability; the requirement for any authority's sanction violated *Roe v. Wade* and was anathema to the concept of privacy. More practically, Oritt and Lundgren found the bill's language vague, and so did the growing number of doctors who would file suit against it. What constituted "grave harm"? How would "good faith and best medical judgment," as Bangerter described it, be interpreted in actual situations?

"We had no guarantee that some prosecutor in Juab County or somewhere wouldn't feel that a woman who was [clinically] depressed due to the pregnancy was not suffering enough to have an abortion," Lundgren said. "Our position was that this was the most restrictive law passed in the country and provided a ban on virtually all abortions. Furthermore, it was passed with the special purpose of challenging *Roe v. Wade*."

Not only did the medical definitions cause concern among some doctors, but the ACLU objected that legal standards imposed on victims of rape or incest were almost impossible. "The reporting requirement killed one's realistic ability to obtain an abortion because of the data showing that many, many women don't report those crimes, and that reluctance to report is a psychological after-effect of that type of assault," Lundgren said.

The lawsuit prevented the new law from being enforced. On April 6, 1991, the *Tribune* announced: "Showdown Set: ACLU Files Suit Against Abortion Law." Staffer Dawn House wrote: "The ACLU has filed a federal lawsuit challenging the constitutionality of Utah's new anti-abortion law, believed to be the toughest in the nation." Filed in U.S. District Court, the suit represented ten physicians, ten religious leaders, four counselors, Planned Parenthood, the Utah Women's Clinic, and a pregnant woman whose name was not used.

Under the pseudonym Jane Liberty, the central plaintiff wrote, "I know the state of Utah wants me to have another baby. But the state is not raising my two children, I am." Liberty did not claim rape, incest, a deformed fetus, or grave danger to her health or mortality. She did not claim, as the governor had explained, "a medical person who says there is a need for it."

Certain doctors joined the suit due to the law's broad language. Technology enabled *in utero* surgery to mitigate fetal distress and the use of fertility drugs to encourage pregnancy. Once a cluster of embryos developed within a uterus, typically some were interfered with so that the rest could develop. The old abortion law—already problematic given these new procedures—was also challenged in the lawsuit. Doctors wanted to know exactly what procedures would be considered illegal. Quickly the medical issues became some of the most difficult to solve, sparking litigation for years. But the confusion did not end there.

As the ACLU sought temporary restraining orders and preliminary injunctions against the Criminal Abortion Law, the question arose whether the law was worth a million dollars from taxpayers to defend it. The *Tribune* reported: "Governor Bangerter said he would not attempt to enforce the law until the Supreme Court reviews it." Bangerter referred reporters to Utah attorney general Paul Van Dam, in charge of coordinating the law's defense, despite Van Dam's earlier opposition to the legislation.

Bangerter's aide Bud Scruggs defended the potential cost, saying that "sometimes principles have price tags," which seemed to summarize the pro-life feeling in the state. However, Scruggs's comment annoyed those whose principles led them to oppose the ban.

For instance, the lawsuit objected to spousal notification, which required even a battered woman to tell her abusive husband. A woman must inform her husband no matter what, even if another man had fathered the child. In addition, the ACLU raised the rights of counselors and clinics who might advise women. Could they, too, be prosecuted under the new law?

While the Utah affiliate undertook litigation, the ACLU National Reproductive Rights Project stirred the public. They ran a large advertisement in the *New York Times* that broke waves of shock and resentment in Utah. In big type, the ad began: "IN UTAH, THEY KNOW HOW TO PUNISH A WOMAN WHO HAS AN ABORTION. SHOOT HER." The smaller print explained that on April 28, a new law would go into effect. "Under it, a woman who has an abortion could be sentenced to the death penalty. In Utah, that means the firing squad. (Or she may choose lethal injection as an alternative.)"

It continued: "Virtually no woman will be able to escape this law. Because it prohibits virtually all abortions—even in most cases of rape and incest." The ad gave background, then quoted the bill's sponsor, Senator LeRay McAllister: "It isn't as serious as it appears." "Not serious?" the ad jeered. "Maybe they had some less serious penalties in mind. Life imprisonment, perhaps."

The ad announced the lawsuit and included a donation slip for readers' convenience. It suggested that people write to Utah's governor and lobby their own representatives in Congress to protect reproductive rights. With devastating insight, the message combined the new abortion law, the state's death penalty, and the sentiments and beliefs underlying them, then projected the extreme result.

As politicians and LDS officials scrambled to explain that no Utah woman would be shot for having an abortion, national boycotts sprang up against conventions and other activities in Utah. Civic leaders and economic gurus voiced concern. Scruggs shrugged off the threat with, "We believe the ACLU and NOW talk to the fringes. They reach the kind of people we don't want to come to Utah anyway."

This flippant remark provoked a local uproar which echoed as the statement was picked up by the national media. It seemed to reinforce the image the *New York Times* ad projected of a place where difference of opinion was unwelcome.

The legislature was summoned to a special session to remove criminal liability for women and their counselors. "We left a penalty for a doctor performing an illegal abortion," Bangerter would say later, "but we tried not to second-guess medical judgment."

Meanwhile the governor emphasized to Scruggs and other aides what he later would tell the International Olympic Committee, then considering northern Utah as a site for the 1996 Winter Games, that the statute allowed reasonable exceptions. He explained, "I can see the pro-choice side; some people can't. I can see a powerful argument for a woman to be the sole determinant for what happens to her body. I lean toward her having the major say, but there's another life at whatever degree of development, and it's entitled to some protection." Both sides, however, continued to see the law as a ban overall and defend or attack it as such.

At the end of May, the *Tribune* announced that Scruggs would be leaving in August "to embark on a career outside the political arena." Scruggs admitted to "getting beaned" by his abortion comment. He said he "always believed public service is best in short doses."

The article concluded: "As the governor's chief of staff, Scruggs has been known to make statements often considered irreverent by the target of the comment, especially the American Civil Liberties Union." Indeed, Parish had written to Scruggs objecting to one of his sallies that characterized her as anti-religious. Nevertheless the two achieved an amiable relationship. Scruggs joined the faculty at Brigham Young University in Provo.

Below the fireworks, the process of readying the ACLU lawsuit galvanized with Janet Benshoof of the National Reproductive Rights Project who would serve as lead counsel. Even after Benshoof left the

ACLU to found the Center for Reproductive Law and Privacy, she continued as lead attorney.

When Benshoof and other New York attorneys appeared in Salt Lake's courts, Lundgren said later, they tended to get a "bad rap" in the city's media. However, in working with them, Lundgren found the attorneys "intelligent, competent, and very aggressive." The New York style didn't defer to the local sensibilities as people would have liked, Lundgren said, "but people forget this was an extremely politically-charged lawsuit." Even some attorneys on the ACLU's local legal panel suggested a more conciliatory approach.

Meanwhile, the State of Utah ran into lawyer problems when the eminent firm Jones, Waldo, Holbrook, and McDonough was forced to withdraw over a conflict of interest. Mary Anne Wood, a professor at BYU's law school, became the strident lead counsel for the state's defense.

In May *Deseret News* reporter Ellen Fagg wrote that scores of doctors had joined the lawsuit. "Dr. Julian DeLia pioneered an intricate laser surgery technique that he performs on unborn babies who have twin-transfusion syndrome," she wrote. This associate professor of medicine developed a "high-risk, innovative technique to fuse shut placenta cells between twins when the blood flows just one way. Technically, the surgery is against Utah law, which prohibits experimentation on unborn children, except for genetic testing."

Due to concerns over these types of procedures, the article explained, 177 members of the American College of Obstetricians and Gynecologists had joined the ACLU lawsuit against the new and the previous abortion laws. "The association says the doctors fear prosecution under the criminal statute."

The next day, May 18, 1991, the *Salt Lake Tribune* reported that about 34 percent of the active Utah members in the American College of Obstetricians and Gynecologists had voted against joining the lawsuit but were outnumbered by 65 percent of their colleagues. One percent remained undecided. The minority were angry at being outvoted.

The newspaper cited Parish's belief that the state had declared "open season on doctors." According to Parish, "Even by taking away the homicide penalties in the last legislative session, the law can still imprison doctors for up to five years."

E. Reed Heywood, chief of obstetrics at LDS Hospital, objected to Parish's characterization. "I agree with the law," he told the newspaper. "For the twenty years I've practiced medicine, I've believed a woman should have an abortion only for rape, the life or health of the mother, or grave fetal defects."

The article continued: "Dr. Heywood says he also objects to the Utah medical organization joining the lawsuit. 'I don't want my name associated with it, and I don't want to be a part of any lawsuit that has anything to do with the ACLU.'" Nevertheless the article cited ten doctors who had joined the lawsuit as individuals, claiming their patients included women who had been impregnated as a result of rape or incest but were unable to report the crime, women carrying anomalous fetuses, women needing experimental fetal treatment, battered wives, and women being aided by fertility drugs.

Words flew between doctors now, as well as between attorneys. While the contested procedures would have an impact on families' options, one doctor told the newspaper that restricting medical procedures would not necessarily have the desired effect of ceasing abortions. "'Women who believe that their pregnancies endanger their physical or mental well-being will find a way to obtain abortions regardless of the law,' said Utah Women's Clinic physician Madhuri Shah," adding: "And worse, 'they will abort themselves or turn to the back alley for illegal abortions.'"

The ACLU importuned federal court to add other plaintiffs to its lawsuit. "Jane Freedom" was hoping to "save her diseased unborn child with experimental drugs," according to a *Deseret News* report, and "Julie Spouse" did not want her estranged husband informed of her abortion.

Quickly a state official objected to the pseudonyms used in the lawsuit, and the matter went before federal judge Thomas Greene, presiding over the case. The ACLU claimed the pseudonyms were neither "impertinent" nor "scandalous." The attorneys wrote: "Liberty's right to name herself is a freedom of speech protected by the First Amendment." They explained that the "anonymous woman who chose the name Liberty eschewed a pseudonym like Doe precisely because that name, rather than being neutral, has connotations of weakness and victimization with which she does not want to be associated." Ultimately the lawsuit became known as *Jane L. v. Bangerter.*

Religious leaders joined the women, doctors, and counselors named in the lawsuit, and clergy continued to object to the Criminal Abortion Law on religious grounds. Roy I. Sano, leader of the Rocky Mountain Conference of the United Methodist Church, spoke in Salt Lake City in May and claimed that the new law overrode religious perspective. "Governmental laws and regulations do not provide all the guidance required by the informed Christian conscience," he said. "Therefore, a decision concerning abortion should be made only after thoughtful and prayerful consideration by the parties involved, with medical, pastoral and other appropriate counsel."

Oritt and Lundgren worked long hours throughout 1991, producing a lengthy pre-trial document summarizing the testimony of forty prospective witnesses and listing more than 280 exhibits. The state's attorneys, the affiliate newspaper reported, "who had previously accused plaintiffs' attorneys of withholding information, filed a much more limited document with the court." Oritt estimated he donated $90,000 in fees to the case and Lundgren between $40,000 and $50,000.

In the midst of the fray, the ACLU *Reporter* reprinted a Pat Bagley cartoon from the *Tribune*. It showed Bangerter and legislators loading a missile with a beehive logo and labeled "abortion bill" on to a truck marked "Anti-*Roe v. Wade* Super Patriot Missile." Said the governor to an observer, "It's never been tested, but with my luck it will reach the Supreme Court and cost a million bucks."

Ironically, the controversy around the abortion issue would convince one frequent visitor to Salt Lake City that this was a place she could live. Formerly a social worker in Wisconsin, Carol Gnade (pronounced with a hard "g" to rhyme with "karate") frequently visited a friend, Peter Boam, whose work had recently relocated him to Utah. Gnade did not originally think she could make a home in the Beehive State. "Too many white people," she would explain, though Anglo herself.

"Then I came one weekend when they were having one of the first abortion rallies. As I listened to the speakers, I realized there were activists here and people interested in the same issues I was. One participant was also on the ACLU board of directors. I said, 'I think I can make this decision now.'"

Gnade called the ACLU office and volunteered her services. As she recalled, "the secretary said, 'Could you come in tomorrow morning?'" She found that Parish needed help organizing the 1991 annual dinner, so Gnade began coordinating volunteers. Sometimes she worked as many as fifty hours a week as a volunteer and then stayed in touch with Parish from Wisconsin.

A major grant allowed the Utah ACLU to hire its first staff attorney, Kathryn Kendell, at the outset of 1992, and funded Gnade as the first development director. By this time Parish was so embroiled in controversies that Gnade's job became getting the finances in order and running the office. Consultant Barry Shane, whom Parish had met at an ACLU conference in Vermont, helped develop a fund raising model for Utah. The affiliate budget, as well as the expenses, had increased dramatically, and Gnade now applied her skills to organizing and managing the resources.

Kendell recalled her initiation as staff attorney with a "climb up a very steep learning curve because the issues were all over the map. Within a four hour period," she said, "I'd be consulted on church/state, police abuse, sexual harassment, free speech, and prison violations. I had to have answers to all of those issues. I felt spun around." She depended upon cooperating attorneys such as Brian Barnard, Ross Anderson, and Dave Eckersley while she found her moorings. However, her own background and experience also provided strength.

Kendell had graduated from the University of Utah Law School in 1988 with fifteen years of debate experience. She began private practice handling employment, domestic, and personal injury issues, though constitutional law was her primary interest—a type of law raised only occasionally in the corporate world. In a couple of years, to her dismay, Kendell had found herself getting bored with her law practice.

"This can't be," she had told herself. "I need to do this for another forty to fifty years." She watched her peers thrive on the same cases that sparked less and less interest in her and finally concluded that "for me, law alone was not enough." The new staff position at the ACLU seemed ideal.

Her interest in civil liberties had begun early. In 1978 she had been in Evanston, Illinois, for a national high school debate tournament and heard news reports of the American Nazi Party march in nearby Skokie. She found the Nazis objectionable but "was intrigued by the idea of supporting everyone's right to free speech, even if you disagreed with them." That incident made an impact, and on the way to the airport Kate had pointed out the town of Skokie to the cab driver.

That split between liberal and libertarian viewpoints would continue within the ACLU, and so would Kendell's fascination with the issues. By the time she became staff lawyer, she was watching the national debate on pornography. The ACLU stand, vigorously promoted by President Nadine Strossen, was that the First Amendment was absolute in allowing the market and other forces to control pornography, rather than censorship. However, many within and without the organization disagreed because women, children, and sometimes racial minorities were exploited and debased in that medium.

"It's a tension nationally," Kendell said, "maybe a dynamic. I think the debate is good. Disagreement is one of the most charismatic things about the organization. There's not really a party line. The board may vote on an approach, but there's always room for dissent. Some say, 'Oh, the organization is coming undone and losing its way,' but I see it as a necessary dynamic."

Kendell immediately became embroiled in the 1992 legislative session in which proposed amendments to the Criminal Abortion Law were hotly contested. On January 25, 1992, reproductive rights protesters filled the Capitol Rotunda. As part of the Utah Pro-Choice Coalition, the ACLU lent its efforts. The coalition included Planned Parenthood, the League of Women Voters, *Network* magazine, the NOW Utah chapter, the Utah Women's Health Clinic, the National Abortion Rights Action League, the Salt Lake branch of the National Council of Jewish Women, the Coalition of Labor Union Women, the Utah Women's Political Caucus, the Socialist Workers Party, Utahns for Choice, and the YWCA.

During a planning meeting, Gnade had suggested that the coalition find a pro-choice Mormon speaker. That week she picked up the telephone and began calling BYU faculty until she reached English professor Cecelia Konchar-Farr, who had helped BYU coeds organize against campus rape. "Well, maybe it's my time to do this," Gnade would remember her saying.

Other speakers included Debara Threedy, a University of Utah law professor and a member of the ACLU board; Kathy Warner, who led the group in "singing for our lives"; and Annette Cummings, representing Utahns for Choice. The affiliate's winter 1992 *Reporter* ran a list entitled "Legislators Who Voted Pro-Choice" and reported the pro-choice rally as its lead story.

"Almost 4,000 were in attendance, nearly double that of last year's rally," the article stated. "Young and old lined the balconies on every floor to show their support for pro-choice political candidates and their extraordinary list of guest speakers. . . ."

Konchar-Farr would suffer serious repercussions as a result of her participation. Quickly called to account by LDS authorities, she was compelled to decline further speaking invitations related to the abortion question but did allow her comments at the rally to appear in *Network* magazine. The following year she would be fired from BYU for "citizenship" reasons, following a third-year academic review, despite outstanding scholarship. She hired an attorney and appealed the decision, finally reaching an undisclosed settlement.

When Gnade later ran into Konchar-Farr, she reminded her of their acquaintance. "Oh, right," Konchar-Farr quipped, "you're the woman who helped end my career."

The firings of Konchar-Farr and another BYU professor after speaking on sensitive issues highlighted a widespread purge of Mormon writers, intellectuals, historians, and feminists. While many of these people would rest their outspokenness on First Amendment rights, and some would call on the ACLU, the affiliate took no issue with the inner workings of any religion.

Konchar-Farr was not the only Mormon to find herself among "strange bedfellows" around the abortion issue, a fact that religion writer Peggy Fletcher Stack gleaned for *Salt Lake Tribune* readers. She reported that Apostle Dallin Oaks, too, found himself among surprising allies. "Abortion Issue Pits Mormons, ACLU Against Catholics" read a front page headline on May 14, 1992. The article began: "It started off as a fight for religious freedom. Now the issue is abortion and it has forged an unusual alliance: The LDS church and the ACLU versus the Catholic church."

The primary issue involved an Oregon lawsuit that found its way to the Supreme Court after two members of the Native American church were found using peyote in religious meetings. The ACLU befriended the case, which later led to the Religious Freedom Act. Various denominations lent their support, including the LDS church which had no sympathy for the use of peyote but was interested in protecting religious freedom. The Roman Catholic church, however, the *Tribune* article explained, "saw a potential loophole: the bill could be used by abortion-rights advocate to claim they were having an abortion for religious reasons."

Nadine Strossen, ACLU president, testified in Washington, D.C., in concert with Oaks, the *Tribune* reported. A parallel story in the *Deseret News* reported Oaks's testimony without mentioning the ACLU or Strossen's testimony. The first woman president of the ACLU, Strossen would later visit Utah and speak in several cities along the Wasatch Front. In 1993 the Religious Freedom Act became law, encompassing a far broader scope than the question originally raised by Native Americans.

Even as issues of church and state swirled around the abortion issue nationally, the Utah ACLU met with a significant defeat that spring. On April 21, 1992, Judge J. Thomas Greene froze the privacy issues in the lawsuit until *Planned Parenthood v. Casey* could be decided by the U.S. Supreme Court. He ruled against the ACLU, Planned Parenthood, and pro-choice plaintiffs on several counts. "In this case there is no free speech violation because there is no free speech right to solicit criminal acts (abortion)," he said, regarding those counseling women on abortion.

"I hope the above ruling by Judge Greene sends shivers up your spine and rattles your bones," Parish wrote in the summer *Reporter*. "If Greene's ruling is allowed to stand, anyone who tries to help a woman or girl could be charged with conspiracy to commit a felony." This could include family, counselors, or individuals "who tell women where to get abortions—legal or illegal—or who actively participate, such as in driving the 'getaway car.'. . ." Clinic advertising might well become illegal.

Furthermore, Parish continued, Greene had "denied religious freedom and freedom of conscience" for Utahns who affiliated with a religion other than LDS, particularly those "who believe it is their moral and spiritual right to choose abortion and their pastoral duty to counsel their members concerning abortion." The ACLU had argued that the law's similarity to LDS policy constituted an establishment of religion within the state. Greene had ruled against this as well, saying that the abortion ban was "consistent with society's traditional moral framework."

Greene refused to hear testimony from a long list of witnesses, including experts, religious leaders, and women who had experienced illegal abortions or problem pregnancies. "The judge said he already had more information than he needed to make up his mind," Parish wrote.

These losses represented skirmishes compared to the central battle around the issue of privacy, which ended with the opposite result. The tensely-awaited *Casey* decision by the Supreme Court brought legal clarity to Utah. The high court was far more conservative than when *Roe v. Wade* changed the political landscape, but the justices decided to keep abortion legal nonetheless. In deciding *Planned Parenthood v. Casey*, the court upheld the core of *Roe v. Wade,* though it maintained abortion was not a fundamental right. States could not prohibit abortion in the first trimester during pre-viability but could regulate it. A twenty-four-hour waiting period was allowed, spousal notification was not. The court later refused to reinstate a Louisiana law that criminalized most abortions.

The message was clear in Utah. With this decision, the core of the Criminal Abortion Statute crumbled. "The Supreme Court is not divine, just supreme," quipped former governor Norm Bangerter. In his opinion, the *Casey* ruling took aim directly at the Utah law and made it clear that the Supreme Court would not reverse *Roe v. Wade*. "This was our attempt to do that." Although Bangerter did not like calling the Utah bill a ban, he agreed that the high court's ruling differed significantly by allowing abortion with restrictions rather than disallowing abortion except in select instances.

So significant was the *Casey* ruling that the ACLU affiliate celebrated with considerable relief. Not surprisingly, on December 18, 1992, Greene struck down the core of the Criminal Abortion Statute, holding that any ban on abortion during pre-viability was clearly unconstitutional. Greene also struck down the spousal notification provision of the Utah law but upheld medical restrictions and choice of the method best for the fetus in post-viability abortions. He then adapted the exemptions in the Criminal Abortion Law to fit post-viability abortions. The ACLU and the Center for Reproductive Law and Policy readied an appeal on these points.

During 1992 Michele Parish's honors and efforts continued to accrue. They ranged from becoming an alternate representative to the pensions committee at the national ACLU executive directors' conference to being elected to the Utah Women's Forum. Her picture and a question-answer profile appeared in *Salt Lake City* magazine. In it, Parish described herself as "a warrior." The most challenging part of her job?—"That it can make a difference, and it is always in the middle of whatever is really hot. I like being in the eye of the storm." She said the secret of her success involved being "coached by people who may very well consider themselves my enemies. I listen to them and get value from what they're saying. Also, I don't sleep."

Her biggest pet peeve? "Being misquoted." When asked what three people in history she would like to have dinner with, she named Susan B. Anthony, Thomas Jefferson, and Mary Magdalene. Her greatest passion?—"Freedom and fairness for everybody everywhere."

As the year climaxed with a U.S. presidential election, the mood of the Utah affiliate shifted as well. Significant victories, a high public profile, substantial donations, a dramatic increase in membership, and soaring costs had transformed the organization. No longer did it run on a shoestring. The board no longer wanted to be in a reactive stance either financially or politically. As Gnade sorted financial affairs, Parish felt increased pressure from the board to pay more attention to administration and less to political warfare.

In November 1992, when Democratic candidate Bill Clinton won the presidency, the effect nationally and locally was enormous. The eight-year assault on civil liberties appeared to be over. Civil libertarians throughout the country breathed a collective sigh of relief.

In Utah the board of directors turned its attention to solidifying and extending the organization's growth. If administration and fund raising were hallmarks, Parish decided, the position of executive director did not "sound fun any more. I'm really more of an activist." Also, with a staff attorney on board, the executive director no longer worked with cooperating attorneys in the same way. "Working on cases was my favorite part." Attracted by the promise of the Clinton administration, Parish told the board she planned to move to Washington, D.C., after the first of the year.

By her tenure's end, Parish's office walls were covered with cartoons and awards. A colored postcard hung directly behind her desk. Taken at night, it juxtaposed the illuminated State Capitol and LDS temple, visually combining the eminent symbols of church and state. "I meditate on this," she said wryly. She noted that prison reforms were underway, the issue of school prayer resolved, and the question of prayer in government meetings before the Utah Supreme Court; lastly, with his ruling overturning the Criminal Abortion Law, Judge Greene had handed Parish a significant farewell present.

Shortly before leaving Utah, Parish recalled the "vision" she received at her first biennial ACLU conference. "This last year I've used the keys of knowledge more than the sword, and that's been a different kind of learning," she said.

The media responded to Parish's exit with several features. In one photograph, printed on the front page of the local section of the *Tribune*, Parish was shown against the wall bearing her collection of framed cartoons. Her arms were spread and drooping in a mock-crucifixion, and she was laughing.

Cartoonist Calvin Grondahl sent her a final farewell in Ogden's *Standard-Examiner*. It showed a family praying in their living room, a framed print of the LDS temple on the wall, the mother pregnant, and two children with bowed heads. The baby, whose diaper drooped, peered out the snowy window at Parish, toting her suitcase labeled ACLU. The caption read, "We give thanks for the snow's coming and Michele Parish's going."

Former board president John Morris later noted the impact of the affiliate's most controversial executive director. "Michele's particular personality and style reshaped the conflict in a way that had a very positive impact on the organization. It's different now, and that's good. The media exposure and the litigation successes gave the organization a kind of credibility that now makes it possible to move the debate without the same pyrotechnics."

8.
Scene Change

The scene shift, as 1993 began, was dramatic. Set, action, and protagonists all switched within the ongoing drama of the Utah ACLU. On a broader stage, the nation adjusted at many levels to the Democratic administration of President Bill Clinton. In Utah Democrats remained a minority, for defeated Vice-President George Bush had carried the Beehive State, reflected in the election of Governor Mike Leavitt and continued Republican dominance in the legislature.

Nevertheless, Utah politics changed in certain respects, too. Michele Parish's sense of being the only woman "playing with the big boys" no longer applied in the larger political arena. Several women achieved election to visible public office including Congresswoman Karen Shepherd, lieutenant governor Olene Walker, state attorney general Jan Graham, and Salt Lake City mayor Deedee Corradini, as well as a number of councilwomen and mayors in smaller cities.

The Utah ACLU had gained a level of security and success that guaranteed the respect and attention of government, the media, and the public, however reluctant. Before leaving, Parish had enjoyed a cordial telephone conversation with Bangerter. Now the new governor proved eager to establish and maintain diplomatic relations with the Utah affiliate in ways that had not occurred before.

No longer was the Utah ACLU the smallest and most impoverished affiliate in the United States, as it had been thirty years earlier. Now it needed an administrator to handle a quarter-million-dollar budget; who could reduce costs to manage an expected loss in donations as liberals breathed easier with the end of the Reagan-Bush regime; who would not only "wage war" but attend to "domestic tranquility," from solidifying and educating the ever-changing board to completing necessary paperwork.

Two capable, outspoken women were already employed, and Parish knew when she left that the board of directors would not look far for her successor. Very quickly Carol Gnade was asked to become executive director while Kathryn Kendell continued as staff attorney and was appointed spokesperson as well.

Despite the abilities of both Gnade and Kendell in forthrightly addressing issues, neither would spark the tumult that had marked Parish's years. Parish defined herself in ways Gnade and Kendell did not, yet the difference in approach probably depended more on the reality that the issues and setting had shifted than it did on personalities.

What remained true on any stage hosting the ACLU was the adage that no civil liberties battle ever stayed won. The major victories of Parish's time began, almost immediately, to fray around the edges. The prison lawsuit offered an example, for the state appealed the awarding of attorney fees even as medical reforms began at the Utah State Penitentiary. A mental health unit opened at the prison, and medical procedures were aiming for compliance with the court stipulations. The affiliate assumed oversight in seeing to it that the court requirements became reality.

The controversy around public prayer had altered but not ended. The types of prayers at graduation ceremonies and before other public school events that were found unconstitutional by the Supreme Court were discontinued overall. Many civil libertarians expected the Utah Supreme Court to rule similarly when it came to prayer in government meetings. But the public prayer bogeyman threatened to become a beast, with a growing effort to amend the state constitution.

Judge Thomas Greene's ruling at the end of 1992 thrust a stake through the heart of the Criminal Abortion Statute after the Supreme Court upheld the essence of *Roe v. Wade*. However, the ACLU still fought a running battle over state restrictions. Although both Parish and Bangerter scored Greene's ruling on the ACLU side of the tally sheet, the state's attorney and sometimes the media posted the state as the victor because of limitations that were upheld. Meanwhile, a long struggle for the awarding of attorney fees—the true marker of loss or triumph—lay in the making.

Despite these continuities, if ever a line of demarcation manifested itself in the history of the organization, that line appeared with the advent of 1993. The issues, the politics, the faces, and the tactics all rotated and adjusted. Clearest of all was the emergence of the affiliate as a power to be reckoned with.

That public perception, in itself, was enormously powerful, board president John Morris would remark. While the grandstanding had worked, he said, "the maximum efficacy for Michele's style is past. The organization couldn't sustain that level of antagonism indefinitely." Nor had the board of directors wished it to.

As with any change, this required considerable internal adjustment. Throughout the first half of 1993, Gnade learned to juggle a variety of new and old issues. Although she would keep a lower profile than her predecessor, she, too, had to accustom herself to being a public figure.

One Sunday soon after she took the affiliate's helm, Gnade stood at a large window in her new home below Brighton Canyon. Her neighbors were strolling home from church in groups, many holding hands. Gnade watched as a Fox News van came weaving through the people in the street and approached her house. She went outside to tape an interview on the question of censoring computer pornography as her neighbors stared. "Welcome to the neighborhood," she told herself.

Throughout her first year at the helm, Gnade repeatedly felt that sense of being an immigrant. Fascinated and challenged by the state's peculiarities, she concluded, "If you're not nice to people who are used to being nice, you're considered a New Yorker."

From the outset, Gnade set her own course. Her background lay in administration, managing volunteers, and working behind the scenes. Instinctively she shouldered those roles first. During Parish's last few months in office, Kendell had assumed responsibility for dealing with the media regarding abortion and several other issues.

"Kate is excellent at church/state issues—excellent," Gnade would say. "With abortion, she handles 99.9 percent of it."

171

Meanwhile, with a beginning salary of $34,000, Gnade excelled at administration. "You grow every day in this position," she would say, but she drew nourishment from personal roots that extended deep into the fertile soil of civil liberties and religious tradition.

The grandparents who had cared for Carol in New York City during much of her childhood were associated with the United Council of Churches. Her grandfather was a theologian and member of the Dutch Reformed Church. He left a vice presidency at Standard Oil because he felt a calling to religion. Her grandmother became known as "Tugboat Hazel" because she would sail into the harbor to meet domestic missionaries, then host them while they studied or worked within their religious communities.

During the years Carol lived with her grandparents, while her parents attended medical school, she relished the rich exposure her grandparents gave her to various beliefs. She also felt comfortable within the wide racial and ethnic variety among the citizenry of Manhattan.

Finally, when her father graduated from medical school, Carol climbed into her grandparents' car and they drove to Chicago, sometimes singing a favorite song, "Jesus Loves the Little Children," to pass the road time. "Red and yellow/ black and white/ they are precious/ in His sight," Carol sang as the scenery swept by.

Gnade continued her education in Chicago, became a social worker, married, reared a family, and later divorced. After she became involved with Utah and decided to resettle there, she missed the racial and ethnic diversity of the eastern cities.

She was shocked when she realized that what she missed wasn't missed at all by many Utahns. The insight came as she drove her tennis group to Liberty Park in the Central City area of Salt Lake. One woman said, "Oh, I don't like to play at Liberty Park."

"Why not?" Gnade asked.

"The people there all look so different. That's the thing that's so nice about Utah—we all look the same."

Later, in her Boston Building office, she would muse, "It seems so paradoxical that I would end up here fighting this lack of understanding." Gnade was also slightly disoriented when she spoke to classrooms of students and addressed white faces almost without exception.

She began her tenure as executive director with several broad challenges, as well as a variety of issues. She was determined to understand Utah. She began making significant budget cuts to contain costs and solidify the affiliate's resources. She sought to stabilize the affiliate's approach to issues.

"It's a total change in the way we operate, and more on the conciliatory side," Gnade commented. "Some people get turned off by that; some like it. Michele used to say the money coming in was in proportion to the time during which the ACLU appeared on the news." However, Gnade concluded, the incoming funds depended more on the issues picked up by the media. "The issues that made ACLU work were abortion and the Reagan/Bush onslaught on civil liberties. Both are neutered now as money raisers."

Gnade and the board of directors tackled the new ACLU scenario at a retreat early in 1993. The affiliate made education a high priority, as well as keeping on top of current cases. The board decided to organize a speakers bureau and workshops and seminars for school teachers. Most affiliates had a large percentage of teachers in the ranks; for example, Massachusetts teachers comprised about 80 percent of that affiliate. "Here, most teachers are hostile," Gnade said. Using a Connecticut model, the Utah affiliate also began producing a video for high school students to acquaint them with their First Amendment rights, as those freedoms influenced young lives.

The board's concern with internal matters came across, as well. Gnade had been handed a stringent budget cut with the prospect of a drop in donations. During the years of expansion, costs had skyrocketed. Now Gnade faced the unenviable task of cutting by 20 percent. Before long the affiliate would move from the fourth to the seventh floor of the Boston Building, squeezing temporarily into much smaller quarters to save on rent.

Despite changes, Gnade felt the causes were not diminished. "Most people are feeling protected by the Clinton administration, but that's a faulty conception both in Washington, D.C., and here. With a new administration, there's not that much effect on civil liberties; those issues don't change overnight. But the money will change because there's no crisis. We'll still work on civil liberties in the war on drugs, searches and seizures, and overcrowding in prisons."

The tightened focus both internally and publicly had been discussed just after the 1992 election at the biennial executive directors' retreat in Santa Monica, California. There, Leslie Harris, of the Washington, D.C., Legislative Office, told a diverse group that the time had come for the ACLU to "move back to an affirmative agenda. We won't be operating in back rooms, but rather figuring how many votes we have. A lot of people you know have suddenly become more powerful," she said, noting that the legal community had backed Clinton. "We need to seek out moderate and liberal Republicans who are newly important."

National executive director Ira Glasser then confronted the bad news—the financial strictures indicated in a current committee report. During the 1980s, Glasser said, the ACLU had prospered "like an undertaker—the worse things got, the more business we had." Under Reagan and then Bush, he said, "Everything was attacked simultaneously and from the highest levels of government." Donors had responded throughout the "siege" with increased contributions. "You don't function at the same level when the siege is over," he added.

Nevertheless, Glasser continued, although donations were expected to drop, good times for civil liberties were not necessarily at hand. "The good news and the bad news is that the siege is over. The ACLU can't continue at pitch level; it has to draw back."

The Supreme Court ruling on the abortion issue would have a great effect on finances, he said, even though in some states restrictions were still severe. Abortion would "become a subset of the race and poverty issues," Glasser predicted. "Five hundred thousand white middle-class women won't come to Washington, D.C., any time soon" to lobby.

Now, Glasser asserted, was the time for the ACLU to recover ground lost under Reagan and Bush in the areas of civil rights, criminal justice, church and state issues, and rights for homosexuals. He reminded the group that the Christian Coalition was a stronger and more effective voice on the right than the Moral Majority had been during the

1980s. "The Christian Coalition basically controls the Republican Party."

In February 1993 the national ACLU voiced these concerns in a pamphlet titled, "A liberal letdown?" written by Naftali Bendavid, in *Legal Times*. He began:

> When presidential candidate George Bush called his opponent "a card-carrying member of the ACLU" in 1988, the result was dramatic: 50,000 people rushed to join the American Civil Liberties Union. Each new inductee brought in as much as twenty dollars a year. Everyone was talking about the ACLU. People wore pins pronouncing themselves "card-carrying members." Now, without an enemy in the White House for the first time in more than a decade, ACLU leaders are retooling their appeal.

The article quoted Glasser saying: "We must neither weaken nor sit back.... We must turn our new opportunity in Washington into victories for civil liberties. At the same time, we must fight the growing and virulent strain of reaction at the grass-roots level before it can do more damage."

The religious right found a voice with the Rutherford Institute in Virginia, which criticized Glasser's recent depiction of their ranks as the "re-emergence of the grassroots forces of darkness." In September 1993 the Rutherford allowed Glasser to respond.

He succinctly defined the ACLU's policy of protecting free speech, then wrote: "The ACLU supports everyone's free speech rights, including yours. But supporting someone's right to speak doesn't mean you have to support what they say." Glasser told readers of the ACLU's support of the Ku Klux Klan's right to march, adding, "But we have also opposed the goals the Klan stood for and we have regarded the Klan as a 'force of darkness.'" He concluded with:

> Advocate as you will, and if any branch of government tries to stop you, call on us to protect your free speech rights in exactly the same way as we have protected everyone else's free speech rights since 1920. But do not expect us to endorse your goals or to refrain from characterizing them as a "force of darkness." That is, in our view, an

appropriate way to characterize a program such as yours, which seems designed to abandon the most traditional American values—the values codified in the Bill of Rights.

The change in scene nationally highlighted Utah's tendency to differ from the norm. National would prioritize workers' rights and oppose the religious right. These did not fit in Utah, Carol Gnade realized. Utah's long tradition as an anti-union state fostered weak workers' rights but nurtured little impetus to improve them. "There's not a state that has worse workers' rights, or where they don't respect workers," she said. As far as warring with the religious right, she quipped, "Let's face it: we are the religious right in Utah."

Utah sported its own brand of conservatism and tended to spurn advances from the religious right, just as some Christian denominations rejected Mormonism from their theological fold. In discussing this with LDS public information officer Stuart Reid, Gnade learned that the church would resist minister Pat Robertson's Christian Coalition setting up shop in Salt Lake City. For one thing, many religious rightists—including the Christian Coalition—hated Mormons. Utah had plenty of inherent church/state issues, but the ACLU need not anticipate the Christian Coalition wielding power in local governments.

Reid himself illustrated the Utah style of religious influence in government, Gnade said, when he gained a seat on the Salt Lake City Council and quickly advocated reinstituting prayer at council meetings. Simultaneously he was reassigned at the Church Office Building, no longer dealing with legislative issues. But all that came later.

As she tried to get her bearings, Gnade cemented her relationship with Reid and other LDS emissaries who worked under the direction of the church's Special Affairs Committee, led by church authorities. The ACLU's relationship with the religious community had developed significantly.

The autumn before she left Utah, Michele Parish had heard from a variety of religious leaders about how distraught they were that the ACLU and the Society of Separationists had sparked a constitutional crisis by objecting to prayer in schools and in government meetings. The practice that perpetuated an LDS viewpoint at least had been unofficial. Now it might become not only legal but mandated.

In response, Parish had organized a private roundtable of clergy, and John Morris asked former University of Utah president Chase Peterson, a liberal Mormon, to chair the meeting held at the Episcopal church. The roundtable included a variety of denominations, but also Parish; Chris Allen, head of the Society of Separationists; and an unofficial representative of the LDS Special Affairs Committee. The leaders drafted a letter to the governor opposing a special session to amend the state constitution.

Later Parish was invited to speak to Capitol Hill's Democratic caucus, which was not out-of-the-ordinary, and then to the Republican caucus, which was a first. The Republican men not only questioned her about her own religious beliefs, she said, but told her the letter from clergy had borne significant weight with the governor. This led to Parish's only direct conversation with Bangerter, a telephone call during which she thanked him for not calling a special session. "I said how odd it was that during all these years we'd never met. And he said something like, 'I've kept up with what you're doing. Bud [Scruggs] and Steve [Mecham, later chief of staff] have kept me briefed.'"

The roundtable led to a meeting between LDS church authorities and the outgoing and incoming executive directors of the Utah ACLU. At the Church Office Building on North Temple Street, the two met with Reid, Bill Evans from the Special Affairs Committee, and recently-ordained apostles Russell Ballard and William Nelson.

For Parish, this meeting—like her conversation with Bangerter and her parting letters to Elder Oaks and first counselor in the First Presidency Gordon B. Hinckley—represented a diplomatic victory and a sense of completion. Gnade viewed the meeting as a beginning rather than an end, and gauged the men's attitudes cautiously.

Concerned with the energy gathering around the Religious Liberties Amendment as the legislative session approached, Gnade was particularly interested in working with LDS emissaries and officials. Yet, to Gnade, the meeting on the twenty-eighth floor of the church tower seemed bland.

"The first thing one of the apostles said was that we should understand that their 'oversight' was the world. Local issues occupy a very small part of the planet, a handful of the many things they have to deal with." Bland or not, the meeting's importance lay in its occurrence. Historically it represented the first formal meeting between the ACLU and LDS leaders. Likely it was the first direct and friendly contact between an affiliate leader and a general authority since Mickey Duncan had tried to enlist the support of Marion D. Hanks for his civil rights bill.

As the 1993 Utah legislature convened, with Mike Leavitt in the governor's office, the sense of change persisted. As Kate Kendell put it, "The legislature had just come away from some major spankings in Supreme Court rulings on abortion and school prayer. It was clear that our agenda was supported by the people who would ultimately decide the issues." Nevertheless, when it came to the abortion question, the plot remained thick, for legislators clearly intended to capitalize on the high court's allowance for certain restrictions.

With a year's experience behind her, Kendell was well grounded and upbeat. She talked with every legislator who would listen to the affiliate's concerns regarding "the attempts of the state to infringe on a woman's reproductive choices and to dictate when, where, and by what method a woman may exercise this fundamental right."

She soon found, as had Adam Duncan and Spencer L. Kimball long before her, where her greatest asset lay. "I've found it's a tremendous advantage being from here. When legislators or others find out I grew up here, their entire demeanor changes." Kendell noticed that if she did not make that point early in a conversation, the person introducing her often would.

In one conversation with a high-ranking senator, Kendell recalled, she had commented that she would like to see the abortion issue resolved because she had grown up in Utah. "His face completely changed. He asked where I grew up, we discussed who we knew in common, and so on. It has an incredible effect for good and cannot be overestimated." Nativity would remain important, she said, as long as most of the population living in Utah hailed from Utah. Once her roots were established, Kendell said, her new acquaintance would then ask the equivalent of, "How did a nice girl like you get involved with the ACLU?"—an opening to discussing business.

Two key reproductive rights issues involved a twenty-four-hour waiting period and pre-abortion counseling and the allowable medical procedures for doctors who practiced high-risk obstetrics and maternal-fetal genetics. Of the latter, Kendell would write, "It is critical to remember that these doctors do not perform elective abortions. . . ." Rather, she explained, they assisted conception and "helping those women to maintain healthy and viable pregnancies. Unfortunately, some women are not able to . . . and must, late into their pregnancies, make very difficult decisions. . . ."

Because some doctors felt Greene's ruling had rendered their practice unfeasible, ACLU attorneys Howard Lundgren and Jeff Oritt joined with lead counsel Janet Benshoof to seek a legislative solution. A series of meetings followed involving the doctors, the governor's office, the attorney general's office, key legislators, and attorneys on both sides, with the hope of concluding negotiations before the session ended.

The House Human Services Committee considered the twenty-four-hour waiting period. Mid-session a *Salt Lake Tribune* article effectively captured the lingering complexities of the quarrel. "Mary Lou Tripp sees abortion in terms of black and white," the piece by Dan Harrie and Michael Phillips began.

"'I believe it's murder,' the anti-abortion activist told the House Human Services Committee.' . . . If you truly believe in God—any of you—you do too. We have no right as women to murder unborn children. God sends children. We do not.'" The article noted that the committee chair ruled Tripp out of order for failing to restrict her comments to the bill, which merely added a restriction.

"The abortion debate in the Utah Legislature is much narrower than it was two years ago," the article remarked, since the core of the Criminal Abortion Statute had been found unconstitutional. "But the issue still sparks the kinds of emotions exhibited . . . in Friday's packed committee hearing."

The committee considered a compromise that allowed nurses, physicians' assistants, and certified nurse midwives—as well as the doctors originally specified—to give mandatory pre-abortion counseling. Limiting such counseling to doctors, the ACLU and others of the coalition argued, discriminated against rural women who had to travel long distances to a clinic in Salt Lake City.

The medical restrictions were also discussed by the committee. "A group of University of Utah obstetricians and geneticists said earlier this week they have no choice but to appeal" Greene's ruling, the article read. "They claim the law forces them to perform Caesarean sections in some cases even when it may endanger the mother's health."

That claim was rebutted by the state's attorney, Mary Anne Wood, who said the doctors were spreading misconceptions. The *Tribune* quoted: "'Doctors have all the discretion they need to do what is best for their patients,' she said. 'In no case does the law or the ruling require Caesarean section deliveries where it would endanger a woman's health.'"

Wood insisted that no amendment should be made to the 1991 statute unless the ACLU would agree not to appeal the case and "rack up attorneys' fees by claiming their suit forced an amendment." However, the ACLU fully intended to appeal to the Tenth Circuit Court if the issues were not sufficiently settled through negotiation.

The quarrel over attorney fees only illustrated the larger question of who had won the abortion battle. Greene upheld what he could of the abortion statute, given the Supreme Court's decision. A few days after the committee met, attorney general Jan Graham appealed Greene's ruling that the privacy element had been found unconstitutional, hoping to give the state legal turf in case the ACLU would not back away. The *Tribune* reported: "In fact, closed-door negotiations between politicians and attorneys to settle the case through a compromise amendment to the law are proceeding at a furious pace. The legislature adjourns today at midnight."

The ACLU offered to drop its appeal if the medical issues were resolved, but no compromise came within reach. The arguments extended through 1994 and into 1995. One compromise solidified. Both sides agreed to a provision that a woman seeking an abortion would receive counseling by medical personnel at least twenty-four hours prior to the procedure, but not necessarily by the attending physician. Kendell felt this represented a significant concession by the ACLU, for the Supreme Court decision on *Casey* already had allowed counseling to be given either by the referring or attending physician. On the other hand, *Casey* had also required parental consent—which was upheld by the court—and Senate Bill 60 did not insist on that. At least the compromise would not place a hardship on rural women.

On February 10, 1993 the *Tribune* praised the compromise, editorializing:

> Opposing sides in the Utah Legislature's endless abortion debate deserve praise for reaching agreement on a proposed twenty-four-hour waiting period. Here's hoping this spirit of compromise can be extended to other facets of the abortion controversy.
>
> Though the U.S. Supreme Court has upheld a woman's constitutional right to choose an abortion prior to the time a fetus has a reasonable chance of surviving outside the mother's womb, the high court also has held that requiring informed consent at least twenty-four hours prior to an abortion does not amount to an undue burden on a woman's abortion rights.

Even as the conflict continued, the Utah ACLU hailed the 1993 legislative session as "a banner session" in the spring 1993 *Reporter*. A resolution seeking to soften the state's exclusionary law for evidence seized illegally had been tabled by the House Judiciary Committee after "sailing through the Senate with very little opposition." The affiliate counted this as a fortunate victory. It also announced that the affiliate would work more vigorously to reduce abortions through education "and to empower women so that an unplanned and unwanted pregnancy does not occur; or if it does, carrying the pregnancy to term is actually a possibility to consider rather than the incredible emotional, financial, and social burden it now is."

During the months following the legislative session, the argument over abortion continued despite the compromise reached. On June 22, 1993, the *Tribune* reported that New York lawyer Janet Benshoof and other attorneys from the Center for Reproductive Law and Policy challenged Utah's 1993 twenty-four-hour restriction, listing several cases in which women in Wyoming and Idaho found it difficult to travel repeatedly to Salt Lake City or stay long enough to meet the requirements. Another instance involved a homeless woman.

The pro-choice lawyers asked United States magistrate Ronald Boyce to recommend an injunction against the new statute. Assistant attorney general Mark Ward argued that the clinics' own literature recommended three trips, and that the women simply were not arranging their affairs efficiently. Boyce said he would make a recommendation to U.S. district judge Dee Benson soon.

The Utah-ACLU withdrew from the battle after Kendell received assurances that the rules would be stretched a bit for women in rural areas. However, Benshoof and the center continued to press for the injunction but lost in court. The twenty-four-hour waiting period went into effect. This affected the Utah Women's Clinic and the Wasatch Women's Center in Salt Lake City and, by extension, women throughout the Intermountain West. The Utah Department of Health replaced rough sketches in the consulting material with actual photographs of developing fetuses and included a detailed list of resources available to women who changed their minds about having an abortion.

From the Supreme Court to meeting rooms on Utah's Capitol Hill, a number of abortion issues were settled. Yet the definitive judgment came with the bottom line—awarding attorney fees. By the end of July 1993, the Associated Press reported that Greene had awarded almost equal fees to each side, describing both as "prevailing parties." The state was to pay the ACLU $71,663 in attorney fees and the ACLU was to pay the state $68,957. In other words, the ACLU netted only $2,706 for challenging the nation's most restrictive abortion law. In win-lose terms, the judge ruled the outcome a tie.

While Oritt and Lundgren had volunteered their time, the ACLU had sought more than $700,000 to pay the New York-based attorneys who argued the case. The judge criticized how the attorneys had documented and justified their time, as well as the higher New York billing of $355 an hour.

The ACLU appealed to the Tenth Circuit Court. The *Tribune* quoted Kathryn Kendell saying, "The award of fees to the state not only flies in the face of our view of who won, but jeopardizes future civil-rights litigation across the range of issues." Legal precedent denied fees to defendants (the state) in civil liberties cases, Kendell explained, unless the plaintiff's case (the ACLU et al.) was found frivolous.

Mary Anne Wood told the *Tribune* that Greene's decision was "well-reasoned and well-supported and it will be difficult to sustain an appeal."

The ACLU disagreed and appealed the award of attorneys' fees along with the medical issues. "They think they won the battle," Carol Gnade remarked, "but we definitely won the war. Abortion is still safe and legal. There are some extraneous issues we're not happy with, but that's all."

Attorney general Jan Graham noted that the ALCU appeal would mean more cost to taxpayers, and in 1994 the parties met again to try to settle. However, Wood opposed settlement on several scores so vigorously that the ACLU attorneys threw up their hands. "Usually in a lawsuit there is a certain amount of mutual respect between lawyers, and courtesy shown," Lundgren said. "That's not Mary Ann Wood's style. She was morally outraged and personally indignant that anyone would even challenge the statute."

Attorney general Graham fired Wood in an attempt to get the issues resolved, saying that Wood's arguments presented an immovable obstruction. But even as Graham met with legislators to defend her action, Governor Leavitt nullified it by hiring Wood as his personal counsel.

The *Deseret News* reported that the governor liked Wood's argument that "the proposed settlement could have exposed the state to hundreds of thousands of dollars in legal fees being sought by the American Civil Liberties Union." Leavitt told the newspaper, "We were anxious that we not compromise our law or our legal position."

The article continued: "'I am doing the negotiating on the settlement, and I have retained Mary Anne Wood as my legal counsel,' Leavitt said. 'I continue to have a very good relationship with Jan Graham and I continue to feel a need to have Mary Anne Wood involved in this case.'"

One close observer interpreted Wood's firing and rehiring this way: The governor had to work with legislators, and many of them had supported the abortion statute and appreciated Wood's efforts to defend it. Leavitt's action, the observer suggested, pacified Wood and the pro-life side while slapping the wrists of the personally pro-choice attorney general. Officially, Leavitt maintained his support of both women, and he and Graham publicly insisted they wanted the appeal resolved outside of court. It never happened.

Four and a half years after the Criminal Abortion Law passed, the U.S. Tenth Circuit Court of Appeals on August 2, 1995, handed the ACLU a hard-won and significant victory. In the decision, the panel of three judges restructured the abortion debate, reversing much of Greene's ruling and remanding it back to his court. The higher court strongly disagreed that both the ACLU and the State of Utah had prevailed and should both be awarded attorney fees.

"Although *Casey* realigned the law," the decision read, "it reaffirmed the central tenet of *Roe v. Wade* that state regulation of abortion impinges on a woman's right to privacy. Utah's attempt to play a significant role in toppling *Roe v. Wade* did not succeed, and we can now assess the constitutionality of the remnants of Utah's pre-*Casey* legislation."

First, the appeals panel reversed Greene's application of the Criminal Abortion Law to post-viability abortions. Although Greene had used the *Casey* decision by the Supreme Court to invalidate the core of the Utah law, he then banned post-viability abortions except in documented cases of rape or incest, to save a woman's health or life, or in case of a child with grave defects. "Re-writing" the Utah law to fit constitutional requirements was deemed an improper imposition of judicial judgment.

Second, the appeals court ruled that the language restricting fetal surgeries and medical procedures was unconstitutionally vague and therefore unlawful. This essentially freed doctors from worries about criminal liability in treating infertility and aiding troubled pregnancies.

The court of appeals reversed Greene's ruling that the means chosen for a post-viability abortion must offer the fetus the best chance for survival. Requiring a woman to suffer "grave damage" before her interests predominated violated her protected right to privacy, they wrote, and "unconstitutionally devaluated her rights."

Overall, the appeals court wrote, the ACLU attorneys' proportionate victory considerably outweighed the credit Greene gave them for his favorable rulings on two of eight claims. In quantifying their "lodestar" success this way, the panel wrote, the judge had discounted "the relative importance of the plaintiffs' successes and failures." The reality was that the law had gone down. This should weigh heavily when Greene re-awarded fees, the judges ruled.

"The Utah abortion law was designed to test *Roe* in this time of great uncertainty," the decision explained, "attempting to force a sharp turn in abortion jurisprudence that would permit a state to ban abortions during pre-viability. Plaintiffs framed the present lawsuit against this backdrop of expressed hostility toward *Roe*. Just as defendants may have hoped to chart a new course for abortion jurisprudence, plaintiffs hoped to preserve a woman's right to an abortion . . . [and] therefore reached for alternative theories that the Supreme Court had not squarely rejected." While these theories did not persuade Greene, the appellate panel ruled, the ACLU was not frivolous in presenting them.

After rejecting certain ACLU arguments such as the similarity between the Criminal Abortion Law and LDS policy, Greene, in fact, had penalized the attorneys. The Utah law's "exceptions directly track the official position of the Church of Jesus Christ of Latter-day Saints regarding when an abortion is permissible," the appeals court ruled, concluding, "We are persuaded that the district court erred in holding this argument frivolous."

The appeals court upheld certain aspects of Greene's ruling, including paying New York attorneys at Utah rates. But it declared a winner, not a tie. Greene must re-award attorney fees to reflect the metaphorical trophy won unequivocally by the ACLU.

During the years of contention over abortion, the perennial issue around separation of church and state continued to smolder. The school prayer question was largely resolved in a legal sense with negotiations involving the Granite School District. To the north, the Davis School District decided not to risk prayers at school although board members publicly bemoaned their "liberties being taken away."

The question of government meetings, specifically Salt Lake City Council meetings, still pended. The Utah Supreme Court had yet to rule on the *Society of Separationists v. Whitehead*. Brian Barnard and Kathryn Kendell, both of whom had argued before the state's high court, watched with guarded optimism as the justices continued to deliberate.

In 1992 the pro-prayer camp pushed for an amendment to the state constitution to allow prayer in government meetings. Cole Durham, a

BYU law professor, urged the referendum, as did Gayle Ruzicka, leader of the ultra-conservative Eagle Forum. On August 25, the *Salt Lake Tribune* reported that the House Judiciary Committee had voted eleven to six "against racing through a series of public hearings in time to get the explosive issue on the November 3 ballot," adding: "The action effectively kills any prospect that Utahns will vote on changes to the Constitution's church/state separation clause before 1994."

Michele Parish's comment was boxed at the top of the article: "The circumstances of the current amendment drive reveal haste and lack of proper reflection. This process," she predicted, "will result in a statewide debate over a broad range of church/state, religious discrimination, and other extremely volatile issues, pitting neighbor against neighbor."

Thus when the Religious Liberties Provision reached the 1993 legislature, the ACLU—now under Gnade's direction—and other groups dug in their heels to again delay any action. The amendment proposed rewriting Article One, Section Four, of the Utah Constitution in a way that smudged the line between church and state.

The Religious Liberties Committee included representatives of most religions in the state. Gnade met with the committee well before the legislative session, finding a group "who seemed burned out and felt that people were very condescending to them." She concluded, "We have to do more to keep people's morale up on those issues, and make it easier for burned-out people to be active."

While the *Deseret News* had editorialized earlier in favor of an amendment, the *Tribune*'s Sunday editorial on February 21 was headlined, "Utah Must Not Alter Religious Freedoms Guaranteed by Its State Constitution." It began: "Republicans in the legislature are determined to fire the first shot in a holy war to weaken the church/state separation provisions of the Utah Constitution. This crusade will only further divide the people of Utah along religious lines. . . ."

The editorial quoted the Constitution's key sentence: "No public money or property shall be appropriated for or applied to any religious worship, exercise or instruction, or for the support of any ecclesiastical establishment," then continued, "Senator Lyle Hillyard, Republican-Logan, has proposed two alternative amendments, both of which would strike this provision from the law."

Despite the newspaper's warning, the Religious Liberties Provision passed the senate and went to the House of Representatives, as both Kendell and Gnade lobbied vigorously against it. Kendell asked Chase Peterson and others to call legislators and discuss the economic impact of such an amendment. Gnade procured the signatures of ten clergy on a letter urging legislators to:

> delay consideration until the implications for the spiritual welfare of our State have been fully considered. We welcomed the atmosphere of cooperation that was beginning to develop in the Religious Liberties Committee, and deplore the antagonism that has arisen over this issue. We ask for further opportunity to dialogue with all the concerned parties. . . . If this amendment passes the legislature in the present atmosphere of antagonistic confrontation, we fear it will bring religious conflict in its wake. We believe that given sufficient time and the right public atmosphere, a fair solution to the concerns of all—for the freedom of an individual to pray, and the right of inclusion for both secularists and people of every religious faith—can be found. Please give us the opportunity to find a solution without making prayer to almighty God the political football it has become.

Signatories hailed from the Catholic Diocese of Utah, Shared Ministries of Utah, Our Savior's Lutheran Church, Trinity A.M.E. Church, the First Presbyterian Church, South Valley Unitarian Universalist Church, Congregation Kol Ami, and Ogden and Orem Unitarian churches. Conspicuously absent was the signature of an LDS church representative although Elder Marlin Jensen, a member of the First Council of Seventy, had been present in committee meetings. He had made it clear he attended in an *ex officio* position.

Jensen's presence but insistence on a low-key approach were significant. Opponents of the amendment understood that if the LDS church gave the nod, the amendment would pass immediately. Similarly a declaration that the amendment should not pass would kill it. However, *Deseret News* editorials, the church's voiced concern over the ACLU's opposition to prayer in the schools, and speeches by apostles Oaks and Ballard had already clarified the church's position. Therefore, those opposing the amendment appreciated the church's restraint.

Ultimately the ACLU and the others succeeded in turning three crucial Republican votes against the amendment. In doing so, they surprised even themselves by defeating the bill. The March 3, 1993, *Tribune* reported that the "volatile mixture of religion and politics brewing under the surface in the Utah Legislature for weeks finally erupted Tuesday on the floor of the House" when the bill failed. "Lawmakers turned down by a thin two-vote margin a proposed constitutional amendment that would have protected prayer at government meetings. The vote did not kill the prayer issue, just delayed it a year."

As this constitutional crisis took a breather, heads turned once again to the silent Utah Supreme Court for a sign, found none, and tensions eased. The ACLU had kind words for the LDS church's political representatives. Kendell was acquainted with Jensen, an attorney, from her VanCott-Bagley days in Ogden before Jensen became a church authority. She considered him and lobbyists such as Stuart Reid and Bill Evans as people with "an abundance of reason and good will." To Kendell's regret, the church sent Jensen on a mission to Rochester, New York, several months after the legislature adjourned. "The slice of the LDS hierarchy I've dealt with," she said, "are people of real intelligence and wisdom who have a love for the state and for diversity."

Other encounters were less sophisticated. As she visited high school classes, Kendell learned that her status as an "insider with outsider views" confused many students especially on issues such as graduation prayer. "Did they pray at your graduation?" a student would typically ask.

"Yes, they did."

"Did it make you feel uncomfortable?"

"No, not at that point. Then I was completely part of the mainstream."

The resulting head shaking clearly asked, "Then why can't you understand how we feel?"

Kendell realized that the issue had become less clear over the past year. Prayer advocates had gained a little "wiggle room," as she put it, due to a Supreme Court decision on a Texas case allowing prayer if it was entirely student led. For the time being, *Lee v. Weisman* still disallowed prayers in Utah schools, but Kendell expected other challenges might be raised in the future. To some degree, that depended on the Utah Supreme Court decision regarding prayer in city council meetings; also, it rested on the future of the Religious Liberties Amendment.

Gnade summarized her first eventful year leading the Utah affiliate in the December 1993 *Reporter*. They had, she wrote, responded to 749 written and approximately 7,300 telephone complaints during the year. The legal docket increased by seven cases. ACLU representatives had visited classrooms and colleges and worked closely with other agencies on community issues, fund raising, and lobbying efforts.

She wrote: "We developed a productive and dedicated education committee that has assisted in the production of a new video for high school students and educators. A goal has been set to present the video to twenty-five schools in 1994." In addition, "We activated a strong ... Gay and Lesbian Rights Project with a commitment to building coalitions to improve an environment that is increasingly hostile to lesbians, gay men, and bisexuals." With typical tact, Gnade ended the list of accomplishments with: "Please note that the 'we' that I refer to is not only our staff of three, but an increasingly active board of directors, extraordinary volunteers, and dedicated cooperating/volunteer attorneys to whom we owe so much for the vigorous defense of our civil liberties this past year."

A summary of two of the ACLU's primary issues that year was portrayed in a *Tribune* poll published March 1: "Do you feel Utah needs to amend its Constitution in order to permit prayer at public meetings?" Fifty-six percent of those questioned said yes. Another 37.5 percent said no, and 6.5 percent were unsure or refused to answer the question.

The second question read: "Is it worth additional state tax dollars for court battles to get a stricter abortion law for Utah?" This time 27 percent said yes, 66 percent said no, and 6 percent were unsure. Conducted by Valley Research, the poll admitted a 4-percent margin of error.

The Religious Liberties Amendment appeared to be supported by a majority of Utahns, yet the minority vote was significant considering the state's religious demographics. The definitive word on abortion still lay nearly two years in the future, but most Utahns were unwilling to pay for another battle.

9.
The Prison Medical Ward the ACLU Built

As Michele Parish moved away from Utah, she presented attorneys Cullen Battle and Kathleen Switzer with a bit of memorabilia—a framed cartoon by Pat Bagley labeled "ACLU Medical Lawsuit." It depicted corrections chief Gary DeLand pouring himself a dose of Maalox—the prison's prescription for an inmate's bleeding ulcer. The inmate died vomiting blood in his cell.

A hearty anti-acid might well have been prescribed for those on all sides of the issue. The medical lawsuit against the Utah State Penitentiary never went to trial yet was battled down to the wording of the last stipulated phrase and the awarding of the last contested penny. Corrections issues flared elsewhere as the state's youthful offenders drew increasingly into armed street gangs and, once locked up, rattled the bars of an overcrowded and understaffed system.

The law enforcement system showed itself still struggling with endemic racial bias, including the "profiling" of suspected drug runners partly by race or ethnicity in performing random searches and seizures. In 1994 profiling complaints and racial issues would prompt the Utah ACLU to sue several eminent law enforcement agencies—the Utah Highway Patrol, the Federal Bureau of Investigation, and the Bureau of Indian Affairs police. The questions involved had changed with the times and the personalities involved but remained consistent made-for-the-ACLU issues nonetheless.

The outcome of the conflict between the affiliate and the Department of Corrections revealed much about the litigants, their philosophies, and the issues involved. The most prominent case, *Henry v. DeLand,* represented a three-year struggle to improve the prison's medical, dental, and mental health services. Filed in December 1989, certified in April 1990, and negotiated in spring 1993, the suit did not reach its conclusion until attorney fees finally were awarded early in 1994.

Behind every lawsuit initiated by the affiliate before Kate Kendell became staff lawyer in 1993, and to some degree afterward, volunteer or cooperating attorneys and their law firms offered assistance. While the executive director fronted the issues in the media, the lawyers researched, strategized, filed motions, attended hearings, and commented circumspectly outside court, if at all.

When Cullen Battle of Fabian & Clendenin had agreed to shoulder the medical lawsuit, he'd considered it a lawyer's duty. Before the case reached resolution, he would muse, both the times and the national climate had changed. The legal profession became more business-driven and less idealistic, he believed, accruing a general disaffection toward traditional liberal values.

During the years consumed by the suit, Battle learned that association with the American Civil Liberties Union had its discomforts. If the union only fought for prisoners' medical rights, that would present no problem, he explained. But when they took on issues like abortion, litigating any ACLU lawsuit produced tension.

"With abortion," Battle said later, "people on both sides have sincere beliefs in human rights. With the prison issue, the other side is morally bankrupt. They can rationalize about money and prisoners and school kids, but there is no real moral ground."

Particularly awkward was his law firm's involvement at the time the ACLU ad ran in the *New York Times* attacking the 1991 Criminal Abortion Act. "Being associated with the ACLU on anything put us in a terrible light and had an impact on us," Battle recalled. "Michele would say what she liked, and the press would serve it up."

Switzer agreed. "In most people's minds, tactics like the newspaper ad didn't comport with the idea of a higher calling," she said. "It made what we were doing suspecting."

The attorneys were pleased, however, with the eventual media coverage of their successful chief plaintiff, Sandra Henry. In one example, a photograph of the diminutive AIDS patient appeared on the *Salt Lake Tribune*'s front page above the headline "Ex-Inmate with AIDS Wins Her Battle to Upgrade Health Care at Utah Prison." In the article Henry, who died in 1996, was described as "a savior to inmates at the Utah State Prison." The article continued:

> On Friday, she won a hard-fought lawsuit in federal court that improves health care at the prison, where she was housed from September 1988 to September 1990. "This is a woman who put up with harassment and threats because she filed a lawsuit while she was in prison," said her attorney.
> ... Henry served time for receiving stolen property and possessing heroin. When she entered the prison, her disease was well along but prison doctors denied her therapy. She got it—eventually.

When released from the hospital after a downturn in her health, Henry told the newspaper, "Experts said the earlier the AZT treatments, the better chance of staying healthy longer. As it was, the prison denied inmates the drug until they had at least one bout of pneumonia." The newspaper noted the improvement in mental health standards at the penitentiary, then added: "On Friday, prison officials also agreed to provide better medical care. More doctors, nurses and emergency medical technicians will be at the prison round the clock."

Battle and Switzer were currently engaged not with public opinion but with the difficulties involved in documenting the new prison policies in agreement with the state. The process was especially arduous due to DeLand's appeal based on an administrative rule he believed had relevance. DeLand later admitted that he became "very rigid" on the wording so as not to lose ground. Finally Battle and Switzer told attorney general Paul Van Dam they simply would not sign the documents as written. Gradually acceptable language was hammered out.

Even as the attorneys argued over wording and meaning, conditions continued to change at the prison. The first improvement, as both sides would agree, came earlier with a staff physician, Dr. Robert Jones, whom DeLand described as "proof there is a God." Under the court's oversight, a quality assurance program developed, the "by-the-book" approach that had been lacking. A computer program began charting each inmate's medical condition, tracking health problems, monitoring care, and ensuring a certain level of competence. In addition, the new mental health facility began operating, the pharmacy improved, the infirmary was remodeled, and more medical staff hired.

As the policies altered, both corrections and the Utah ACLU had undergone changes in leadership. Not only did Department of Corrections executive director Lane McCotter's style differ from DeLand's, but now Nick Morgan served as inspector general and Kim Thompson directed operations, dividing the turf Scott McAlister had once dominated. The ACLU found both to be reasonable. Kendell would say, "Our relationship is adversarial—that's our job—but not at all hostile."

By the summer of 1993 Kendell was accustomed to visiting the penitentiary approximately every six weeks. Prompting only "mild disparagement" from the staff, she liked to refer to the new facility in the Wasatch building as the "mental health unit the ACLU built." With thirty-three beds, the ward usually operated at capacity under the direction of Evan Shapiro, supervising psychologist.

The mental health stipulation detailed each procedure, involving screening, staffing, crisis intervention, and inpatient services. Staff training and "structured, out-of-cell daily activity" were specified. As the mental health unit approached compliance with the court stipulation, Kendell expressed optimism. "Eventually, it will be adequate."

Nevertheless throughout 1993 Kendell wrote hundreds of letters for individual inmates and followed through to see that they received help. During the first quarter of 1994, the Utah affiliate would process 236 complaints, more than half of them involving prison issues. This represented an increase in complaints over the previous year.

There was a difference, however. Her correspondence and telephone calls to the prison appeared to be unimpeded. If a complaint sounded urgent, she would call Dr. Jones instead of writing. Either way, results were forthcoming. "The medical department has been adequately responsive," Kendell said with an attorney's caution.

She placed her experience with the penitentiary into a larger context as she amassed statistics while preparing to teach a university class on prisoners' rights. She found that the U.S. incarceration rate ranked higher than any in the world including Russia or South Africa, she said. Also, 30 percent of the population in state prisons and 50 percent in federal prisons had been convicted of drug crimes that would not have meant incarceration a decade earlier.

When Carol Gnade met with Kim Thompson to review the new mental health hospital, she found their discussion disturbingly nostalgic. Gnade had left social work twenty years earlier when, as drug therapies became available, mental hospitals had decided to deinstitutionalize their patients. Social workers were supposed to watch over them, supposedly at a ratio of one social worker per ten patients, a number that, in reality, rose to around one worker to 200 clients, she said.

"The prison is glad we brought suit, or they never would have gotten the mental hospital," she said. "It was just interesting to me that twenty years ago they let everyone out of the hospitals. Now they're building mental hospitals behind prison doors."

If certain prison officials and staff felt relief at the success of the lawsuit—as Gnade, and earlier Parish and Christopher Smart, had reason to believe—that welcoming found no expression in the legal dispute. The opposite was true. The final word on who had won the lawsuit rested with U.S. district judge Bruce Jenkins when the state appealed the awarding of attorneys' fees.

In the appeal DeLand claimed the ACLU should not be awarded attorneys fees on the basis that no changes in medical care had resulted from the lawsuit. Essentially, he claimed, he had been directing the medical reforms when the ACLU, in a show of bad faith, had brought suit. Simply put, his tactic held true to his approach throughout the conflict and could be summarized in three words: blame Michele Parish.

Regarding the medical and dental complaints, DeLand described for the judge a cordial relationship with Robyn Blumner and the evaluations by prison expert Bonnie Norman. "Prior to the evaluation, I agreed to accept Norman's findings and recommendations in their entirety, and Blumner was fully satisfied with this solution," he wrote. "In addition, I asked Norman to meet with representatives of the ACLU and Legal Center for People with Disabilities prior to her on-site evaluation in order to more specifically address each of their concerns. . . ."

DeLand continued, "In response to Norman's report, I organized a task force to develop a master plan to implement the recommendations. The Medical Master Plan has served as the basis for all of the improvements in the medical system since its adoption."

This Medical Master Plan was not referred to or described in any of DeLand's correspondence with the ACLU during the relevant years. Now, however, DeLand wrote that the plan had been adopted in December 1988 and "followed consistently" ever since.

"Blumner and I worked well together, and there was never any indication from the ACLU that they were no longer willing to work with the department to improve prison facilities," he continued. "However, the ACLU, under the direction of Michele Parish, filed suit in December of 1989. The suit came as a complete surprise in light of the progress that the department had made, and was continuing to make. . . ." DeLand maintained that the prison did not have a mental health plan or unit simply because the Department of Corrections was sued before a plan could be developed in concert with Norman.

"But there was not a damn thing they could force us to do we were not doing," he commented later about the ACLU's intervention. Early on, he related, he had called in an expert to analyze what the prison needed to do to provide mental health service and to recommend "a Chevrolet" plan "not a BMW" plan. He offered this Chevrolet to the other side, DeLand said, and they refused it. This action, he claimed, legitimized his Rule 68 argument that if you offer the other side an acceptable option, they cannot litigate harm beyond that point.

In supporting DeLand's objection, assistant attorneys general Kirk M. Torgensen and Frank D. Mylar wrote that the ACLU lawsuit had been essentially frivolous because "well before plaintiff filed suit, defendants had begun to significantly upgrade the quality of medical services." Rather than using the terms Chevrolet or Medical Master Plan, the attorneys simply said DeLand had made offers "formalizing the improvements that defendants were already working on in an effort to eliminate costly litigation." These offers "were significantly above constitutional requirements. . . ."

However, they continued, once the lawsuit reached settlement "and without even discussing the issues of fees, plaintiff ran to the court with a two-inch-thick motion for fees." Yet, they claimed, the plaintiff "cannot show that she helped remedy any constitutional deficiencies by bringing this suit and therefore, her request for fees must be denied."

"We're hard on trees," Kate Kendell quipped, as the ACLU attorneys vigorously rebutted DeLand's version with a response several inches thick. It detailed the lawsuit's history, claiming it "demonstrates conclusively that this lawsuit was the chief cause of unprecedented reform of the prison health care system, and that plaintiff's claims were anything but meritless." Medical experts' testimony in court hearings established "that serious deficiencies in health care have existed at the prison and have persisted well into this litigation."

In addition, DeLand and his administration had admitted in their reports to the legislature that health care was inadequate and that improvements would be required as a result of the ACLU lawsuit. Based on this argument, corrections had received additional taxpayer dollars for reform.

"Finally, if plaintiff's suit were truly 'meritless' and unsupported by even a 'scintilla of evidence,' defendants could have filed a motion for summary judgment and avoided liability altogether," the brief continued. "Instead, defendants recognized the strength of plaintiff's claims and came to the settlement table."

In short, then, not only had the Department of Corrections agreed to settle out of court but had used the ACLU lawsuit to successfully demand funds from legislative committees. The ACLU lawsuit not only brought medical funding to corrections but required that the increase continue in the budget.

That constituted enormous change, the ACLU lawyers insisted. Formerly DeLand or any corrections director had enjoyed complete discretion as to how much money was spent on prison health care. The funds could be shifted to another part of the department budget or returned unused to the state, as DeLand had done. "As a direct result of this lawsuit, funding for prison health care increased dramatically, and the budget is no longer the director's private 'slush fund' to manipulate at will."

In response to DeLand's contention that he and Blumner had a "gentlemen's agreement" which he kept faithfully, Blumner filed her own affidavit. She stated:

> It was my understanding that DeLand understood that if the deficiencies which existed were not timely remedied the ACLU would commence litigation in order to force improvement of the medical and mental health care . . . [and] that I took the step of directing a draft complaint be prepared . . . in the event litigation was necessary. At the time of my departure, it was my perception that progress toward improving the deficiencies in the medical and mental health care at the prison had stagnated.

Until the day of the judge's decision, both Bangerter and DeLand assumed a victory on the state's side of the tally sheet. The former governor said early in 1994, "The ACLU does some very good things, they protect some things." He summarized with a smile, "I'm not mad at Michele Parish and the ACLU. I just hope they're not mad at us because we beat them most of the time." With a chuckle, he amended, "Actually they beat us on two out of three—on abortion and prayer—but we won the most on the prison."

At that point, Bangerter did not know of Jenkins's thirty-page decision which would award more than $300,000 in taxpayers' money to the ACLU. The affiliate had prevailed without doubt, the judge wrote. "The court finds that the plaintiff's lawsuit was a catalyst in achieving prison health care reform and increases in legislative funding necessary to implement that reform."

Jenkins found DeLand's application of Rule 68 inappropriate to a stipulated lawsuit. Even if the rule applied, the judge said, the plaintiff had received far more relief due to the lawsuit than would have come without it.

The financial breakdown awarded Fabian & Clendenin $228,697 in fees and $3,058.49 for expenses, the Legal Center for People with Disabilities $27,944.40 in fees, and the ACLU National Prison Project $17,704.50 in attorney fees and $2,719.56 for expenses. Once the accounts were settled, the Utah ACLU found itself with more than $96,000 in a money market account while it deliberated various investment plans.

DeLand had a contingency appeal in mind in case Jenkins ruled against the state, but the attorney general's office wasn't interested in pursuing it. For the moment, at least, the conflict had come to a halt.

"It was a very fair award," Switzer said. "We got nearly everything we asked for."

From her office in Washington, D.C., Parish expressed satisfaction. Her experience had shown, she said, that awarding attorney fees was important when a state department approached the legislature for funding. The cost told the legislators that the taxpayers had not only paid for improvements but they would also pay the attorneys who won the reform. When the attorneys donated those fees to the ACLU, they ensured future battles on civil liberties issues.

"DeLand was sitting on a complex and beleaguered system," Kendell commented. As she saw it, he had chosen to pour resources into security at the expense of medical care, rehabilitation, or mental health care, and then warred with the ACLU to defend his decision. "I think it's disgraceful that he became legendary for his sniping match with Michele Parish. The department staffers and the media all still talk about it," Kendell said. "Michele must have been effective to have a powerful department head spending his time arguing in public with the head of a public service agency." Even with all the changes in leadership, policy, and issues, Kendell said, paranoia remained common among the inmates.

Early in her tenure as executive director, Gnade welcomed to her office representatives of an issue that had prompted the Utah affiliate's organization. One March morning James and Tia Jones carried in their infant daughter and told Gnade of James's recent incarceration in the Salt Lake County Jail. Walking home from his cousin's December wedding reception, Jones had been stopped by police and arrested for public intoxication; however, he was actually held on suspicion of rape. While in jail for five weeks, Jones had lost his job, missed the birth of their daughter, and endured the stigma of a black prisoner accused of raping a white woman.

The rape victim did not identify Jones. In fact, she said he was not her assailant. Yet he remained incarcerated pending the results of a DNA test, which finally freed him. By that time, the young family had to seek asylum in the homeless shelter. Not only had Jones been incarcerated unduly for more than a month, but the county attorney's office had not erased the unfounded charge from his record, making it impossible for him to get another job.

While Gnade and Kendell discussed the legal side of the incident, Gnade took a shortcut and called the media. The Jones incarceration became an immediate story. "I still can't believe it," Jones told the *Tribune*. "It's outrageous. It's cruel. And what do I get? Sorry mister and that's it? Look at me. Look at my wife and baby."

The publicity brought immediate results as calls poured into the homeless shelter with offers of jobs, money, and housing. In a follow-up story, Jones told the newspaper, "I don't want all the attention, really. I just want to get back on my feet and support my family."

While the legal system tended to discriminate based on race and income, the times had changed in one respect. In 1958 when the Utah ACLU received its charter, Jones's experience would not have made the newspaper, let alone spark community support.

Several months later the *Tribune* placed Jones's experience in a wider context in a front-page article beginning: "For most people charged with a serious crime, getting out of jail may all come down to cash." Jones, who had worked as a dishwasher, was cited as an example of a prisoner facing too grave a charge with too little backing to win bail. "There are not too many bondsmen in town that will post bond for a poor person," the article quoted Salt Lake County attorney David Yocom.

Kendell's comment followed: "This is an example of justice if you can afford it. . . . If people are well-to-do or have stature in the community, they will not serve time in jail."

Jones's incarceration was linked that summer to the first anniversary of the execution of an African American, convicted murderer William Andrews. Racial disparities in the judicial system highlighted the community uneasiness around the death penalty, particularly in the Andrews case since he had not fired the fatal shots. The shooter in the notorious Hi-Fi Shop torture murders in Ogden, Pierre Selby, had been executed several years earlier.

Now, using the injustice toward James Jones as a point of departure,

James Gillespie, head of the Ogden National Association for the Advancement of Colored People, drew comparisons with the execution the past summer. "There's no way Andrews would have been executed if he was white. No way in the world. [Mormon forger and bomber Mark] Hofmann killed two people—in premeditated murder—and he's not on death row."

So strong had been the African-American community's resistance to Andrews's scheduled execution that the NAACP and other groups asked the ACLU to keep a low profile in the protest. Only when the cause became hopeless, Michele Parish said later, was the ACLU asked to make its presence known. Parish then called the National Capital Punishment Project and wrote to the governor, sorry the affiliate had not been more involved.

"They had me on the stand at the candlelight vigil the night before the execution," she reminisced, "because I knew all the verses to 'Amazing Grace.'" Parish understood the dynamic. Andrews had so much community support that the ACLU's backing was not only less in demand but less desired. "We are the ones who deal with the most despised and rejected people."

The issue of race emerged elsewhere. Two African Americans were arrested in Iron County because, as the arresting officer testified, they were black and had a California license plate and thus fit the profile for drug runners. In this instance drugs were found, reinforcing the profile's stereotype.

"However," Kendell said, "the Fourth Amendment works before the fact. The profiles are developed for a reason. A fair number of individuals, due to socio-economic dynamics in minority communities, are involved in drugs. The problem is that for every person who is guilty who is pulled over and subjected to an illegal search, dozens have their Fourth Amendment rights trampled over."

She added, "The most objectionable thing about profiling is that it places people of color in the position of having diminished constitutional rights. Whites can presume their constitutional rights are okay; a person of color can't." When it came to the declared war on drugs, Kendell said, "I don't care if we end up with more drugs on the highway if we still have a Fourth Amendment that means something. Maintaining that is a more worthy goal."

The ACLU found a plaintiff in Joe Soto, a Hispanic citizen repeatedly pulled over despite an immaculate drug record. A complaint demanding a jury and filed June 11, 1993, stated that Soto, a resident of Salt Lake City, was "readily identifiable as Hispanic." He alleged that he was stopped without justification seven times between June 1992 and March 1993 by Highway Patrol officers Paul G. Mangelson or Lance D. Bushnell, who were named in the complaint along with various John Does. Soto was stopped, the complaint alleged, because he fit a drug-smuggling profile developed by the Highway Patrol, prompting officers to detain drivers who were of minority descent; drove late model, luxury, or rented automobiles; and had out-of-state plates.

"These tactics are the product of an agreement . . . properly termed a conspiracy," the complaint read, which "has the purpose of depriving persons of their right to equal protection or equal privileges and immunities under the laws, the right to be free from unreasonable searches and seizures, and the right to due process of law." The Utah ACLU pursued the Soto case through a number of court hearings during the next several years.

In the meantime the Youth Corrections system seemed to teeter on the brink of an irreparable crisis. In visiting detention centers, Kendell found teens sleeping on the floor, sometimes beneath toilets, and doing without classes, programs, and counseling because the resources were too limited. Kendell attended regular meetings of a legislative detention committee hunting for solutions to the crisis. In June the ACLU filed a lawsuit but continued to work toward a solution.

Both the Salt Lake County Detention Facility and the Moweda Detention Center in Davis County consistently housed more teens than their allowed capacities. The lawsuit alleged that the Salt Lake center was over capacity during 76 percent of the year 1992, while the Moweda center was over capacity 36 percent of the same year.

Late in the summer of 1993, an escalation in gang violence claimed headlines and stirred the public. A fatal shooting of a teenager outside the Triad Center in downtown Salt Lake City, followed by the gunning down of a prime witness in the case, horrified the community. Salt Lake City mayor Deedee Corradini called for gun control and curfews. Police chief Ruben Ortega agreed and proposed searching juveniles at the Utah State Fair and publishing the names of juveniles charged with violent crimes. Kendell cautioned against basing police procedures on race, age, or clothing.

Now that young offenders had managed to capture government attention, the ACLU put the lawsuit against the youth corrections system on hold. Kendell lobbied the governor's office directly and continued to meet with juvenile corrections officials. In a letter dated September 23, 1993, she urged Governor Mike Leavitt to relieve the overcrowding and provide greater resources to juvenile court.

"I am convinced that simply locking more youth up is not the answer to the problem of juvenile crime," she wrote. "Most juveniles respond to less severe sanction, such as probation, community service, or other work programs." The programs would not work effectively, however, lacking another juvenile judge and more probation officers. She closed by thanking the governor for his efforts and indicated a willingness to meet with him or with his staff.

By October the *Tribune* reported that the youth corrections system was overwhelmed. "More than 290,000 children between the ages of ten and seventeen live in Utah," the article stated. "Of those, more than half are ages fourteen to seventeen—the time when juveniles are most likely to have a brush with the law."

Not only had the population risen, but so had the seriousness of the crimes committed. The 1990s saw more juveniles jailed for murder, aggravated assault, and other violent crimes. "Last year, juveniles in detention had an average of 10.3 convictions, according to a report to be released today," the article continued.

While teenagers of all racial and ethnic backgrounds became involved in gangs, some gangs were identified by ethnicity, and minority youths, like adults, tended to fare poorly in the justice system. "The study also shows that Latino, American Indian, Asian and black juveniles are more likely to be locked up than their white counterparts," the report read. "The findings mirror results from a 1991 report, showing no improvements have been made." Minority juveniles spent more time behind bars, the *Tribune* article continued.

"'The problem may be a combination of things,' said John Dewitt of the state Division of Youth Corrections. 'Minority families may not have the resources to send their children to treatment programs or it may be difficult to get them to come to court.'"

The article noted how few minority staffers there were in the juvenile justice system. Whites made up more than 80 percent of the detention staff. Latinos represented 7.4 percent and African Americans 4.7 percent.

The severity and complexity of the problems might have given the 1994 legislature much to discuss. Yet the proposed bills dithered between outlawing spray paint and markers and requiring students in public schools to wear uniforms. Despite a great deal of rhetoric, Kendell concluded that little would be accomplished. The lawmakers seemed unable to come to grips with the scope and urgency of the situation. Following a riot at the Salt Lake County Youth Detention Center, Kendell said the affiliate would pursue its lawsuit.

She wrote Leavitt that providing more beds for youths in detention facilities was critical, yet must be backed by "other meaningful and fully funded alternatives" as well. For one thing, "lightweight" and "hard core" offenders ought to be separated so that a youth who played hookey from school and a youth arrested for aggravated assault would not be housed together. In fact, those committing minor offenses would be far better served by other alternatives.

"Intensive parole and supervision programs, such as exist in other states, must be implemented in Utah if we are to seriously deal with our juvenile crime problem," she wrote. Work camps, home confinement with supervision, and reporting centers were all less expensive alternatives "than the bricks and mortar required to provide more bed space. Moreover, these alternatives often succeed where incarceration does not."

While concern about gangs focused on northern Utah, in Washington County, in the southwestern corner of the state, the ACLU forced the county jail to accommodate female inmates. "I sent three letters to county officials and I personally visited the jail, and everyone agreed that the system needed to be rectified," Kendell said. "But it was clear to me that nothing was going to get done unless we filed the suit."

The county reluctantly consented to overhaul and enlarge a room to accommodate up to eight women. This meant installing windows, showers, toilets, and other facilities, scheduling regular visitation hours and rules, notifying the ACLU if a mass arrest occurred involving more than eight women, and maintaining a ratio of one jail guard for every six inmates. Interestingly, in this and other cases when jail standards were written or revised, the work was contracted to former corrections chief Gary DeLand.

The *Salt Lake Tribune* featured another law enforcement incident involving race that would become the basis of an ACLU lawsuit in 1994, written by a frequent ACLU ally, para-legal Todd Gabler. Beneath a large color photograph of Rosanna Valdez and her son Raymond, datelined LaPoint, the article by Michael Phillips began:

> From her kitchen window, Rosanna Valdez saw a man outside squat on his haunches and scurry across her lawn. Another man, a police officer from the Bureau of Indian Affairs, strode to the front door and cocked his shotgun.
>
> "I caught sight of these guys and thought I was under attack," says Valdez, a Ute tribe member who lives on the Uintah-Ouray Reservation in northeastern Utah. "I was right, only it turns out these guys were police."

The officers were looking for her son, Raymond Valdez, who they said was wanted on warrants. Rosanna told them her son did not live with her and that she had not seen him for weeks. She asked to see the search warrant. No warrant appeared, Valdez alleged. According to the *Tribune*:

> "I told him I had rights, and he started screaming at me. He threatened to kick the door down and arrest me for interfering." Valdez, forty-one, looked up at the BIA officer. "Can he do this without a search warrant?" she asked.
>
> "He can do anything he wants," she claims the officer said. "He's the FBI."

Gnade's interest in this incident had been keen from the start. She contacted ACLU pundit Steven Pevar, a University of Denver law professor and author of *The Rights of Indians and Tribes,* who agreed to assist the Utah affiliate. The newspaper quoted Pevar saying, "It's almost like a legal no-man's land on the reservations. Police out there can do what they damned well please."

Several weeks after the search, Raymond Valdez surrendered to the BIA at his mother's insistence and was later freed on bond. He faced state charges of burglarizing a Salt Lake County home, a second-degree felony, and with third-degree felony theft.

In spring 1994, about five months following the incident, the Utah ACLU filed suit against FBI agent Samuel McPheters, BIA officer Greg Littlewhiteman, and several John Doe defendants. According to the complaint, the officers had threatened Rosanna Valdez, brandished weapons, questioned her house guests, ordered her outside her home where they "yelled at plaintiff" and threatened to shoot her son on sight. Two hours later they returned to repeat the threats and search further. They said they would harass her neighbors, as well, in order to embarrass her.

The lawsuit alleged violation of Rosanna Valdez's Fourth Amendment rights against unreasonable search and her Fifth Amendment rights guaranteeing due process of law. The lawsuit claimed that Valdez had suffered emotional distress and fear for her own physical safety. "Defendants violated plaintiff's rights intentionally and with malice," the complaint stated. "Moreover, defendants knew or should have known that they did not have the right to search [her] . . . residence without a warrant." The suit requested a judgment against the FBI and BIA agents for compensatory damages of $100,000, punitive damages of $50,000 each, as well as attorney and court costs.

All these issues involving race and law enforcement may have been harbingers for a proliferation of complaints alleging prejudice. By June 1994 an increasing spate of "horror stories" reached the ACLU office involving Spanish-speaking immigration into Utah. Immigration was on the rise and was a national concern, particularly in the southeast and southwest where it pressured social systems including law enforcement. Yet the problems came as something of a shock in Utah, as did the prejudices revealed with them.

In one instance a prominent Hispanic Salt Lake City resident was asked for her green card, a permit issued by the Immigration and Naturalization Service, when she visited her father in the hospital. The ACLU tipped off the media, and, following publicity, the employee was fired. Similar complaints continued to flow into the affiliate office. A dark-complected housekeeper took her employers' toddler to a hospital for stitches and was refused service. Hispanic motorists, stopped for alleged traffic infractions, were asked for their green cards. Green cards were confiscated by police in parks, apparently just to create difficulty. Such incidents were not entirely new in the diverse Hispanic community, but the complaints were new to Gnade and she intended to seek remedies.

Another police profiling incident, not involving race, also came to light. A twenty-one-year-old Bountiful resident was stopped one September evening by the Utah Highway Patrol as he traveled past Farmington on Interstate 15. Robert David Fitches's young age, his shoulder-length blond hair, and his older-model vehicle, the ensuing lawsuit claimed, "placed him within the identifiable drug courier profile employed by the defendants [the Utah Highway Patrol]."

Fitches and a friend, Tony Morley, were stopped by Officer Terry Mercer, purportedly for a burned out headlight. After a routine identification check, however, the officer told Fitches that he smelled marijuana smoke. Fitches and his friend denied possessing or smoking marijuana but were ordered out of the car. Since Morley required a wheelchair, the officer allowed him to remain in the car while he tested Fitches for impaired faculties. The young man passed the tests.

Gradually a veritable crowd of law enforcers gathered—up to ten John Does. The officers removed Morley from the vehicle and placed him in his wheelchair. They allegedly called Fitches a liar when he again denied having marijuana, and they searched his friend and the car without consent. A canine unit was called. The dogs found no drugs. The final insult occurred, the lawsuit alleged, when Mercer required Fitches to lower his trousers and place his hands on top of the car. "Defendant Mercer then probed Fitches's genitals with his gloved hands through his underwear," the complaint continued. "This incident took place while Fitches was standing on the side of the road in view of all officers gathered, traffic, and his friend.

"The officers at no time during any of these searches located any controlled substances or any other evidence of illegal activity." After three and one-half hours of threats, searches, and insults, the young men were allowed to leave. Fitches was given a warning ticket for the burned-out headlight.

The lawsuit claimed that the Utah Highway Patrol had violated Fitches's Fourth, Fifth, and Fourteenth Amendment rights, as well as his right to privacy. It requested not less than $150,000 in damages, claiming that the incident resulted in "physical and mental suffering, distress, degradation, humiliation, anguish, loss of dignity, . . . and loss of freedom, which resulted from the substantial length of his detention." The ACLU lost the case in court after the defendants entered a marijuana stem into evidence.

These lawsuits lent considerable energy to the ACLU office. Many of the judicial issues that prompted the organization of the Utah affiliate clearly remained at the forefront forty years later. Progress in protecting defendants' and prisoners' rights was apparent within the legal system and documented in court records. Still, the right of ordinary citizens to be safe from unlawful intrusion or unjust accusation in their homes, in businesses, and on the highways, remained a cause that the ACLU enthusiastically championed.

In addition, both the rise in teen violence and in drug-related crimes burgeoned within the already stressed corrections system. The challenge of preserving First Amendment rights within a society beleaguered by violence promised to keep law enforcement and the ACLU busy in future years.

10.
And Justice for All

At first, under Carol Gnade's directorship, it seemed the affiliate's improved clout and communications formed stepping stones that might converge into a bumpy but convenient road, with litigation an unwanted detour. Yet between 1993 and 1996 questions of how Utahns lived, where they prayed, what they might be taught in schools, where and how legislators performed governmental business, and how murderers were executed all crisscrossed in a busy intersection of church and state. Separating the two in Utah remained as intricate a task as ever and raised the Utah ACLU's own split in approach. Increasingly, Gnade juggled conciliation with one hand and confrontation with the other.

Kate Kendell put it this way: "ACLU is a four-letter word in Utah. In Utah there's a mentality that you don't make waves. When you have an organization like the ACLU, whose mission it is to make waves, it's antithetical to the rest of the population."

In 1993 a friendly spirit promoted conciliation, although major lawsuits remained unresolved. The affiliate had not yet prevailed in the appeals regarding prison medical reform and abortion, and the Utah Supreme Court had yet to rule on prayer in government meetings. However, telephone calls from Governor Leavitt's aides, a cooperative ambience in the legislature, ongoing media coverage, and the scores of supporters who turned up to lobby all bore witness to the affiliate's power.

The year 1993 was the first for the affiliate to remain in financial black ink. In fact, the $60,000 in the bank at year's end might have caused Jim Joy or Shirley Pedler to swoon. "I feel we have to act like a business even though we are activists," Gnade said. She enlisted the ongoing support of major donors, assuring the affiliate's stability for the foreseeable future.

Perennial issues such as censorship took a new tack. Nationally and locally homosexuals had initiated a quest for acknowledgement—if not acceptance—by American society. Executive director Shirley Pedler had discussed homosexual rights with the media a decade earlier, but practical matters had affected Utah very little. With the 1992 election of Bill Clinton, the gay rights movement clarified its issues and showed political muscle, particularly concerning homosexuals serving in the military.

In Salt Lake City several gay and lesbian groups had organized quietly and, with the change in times and attitudes, become vocal. These groups took their turn in the "rights revolution," asserting a small but increasing influence in elections and with the media. This occurred despite a powerful stigma against homosexuality, reinforced by the attitude of many churches including Utah's predominant religion. Certain Protestant denominations grappled with gay issues among parishioners and within the clergy, but the LDS leadership simply denounced any and all homosexual activity as excommunicable sin. In Utah's child-centered culture, the controversy focused on the control of information, especially any tone of tolerance or acceptance appearing in public school textbooks.

The matter erupted in March 1993 when the state textbook commission attempted to liberalize its policy on texts used in high school classrooms. The commission was prepared to approve texts that acknowledged homosexuality as an existing lifestyle as long as it was not promoted as an equal alternative to heterosexual family life.

This seemed a minimal concession to reality, especially given the pressures on teenagers who believed themselves homosexual or wondered about their sexual identity. However, perhaps with those same students in mind, opponents considered any neutral or accepting mention of homosexuality a dangerous provocation.

The state's higher-than-average teen suicide rate was examined by public agencies and within the media from time to time. No firm answers existed as to why Utah teens ended their lives at a higher rate than teens in most areas of the nation. However, Utah's birth rate far exceeded the national average, and the children born to the post-World War II baby boom generation were coming of age. This placed pressure on schools, jobs, activities, and, inevitably, on young people.

In addition, the high value Utahns placed on achievement presented a possible factor; many parents emphasized higher education, sexual abstinence which predicated young marriage, rearing large families, and successful employment. Also, LDS males were strongly encouraged to serve two-year missions in their late teens and early twenties. Ideally incoming missionaries were sexually inexperienced and remained celibate until they returned home to marry. Homosexuality found no place in most people's expectations for the state's youth.

The Gay and Lesbian Youth Group formed in the late 1980s to discourage drug or alcohol use, increase self-esteem, provide a social climate, and issue information through guest speakers and peer counseling. Yet the founders and leaders acknowledged, at root, a grimmer goal—to prevent teen suicide, which to them seemed astronomical among teens who believed they were homosexual.

Commonly these youngsters dropped out of school, where they felt ostracized. Many were banished from their homes when their parents discovered their sexual inclinations. The youth group aligned with longstanding gay community organizations and welcomed disenfranchised youngsters every week. To this community, any tolerance indicated in school textbooks seemed not only a positive step for society, but possibly a lifesaving boon for anxious teens.

A State Textbook Commission meeting in June 1993 saw heated disagreement from individuals and a variety of groups, with the archconservative Eagle Forum strongly present. Recently the forum had been credited with gutting a hate-crimes bill, considered by the legislature following a virulent outbreak of assaults and murders of homosexuals. The forum clearly came to the textbook meeting prepared to resist any softening of the anti-gay line.

A report in the *Tribune* quoted textbook commission member Michael Bennett in explaining the commission's original decision to accept textbooks with a moderate approach short of advocacy. "We were looking at it from the standpoint of tolerance," he explained. "We would not have adopted a book that advocates a homosexual lifestyle. We simply wanted people to be more tolerant of choices made by others."

Such an uproar ensued, however, and by the meeting's end, the State Board of Education decided to continue the prohibition of any text that mentioned homosexuality. This essentially banned updated health and psychology texts. Exactly what could be discussed in the classroom remained vague. The state director of curriculum explained that teachers could discuss homosexuality as long as they did not say "that it doesn't matter what a person's sexual orientation is."

The Utah affiliate began to consider a lawsuit. Kate Kendell viewed the issue as an abridgment of free speech. The policy prevented teachers from disparaging any profession, race, or religion while disallowing any positive or neutral comment on homosexuality. "This prohibits any kind of discussion that's comparative or analytical."

The Utah ACLU viewed Gayle Ruzicka and her Eagle Forum as formidable opponents since she could quickly mobilize a zealous lobby. When the ACLU opposed the forum, the negative, nasty, and anonymous telephone messages left on the hotline noticeably increased. "Instead of the Christian right, we have Gayle Ruzicka," Carol Gnade would say ruefully.

Actually Ruzicka was not far removed from the national Christian right, and the alliance would tighten. For years she had attended the Christian Coalition's national conference. By 1994 a chapter of the Christian Coalition functioned in Utah, boasting more than 5,000 members by the year's end. Reverend Vaughn Milliron, chapter president, told the *Salt Lake Tribune* he was uncomfortable rubbing shoulders with Mormons, given major disparities in their theological views. Yet the coalition fit snugly into the political mix of "pro-family" Mormons, including the forum. The violence and open hostility seen elsewhere in the nation around such groups deferred to Utah's nicer style, the *Tribune* reported. Yet the issues were battled fiercely.

In September, as public schools convened, the textbook question naturally surfaced as teachers and administrators debated the appropriateness and legality of various books. For instance, the text *Psychology:*

An Introduction was proposed, but refused by the commission due to one sentence on page 567: "Homosexuality itself was no longer considered a disorder unless it caused the person significant distress."

Gary Crump, Salt Lake City sales representative for the publisher, Prentice Hall, told the *Tribune*: "You really are out[side] of the twentieth century thinking in this country. Whether [homosexuality] is right or wrong, it is factual information. . . . The state wants to view it as abnormal."

The *Tribune* asked Gnade for comment. She described how the affiliate had already been contacted by parents and teachers who wanted the state board's decision amended. "It seems that educators are being relegated to taking an X-Acto knife to the pages of textbooks to cut out opinions that do not comply with the policy of the board of education . . . ," she told the newspaper. "It is essentially viewpoint discrimination. Given the demands placed upon our young people living in a complicated world, what we should be giving them is more information, not less."

An Eagle Forum curriculum monitor, Debbie Simpson, countered by telling the newspaper that the need to find newer, more relevant textbooks was "not an issue," explaining, "We here in Utah do not want homosexuality as a lifestyle taught to our students when they are young and impressionable, period."

The *Tribune* gave the last word to David Nelson, founder of the Gay and Lesbian Utah Democrats. "The books they are talking about have four pages out of 200 pages that deal with homosexuality . . . ," he said. "If we look at any of those books they are proposing, none of those would be advocating or promoting homosexuality. They are giving explanations."

The textbook controversy evaded any resolution beyond the discussion ban. In May 1994 Kendell briefed the board of trustees on the implications of a lawsuit against the Utah Board of Education. She explained that the guidelines barred a "vast range of material, including most literature and art that addresses or mentions the subject of homosexuality except to condemn it." She concluded the guidelines were "vulnerable to challenge" based on viewpoint discrimination, a recent and largely unlitigated concept. The "guidelines at issue here simply go too far and do too much," she wrote. "While a school may have the power to impose some view, [it] should not have the power to absolutely forbid even the mention of opposing ideas."

That month the State Board of Education approved a parent/teacher guide to help "junior high school students develop healthy attitudes toward sexual behavior." The Eagle Forum again objected to any information on homosexuality, contraception, and abortion even in the guide for adults. (Utah's teen pregnancy rate was also high compared to other mostly white populations.) Others said that teachers needed help in gaining and giving correct information, and that teens should be adequately informed on these topics. Finally board members reiterated the state's policy of promoting abstinence and forbidding teachers to discuss contraception, but approved the parent/teacher guide. Athough the issue would lie dormant for several years, when it steamed into the public consciousness even more forcefully, students would be driving the train. By spring 1996 the board approved a new health text, but still no new psychology text that did not mention homosexuality could be found. In addition, a new history text was rejected due to a description of the gay rights movement.

Quite a different complaint reached the affiliate when students returned to classrooms in the fall of 1994. A Provo parent, who had attended back-to-school night at a junior high, telephoned Gnade. One United States history teacher had explained to each rotating group of parents the areas of study, then added: "Of course, all of these teachings in history will be supplemented by our study of the Book of Mormon because it is the foundation of our people." He later joked, the caller continued, that during lectures he occasionally broke out into "a few Primary songs," the religious music taught to LDS children.

The complaint came, Gnade said, from a practicing Mormon who was aghast at the teacher's approach. Gnade replied that she appreciated his outrage but foresaw difficulty in finding many parents who would participate in a public action due to the social and religious stigma that would follow. "I have to admit," the caller replied, "I'd like to be a John Doe in this, but if you need me, I'll be willing to go public."

During this period, the discussion of public discourse dominated several ACLU affairs. In October 1993 actor and activist Ed Asner regaled the lawyers, community leaders, journalists, and ACLU donors and members who crowded into the Red Lion Hotel ballroom for the annual dinner. He skimmed over dozens of First Amendment triumphs and failures and challenged the group to maintain continued vigilance. Junior high student Maren Larson was given a special award for objecting to the use of degrading cartoons depicting Native Americans in her school's yearbook.

Nadine Strossen, president of the national ACLU, visited that month as well, speaking at Utah State University in Logan and at A Woman's Place Bookstore in Salt Lake City. She not only drew media attention, but an anonymous note threatening to bomb either the bookstore or the affiliate office. Law enforcers surmised a white supremacist group might be behind the threat.

Accordingly three marked police cars parked outside the bookstore on the evening of October 28 while Strossen spoke to an audience of around fifty. She quickly established a national context for the censorship issue, referring to the criminal prosecution of a Cincinnati art gallery, the stringent restrictions on media coverage during the Persian Gulf War, and the political correctness movement on university campuses.

Strossen laced her remarks with humor, emphasizing that no one ever asked her why she defended free speech—only why the ACLU defended the free speech of unlikable individuals or groups, some of whom seemed dangerous. When she described the "arrest" and eventual "acquittal" of a student's painting in Chicago, uniformed police officers chuckled along with the audience. Her point was that defending free speech was very nearly an absolute for the ACLU; the sanctity of any group's rights implied the safety of everyone's rights.

"If freedom of speech is jeopardized for one idea, then it's never going to be safe for another idea," Strossen was quoted in the *Tribune*. "And history certainly proves the veracity of that theory."

Around Thanksgiving 1993 the protection of First Amendment rights joined questions around Fourth Amendment rights when twenty-year-old Mark Wilson came to the affiliate office to complain about housing near Brigham Young University in Provo. He faced eviction

215

because he had hung posters from the swimsuit issue of *Sports Illustrated* magazine in his bathroom. The photographs violated BYU regulations, which were enforced by landlords of approved housing located off campus.

BYU required unmarried students under twenty-five years of age to live in supervised housing, but only about 6,000 could be accommodated in campus dormitories. An additional 12,000 found housing in apartments that BYU approved after landlords added university regulations and prohibitions to their leases. The arrangement benefitted BYU by allowing student housing to expand throughout the Utah Valley while still maintaining the standards required on campus. It benefitted landlords by supplying them a seemingly endless pool of well-behaved tenants.

Wilson was not a student but needed an apartment and had found one in an approved complex. He had signed a lease that included restrictions on decor, alcohol, tobacco, drugs, and allowing the opposite sex into the bedrooms. Then he and his apartment had flunked a routine inspection.

The arrangement between BYU and nearby landlords varied from one apartment complex to another. The landlords segregated male and female tenants, families and unmarried tenants, and sometimes they combined students and non-students as long as non-students signed the lease restricting their behavior. The BYU regulations affected—or protected, as the ACLU saw it—around 1,200 Utah Valley landlords. Together their holdings represented 31 percent of the valley's total housing market and included apartments, condominiums, townhouses, four-plexes, and complexes.

The policy had begun in the 1950s when the number of BYU students exceeded campus housing, and it went unchallenged until 1978. At that time, a young woman hired Kathryn Collard as her attorney, and they appealed to the United States Justice Department. Collard said her client was prohibited from moving into a studio apartment set aside for male tenants. She was required to rent a more costly one-bedroom apartment.

In 1978 the Justice Department and BYU worked out an exemption similar to the regulation allowing universities to provide gender-segregated boarding houses. It rested on BYU's status as a church-owned university and the church's moral code, which prohibited premarital sex. Since that time the housing situation had evolved into various configurations.

Monitoring was performed not only by landlords but by the watchful eyes of other students and tenants. A negative report could bring an inspection, which could mean an ouster for possessing tea bags in the cupboard, beer in the refrigerator, "or, conceivably, the swimsuit issue of *Sports Illustrated*," Kendell would tell a reporter, pointing out that all those items were legal for adults.

Aware of the combined power of the Justice Department and BYU in past deal-making, Gnade and Kendell decided to release their information on the BYU housing situation to the media while they sorted and researched the legal options. On November 24 the *Tribune* quoted Kendell saying the university must modify or remove its policy in the case of non-students.

BYU spokesperson Brent Harker commented, "We're in an interesting position . . . We really try to create a unique atmosphere where people can integrate faith in God with high academic excellence." Part of that, BYU officials would explain repeatedly to reporters, involved supervising student living quarters whether on or off campus.

Kendell called the policy absurd. Such restrictions could legally be applied to BYU students, she said, but they put non-students "in a position of either not getting an apartment or making them promise not to engage in perfectly legal activities, [which] is an unconstitutional choice."

The Fourth Amendment issues rose as Kendell read the lease that the complaining resident brought in. One notice stated: "BYU will inspect this apartment again." The monthly searches of the apartments, occupied or not, were undertaken by the apartment managers in order to keep their status as approved housing. Yet the Fourth Amendment guaranteed every citizen's right to be free of unreasonable searches.

Privately Kendell spoke with a BYU official who said the university was in the process of modifying its policy; he discouraged litigation. Fine, Kendell said, but insisted on seeing a draft of the new policy quickly. Meanwhile, she and Gnade, along with members of the legal panel, debated whether the compliant landlords or the university should be targeted for a lawsuit, if it came to that.

On November 28 the *Tribune* led its coverage with the landlords' position. Datelined Provo, the article by Anne Matthews and Michael Phillips began:

> Brigham Young University has no greater champions of its honor code than off-campus landlords who require tenants to abstain from drugs, gambling, coffee, and even racy posters. It does not matter if the apartment's occupant is a BYU student or not.
>
> "There is no place else in the world like this," says Madeline Hendricks, manager of The Brittany Apartments. "I cannot check on my tenants twenty-four hours a day. We rely on BYU's honor code and on tenants to tell us when other tenants violate it. It's a system that works."

In the same article, Carol Gnade called this system "economic blackmail . . . It's exactly what fair-housing laws are supposed to prevent. Of course, the landlords like it. It's a kind of conspiracy to take away tenants' civil rights."

The article quoted Richard Knapp, owner of the Branbury Park Apartments where the complaint had originated: "Our way of life is threatened . . . The ACLU, in championing freedom, might take away something important here," he said. "We're a group of people living by the standards we have set for ourselves. Other people are free to do what they want, but not on my property."

Early in December the *Tribune* editorialized under the headline: "Private School Housing Rules Go Too Far When Imposed on Non-Student Renters." The column reviewed the situation and closed with:

> This isn't a question of denigrating BYU's honor code, the Mormon religion, or the high moral standards it espouses. Indeed, underage or irresponsible alcohol consumption, to cite one example, is a terrible epidemic on college campuses. Many parents of college students throughout America probably would be grateful for stricter moral standards of the kind BYU enforces for its enrollees.
>
> But it is unfair and probably unconstitutional to impose a religious

code on law-abiding adults unaffiliated with BYU as a condition for obtaining housing in privately owned buildings off campus. Surely a compromise can be achieved that could serve BYU's purposes while simultaneously respecting the civil rights of those renters with no ties to the university.

The ACLU won the initial round without filing a single paper. In January BYU informed the landlords involved that they could no longer impose BYU standards on non-students. That meant landlords could no longer allow students and non-students to share an apartment building—they would have to segregate students and non-students, as well as continuing to segregate BYU students by gender and family status.

Although the new arrangement meant that BYU students would be held to the university's code while non-students would not, it was clear that the landlords would continue to monitor non-students' conduct insofar as possible. Tenants would sign a contract requiring conduct "consistent with basic principles of modesty, decency and privacy in keeping with accepted community morals," according to a BYU statement, as reported by the *Tribune*.

The new policy specifically addressed the sanctions imposed on Mark Wilson and other non-students but failed to satisfy the Utah ACLU, which objected to the overall principle of applying religious rather than legal standards to tenants' lifestyles. Commented Gnade, "We are in total disagreement with this new policy and believe that it still requires a religious test to acquire housing in Provo . . . We are researching our next response to this issue. This is not the end of it."

The other side also expressed discontent, for the article quoted landlord David Freeman saying, "The ACLU didn't do anybody a favor . . . Many single people want to live in the BYU environment and because of the ACLU's actions, they are not going to be able to do that."

The landlord of the Branbury Apartments told the *Tribune* he intended to monitor his non-students to the extent possible under the new policy. "Even non-BYU students are still subject to some of the rules we as landlords are able to enforce, such as restricting smoking, alcohol, and having unregistered guests spend the night," he said.

Kendell communicated for months with BYU attorneys regarding the housing policy, but each new twist seemed to bring a comparative constitutional problem. In May 1994 she wrote a memorandum to the board of trustees outlining the continued regulation of non-students' behavior by their off-campus landlords.

Meanwhile, the affiliate awaited a response from the Justice Department regarding the intent of its earlier decision. By telephone, a Justice Department official had informed Gnade and Kendell that there had never been any intent to allow BYU to monitor housing off-campus, even though the university was allowed to segregate housing by gender because of the church's moral code. The affiliate leaders asked for this statement in writing.

Kendell informed the board that a variety of complaints had spawned from the BYU policy and the earlier accommodation with the Justice Department. Some plaintiffs could not rent in certain complexes because they were not BYU students. Other plaintiffs were refused housing based on gender or because they were not married or were single parents. In addition, the affiliate was collecting leases in order "to determine what privacy violations we can expect as the landlord tries to enforce BYU's morality. . . ." Finally, Kendell wrote, the affiliate would debate the timing involved—whether to pull back and allow more offenses to occur before filing the lawsuit, or whether to press ahead.

Eventually the litmus test for the lawsuit became not the code enforced by the landlords, but the overall approach, which the Utah ACLU claimed constituted a religious test. Essentially, the landlords working with BYU discriminated by church membership, the ACLU claimed, for only 1 percent of BYU students were non-Mormon. Additionally they discriminated by gender and by marital status, both of which violated the Fair Housing Act. Finally, they advertised these discriminations in the effort to attract acceptable tenants.

In August 1994, in a complaint written by cooperating attorney Bruce Plenk, the Utah ACLU sued a dozen Provo area apartment complexes and corporations on behalf of three plaintiffs: Wilson, eighteen-year-old Anne Walker, and thirty-year-old Stan Burnett. The first two defendants had been refused available apartments due to their gender, and Burnett had been refused because he was not a BYU student. In addition, Wilson had applied for an apartment as a single parent and been turned away because children were not allowed.

The lawsuit asked only for attorney fees and costs for the plaintiffs, but demanded change. "The injury suffered by plaintiffs is immediate and irreparable," the lawsuit read, "and there does not exist an adequate remedy at law." If the landlords' policies continued, the lawsuit went on, multiple violations of people's rights would continue, for the landlords' policies were "entrenched and will not change" lacking a court injunction.

The ACLU further claimed that the landlords' actions constituted "a deliberate pattern and practice of violations of the Fair Housing Act" and presented the clear possibility of "irreparable harm and injury" through discriminating by religion, gender, and family status. It urged the U.S. District Court to retain jurisdiction to ensure that the changes became permanent.

Brigham Young University quickly filed a motion to intervene in the lawsuit in support of the landlords and appointed Mary Anne Wood as lead counsel, the attorney who was battling the ACLU on abortion. The ACLU raised no objection to BYU's alliance, provided the university stuck to the housing issues rather than raising religious or doctrinal concerns that were not addressed in the complaint, Kendell said. The university insisted that it complied with all laws, including the Fair Housing Act, and did not discriminate by religion, race, ethnic origin, or disability.

Then BYU president Rex Lee—previously employed by the Justice Department as solicitor general—immediately linked segregation by gender and governance of students to the LDS moral code. Furthermore, BYU attorneys claimed that the off-campus housing policy had been reviewed by state and federal housing agencies and found to be in compliance. Their precedent remained the 1978 case when the Justice Department had ruled that the education amendment to the Civil Rights Act took precedence over the Fair Housing Act.

Attorney Bruce Plenk insisted that during these instances of approval, the federal agencies had not scrutinized the private landlords and their practices. Religious discrimination was not the only offense, he claimed, for the plaintiffs also suffered discrimination based on marital status, children, and gender. The recent attempt to segregate students and non-students by building, Plenk claimed, had worsened matters for non-students, who found apartments scarce in a tight housing market.

Inevitably, the discussion returned to whether the ACLU was attempting to destroy the LDS world view and lifestyle, as provided for BYU students both on and off campus. The ACLU maintained that its concern lay only with the abridgment of rights of people who were not thus encompassed. "The religious beliefs of BYU, its students, and their parents are not at issue here," one brief read. "The question here must focus on the religious beliefs, if any, of defendants [the landlords], since it is their behavior that is alleged to be discriminatory."

In early 1995 U.S. district judge David Winder found entirely for BYU and the landlords. He found no guise of religious discrimination in renting to BYU students, for applicants were not asked their religion. He upheld the university's right to discriminate on the basis of gender due to the church's moral code and right to provide supportive housing, and therefore to advertise it. The landlords turned down applicants, Winder explained, because they were not students, not because they were not LDS. The family status claim also fell, for Winder ruled that since Wilson was not actually a single parent, he had no standing in the lawsuit. (A precedent for sending "testers" into the housing market had existed since the civil rights movement but was somewhat ambiguous.)

The Utah-ACLU could take comfort only in two things: first, that the landlords had been forced by the ACLU protest to remove the BYU prohibitions for non-students, and, second, that Winder ruled the lawsuit had merit and the ACLU would not be charged the other side's costs.

Of course the ACLU disagreed with the judge's literal view of student status not equaling, essentially, LDS membership. The affiliate was particularly upset, however, that discriminating by gender and advertising that discrimination had been upheld. Winder ruled that the landlords had not so discriminated because the applicants were not students and therefore not qualified for the apartments anyway. Had they been students, he said, the discrimination was justified by the 1978 BYU exemption. Since the "BYU-approved for men" and "BYU-approved for women" signs posted on rentals were honest, they were acceptable.

The affiliate's new staff attorney, Jensie Anderson, commented that she believed Winder was "dead wrong" on those rulings. "You can't engage in discriminatory advertising regardless of what your position is." The ACLU attorneys asked Winder to reconsider his ruling on advertising; should he reverse himself, that would grant them a portion of fees. In the meantime, they discussed with Gnade and the board the efficacy of an appeal.

Even the defeated had to chuckle when they learned that soon after Winder's ruling *Sports Illustrated* staffers went to Provo to write an article on two basketball-playing brothers at BYU. The feature would appear in the annual swimsuit issue, amid the kind of photographs that had started the entire ruckus.

While the BYU controversy developed, other church/state questions arose. In December 1993 new guidelines specified the place of religion and holiday celebrations in the public schools. Students would be allowed to express their own beliefs in class discussions or assignments, and they or their parents could waive any part of a course they felt infringed on their freedom of religion. Teachers could discuss religion as related to music, art, literature, law, politics, and history as long as it was presented in context and did not encourage or condemn any religion. High school choirs had a long tradition of performing in LDS sacrament meetings in December; now performances at churches were allowed as long as arrangements were initiated and carried out by students or non-school personnel. However, no prayers could be given at school-sponsored events, and school choirs could not be required to perform in religious meetings.

While red and green bells and chains went up in school windows, a controversy around religious display arose at one site in elaborately decorated Salt Lake City. Both the Society of Separationists and the ACLU protested the presence and placement of a menorah at the Gallivan Utah Center Plaza in honor of Hanukkah. The Separationists threatened to sue the city.

Kendell told the *Tribune*, "The United States Supreme Court has made it clear that any holiday display which emphasizes or implies government support or endorsement of a particular religious perspective is impermissible . . ." She explained, "That standard is religiously neutral. It applies to creches, to menorahs, or to any other symbol in and of itself which is a religious symbol."

The menorah had been erected by Chabad Lubavitch of Utah, an organization designed to strengthen the Jewish identity in the state. The group was also displaying a Hanukkah menorah on private property without sparking any protest. The *Tribune* quoted Rabbi Benny Zippel, director of the Chabad Lubavitch, saying, "The issue of the menorah on public property has been litigated throughout the country . . . The Pennsylvania case says the menorah doesn't violate separation of church and state and is legal."

Salt Lake City mayor Deedee Corradini promised to keep the menorah in the park as a symbol of cultural, philosophical, and social diversity, despite the threatened lawsuit. She said she had recently seen a variety of religious symbols grouped together on public grounds near the White House in Washington, D.C. The city added a lighted Christmas tree in the same vicinity, and the mingling of religious symbols sufficed. "The outcome contributes an even finer ecumenical spirit to this year's mid-winter holiday season," a *Salt Lake Tribune* editorial praised. The ACLU agreed.

The pre-eminent church/state issue, however, had been "on hold" for a year in the prayer case considered by the Utah Supreme Court. Late in 1993 the court prepared to release its long-awaited decision, which would prove, for the Utah ACLU, a holiday surprise.

As attorney for the Society of Separationists, Brian Barnard had no advance warning of what the court would decide—only that it would release a decision on December 10. Throughout the day Barnard's telephone rang steadily with calls from reporters, but no decision came until evening.

The decision on the constitutionality of prayer in government meetings was especially crucial given the movement to pass the Religious Liberties Amendment. Would a decision upholding the district court's ruling that city council prayers were unconstitutional inspire the amendment lobby to even greater efforts? Or would it squelch the impulse once and for all? A decision overturning the lower court would no doubt please those favoring prayer in meetings—but could the high court reasonably allow prayer, given the clear wording in the state constitution?

Interestingly, the court's decision preceded by only five days an Interim Legislative Judiciary Committee meeting on the Religious Liberties Provision. This juxtaposition was not lost on anyone observing the legal course of the prayer issue. Barnard commented later, "It seems clear the court's intent was to issue an opinion prior to that meeting."

The task of the Supreme Court, traditionally, lay in examining the legislative history of the law in an attempt to discover the intent and the implications in the larger context of jurisprudence. In this case, however, a legislative history of the article in question virtually did not exist. In his own research, Barnard had found nothing more than a couple of paragraphs indicating discussion—no newspaper accounts, journals, debates, or conferences revealing the intent with which the provision had been penned at the 1895 Constitutional Convention.

The reason lay within the controversy around statehood itself. In the 1880s and early 1890s, prominent LDS leaders in both church and civic affairs had struggled to convince Congress that the Mormon theocracy called the State of Deseret now deserved statehood. Repeatedly non-Mormons living in the Utah territory fueled the controversy around polygamy and religious autocracy in order to keep territorial officials in charge and to counterbalance Mormon power.

Finally, once polygamy was quelled, the statehood proponents had borrowed language from the constitutions of other western states—language that had already been accepted by Congress and would reveal gross prejudice if turned away. The provision in question more than a century later was lifted verbatim from the Washington Constitution, a state admitted six years before Utah.

Given the Utah State Constitution's unequivocal language, and despite the lack of legislative history, Kendell and Barnard were optimistic as they waited together at the Capitol Building for copies of the high court's opinion. When it came, Kendell began reading from the top, while Barnard thumbed quickly to the end. Hearing him react, she flipped to page forty-two and read, "The judgment of the district court [which had forbidden prayer] is therefore reversed, and the case is remanded with directions to enter judgment for the City Council." Barnard and Kendell had just lost a case that neither had expected to lose.

On December 11 the *Salt Lake Tribune* headlined the front page,

225

"City Councils Can Pray On, Rules the Utah Supreme Court." The article reported that on December 10 the high court had upheld the embattled tradition of opening city council meetings with prayer and had ended a twenty-one-month moratorium. The four-to-one decision had taken one year and fifty-two pages, overturning the March 1992 decision by Third District judge J. Dennis Frederick that council prayers violated the church/state separation clause of the Utah Constitution.

The Supreme Court decision devoted more than twenty pages to dissecting Utah's theocratic roots, with the majority of justices determining that "upholding an absolute ban of governmental support of religious activity could prohibit a resident from praying even in a public park," the newspaper explained. On the other hand, wrote Justice Michael D. Zimmerman, "our history convinces us that direct expenditures for religious purposes are not to be permitted lest the old wounds of church-state entanglement be reopened." The court ruled that the test of legal government support of any religious exercise was that it be "neutral" and "indirect" and available to all religions or secular groups.

Reaction to the decision came quickly, with celebration among those who favored prayer at government meetings. The following day the *Tribune* quoted the reaction of Provo Republican representative Byron Harward: "The Supreme Court has now put things back to the way they were."

The lengthy article included a small but surprising agreement between Harward and Kendell. Harward told the newspaper that while he applauded the decision, he feared the justices "bent over backward" so far that the decision might be overturned by a more literal-minded Supreme Court in the future. "Kathryn Kendell agrees that the ruling relies on a 'torturous analysis' that has little to do with the state constitution's language. The ruling renders the promise of church-state separation 'meaningless,' she said."

Since much of the court's reasoning virtually echoed Kendell's and Barnard's arguments before the justices, the conclusion hit both the ACLU and the Society of Separationists with a shock. Zimmerman wrote, "Government is not to prefer religion to nonreligion, but neither should it be hostile to religion. Religious exercise is to be unfettered, and freedom of conscience is to be supreme."

Each attorney analyzed the decision carefully. Said Barnard, "The bulk of this opinion goes through the history of the trials and tribulations of the Mormons," rather than reviewing the process at the Constitutional Convention. "The justices drew on history, not legislative history, because there is none."

He explained, "Because the Mormons were persecuted in Illinois, Missouri, then in Utah by the federal government, the court decided this constitutional provision couldn't mean what it clearly says." Barnard said he would consider the decision more legitimate had it been based on legislative history.

Explained Barnard, "Because there was a sixty year history of persecution of Mormons, they [the justices] felt the Mormons wanted to support religious activity and didn't mean what they said [in the Constitution]. The interesting thing about Zimmerman's opinion, is you can take the same history and come to the opposing opinion—that the mobs had been sanctioned by government officials and, because of that history, the Mormons were smart enough to want to separate church and state."

While both Barnard and Kendell professed great respect for the court, particularly justices Zimmerman and Christine Durham, their disagreement went deep. Kendell was especially impressed with the dissenting opinion written by Justice I. Daniel Stewart, which contended that the ruling actually constricted religious liberties. The writing of Stewart's dissenting opinion, she learned, had been responsible for the late hour at which the decision was released.

The high court ruled that prayer in government meetings must be open to all and non-restrictive in its content, so the city set about developing guidelines. "If you go into great detail defining the guidelines," Barnard wondered, "how can you say there are no restrictions?"

This outcome, if Barnard read the justices correctly, reflected another instance in Mormon history when church leaders said one thing but meant another. Under crushing opposition from the federal government, LDS president Wilford Woodruff had issued the Manifesto of 1890, which denounced the practice of polygamy. Mormons had commonly considered their prophet's edict an expedient intended for the ears of government officials, and polygamy continued. In 1904 a "Second Manifesto" was announced as a true polygamy ban, subsequently enforced by church discipline of two apostles who continued to take wives.

One prominent prayer proponent understood the distinction between law and intent. Former governor Norm Bangerter explained that the justices had determined, "This is what the Constitution says, but this is what they [its authors] meant." Bangerter added the justices "should get gold stars on their foreheads for doing the practical thing. The Constitution has room in it for common sense, and this was a simpler way to solve the problem." He reflected that during his years in the House of Representatives, the duty to open sessions with prayer had simply circulated through the roster of legislators. Anyone who didn't wish to lead the prayer could ask clergy or someone else to substitute.

Once the Supreme Court ruled prayer legal in government meetings, the Religious Liberties Amendment died a fast and natural death. Barnard did not view this as a coincidence. "We liberals were the victims of judicial activism," he said of the prayer decision. "Conservatives have been complaining forever about justices rewriting or making up law instead of merely interpreting it. In this case, Justice Zimmerman made up the law, and the liberals were the victims instead of the other way around."

The provision in the State Constitution contained two contradicting ideas involving religious practice, Barnard said—first, that government shall not establish or support any religion and, second, that government shall not interfere with the free practice of religion. "Rather than acknowledging the tensions between the two, and the fact that hard decisions sometimes are necessary, Zimmerman in his opinion really made the establishing cause take a back seat to the free practice provision."

Now the intent of the state founders, the desire of the city, and the lenience of the high court had to be translated into policy. On New Year's Day 1994 the *Tribune* reported that the victorious Salt Lake City Council intended to test its triumph. However, the ruling's insistence that government's friendliness toward prayer must benefit everyone equally was already raising questions. The city set about finding answers.

City council aide Ed Snow compiled a list of congregations and potential prayer leaders, soliciting suggestions and even scanning the *Yellow Pages*, the *Tribune* reported. While the city attempted to open the process in this way, Barnard considered it a type of screening. He told the newspaper, "You look through the phone books, and you don't find 'Polygamists' listed in the Yellow Pages." He added, "Santerians aren't listed. So there is a selection process."

Snow declined to comment on whether the city would allow a representative of "an uncommon religion," such as a Wiccan priestess, to open a city council meeting. But the article closed with Barnard's repeated prediction: "Barnard says the city will eventually have to deal with the reality that all religions, no matter how repugnant to the mainstream, must be made welcome under the [Utah] Supreme Court ruling."

He told the newspaper, "This opinion will mean that any municipal meetings anywhere in Utah can have prayer. And that may be the downfall of the opinion." He predicted: "One of these days, somebody's going to stand up in one of those meetings and pray to almighty Satan. According to the opinion, that person is going to have to be allowed."

During an earlier appearance on KUTV's *Take 2* program, city attorney Roger Cutler had scoffed at Barnard's interpretation, adding that exotic offerings would be allowed only if they represented deeply held religious belief.

In relating this, Barnard leaped—lawyer fashion—on Cutler's statement: now the government would have to judge depth of belief. First, the city council had said people would open meetings with prayer; then the council—and now the high court—had told them how to pray; now the city must judge if the supplicants' beliefs were sincere.

Barnard readied the test case after being contacted by Tom Snyder, editor of a small newspaper, the *Utah Xpress*. Together they comprised a prayer that Snyder proposed to offer in the first city council meeting, and they sent it to the council offices. The prayer was addressed to "Mother in Heaven," embracing a tenured but officially unpopular LDS belief. As the women's movement had inspired an effort to recognize the concept of female deity, church leaders had insisted that a Heavenly Mother should not be importuned in any prayer, private or public. At least one church membership was lost and others threatened in the debate.

Since belief in specifically female deity was not held by other Christian-Judaic religions, the prayer seemed destined to offend most Mormons and most non-Mormons with its salutation, if not its content: "Our Mother in heaven . . . We fervently ask that you guide the leaders of Salt Lake City . . . and Utah, so that they may see the wisdom of separating church and state. . . ."

While Barnard prepared to hold the council's feet to the fire, the Utah ACLU appealed to their hearts and heads. On January 19 Kate Kendell and Carol Gnade wrote to the council:

> We are well aware that the issue of government prayer is deeply felt by individuals on both sides of the issue. We understand that some of you feel strongly that prayer should be a part of your formal meeting. Nevertheless, we request that you consider, as an alternative, the adoption of a moment of silence as a proper way of solemnizing your official meeting. The Ogden City Council recently voted in favor of this approach. Their public statement indicated that they approved a moment of silence, not because of any hostility to religion or prayer, but rather, out of a profound respect for religion and the proper role of government in protecting religion. Moreover, those supporting a moment of silence recognize and celebrate the diversity which makes Utah great and which demonstrates that we do not all worship the same God, nor do we all worship.

Whether this letter or the prospect of prayer by any and all comers tipped the balance, on February 9, 1994, the *Tribune* reported that the Salt Lake City Council had voted four-to-three *against* resuming prayer. The feelings of the council members and the public were as divided as the vote. But, as Barnard had predicted (and virtually guaranteed), the government found itself in treacherous political terrain—though no longer a constitutional wilderness—by the need to regulate and judge the appropriateness of individual prayers. The "pro-prayer zealots" could not truly win their cause Barnard summarized. "They want comfort in praying, and [having it] will mean no public prayers."

A scorekeeper, then, might give the ACLU a win on the school prayer issue and a loss on the question of prayer in public meetings. Yet the practical outcome suggested a different kind of victory. Public prayer offered in government meetings in ways fair to everyone had proven unworkable, at least thus far. The reality that "fair prayer" constituted a contradiction in terms became apparent only after the Society of Separationists and the ACLU pressed the issue to a literal impasse.

The 1994 legislature bypassed the Religious Liberties Amendment as the prayer question won in the high court and returned to the city council. No sooner had the body adjourned, however, than it posed another church/state challenge by scheduling a town meeting in the LDS Logan Tabernacle. Immediately Kate Kendell wrote to retiring house speaker Rob Bishop that the affiliate would file a lawsuit if the legislature pursued these arrangements. "It not only sends a message of favoritism for the Mormon faith," Kendell wrote, but also constituted a violation of the separation of church and state.

Bishop, in speaking with a *Tribune* reporter, brushed off the conflict as trivial, saying: "It does not rank in my mind with thermonuclear war." However, he added that the legislative leaders would consider other sites and wished to be "as accommodating as possible." Still, Bishop said, he did not relish the appearance of giving in to the "bullying action" of the ACLU.

Kendell responded: "We talked to our national office legal experts and they said this kind of issue has never been litigated before because no other legislature has been stupid enough to do something like this."

Despite Kendell's threats and Gnade's attempts to explain, the legislators pursued their original plan. Democratic legislator Kelly Atkinson told Gnade that they would provide a room outside the tabernacle for people who were uncomfortable meeting in the historic Mormon edifice. "For me, this was so symbolic of the nature of the problem here," Gnade said. She could not understand how the legislators could overlook the implications of holding a town meeting in a church building with a separate space for those who felt excluded. She called LDS church emissaries but raised little sympathy there.

Public speeches by political figures in the Salt Lake Tabernacle, including former President John F. Kennedy, were cited as precedent for the legislative meeting. Gnade was not impressed. "Even the most

231

unintelligent person must be able to see the difference between Kennedy coming to speak in the Tabernacle and the business of government going on there." She was deeply upset by accusations of Mormon-bashing. "They just don't get it," she concluded.

After consulting with legal chair Elizabeth Dunning, the affiliate decided not to sue. Separation of church and state was an obvious problem and so was the open meeting law. Yet given the city's invitation to the legislators and the lack of suitable meeting places, the prospects of successful litigation appeared slim.

Also the LDS church modified its policy of not allowing the distribution of literature on church grounds, and so protestors distributed pamphlets during the meeting without threat of arrest.

The *Salt Lake Tribune* began its report under the headline: "Unorthodox Meeting at Tabernacle: Leavitt and Lawmakers Go To Church To Hear Citizens, Not Sermons." Describing the ninety lawmakers inside the tabernacle and the protesters outside it, the newspaper noted "a dozen other residents [who] watched the proceedings via a televised feed at a restaurant across the street." Gnade told the newspaper she was "willing to rely on legislative good will that this incident will not be repeated."

However, the article continued, her expectation was contradicted Thursday. "House Speaker Rob Bishop ... said legislators will not think twice about holding a meeting in a religious building." Bishop praised the "Logan Civic Center" as "convenient, free, large enough to accommodate a crowd, and air-conditioned." The *Deseret News* gave the meeting a different focus, noting that Cache Valley residents were allowed only thirty minutes for questions after lawmakers spent an hour making political speeches.

Mixed messages persisted when the legislature reconvened in January 1995. Several bills were introduced ensuring a minute of silence in the public schools—a ritual the sponsors said was unrelated to prayer. Carol Gnade thought otherwise. One afternoon on Capitol Hill, she scanned the legislative docket for "Minute of Silence" and found the bill listed farther down—under "Prayer."

In the summer of 1994 Kate Kendell decided to leave the Utah affiliate. Her departure was reported as front-page news in the *Tribune*, where a color photograph showed her beside an American flag. Kendell accepted a position as head of the legal department for the National Center for Lesbian Rights in San Francisco.

"Blending feistiness, eloquence and legal smarts with a disarming sense of humor," the *Tribune* praised, Kendell had played an important role in battles involving reproductive rights, public prayer, and prisoners' rights. Praised by Gnade and a variety of government officials, Kendell found her departure from the Utah affiliate bittersweet. She told the *Tribune*: "I find myself walking around with a big lump in my throat . . . ." She added, "As a lifelong resident of Utah, I have always loved living here and I will always have tremendous respect for the community and the state as an institution." Immediately Gnade began a statewide search for Kendell's full-time replacement.

Early in 1995 Jensie Anderson, of Holme, Roberts & Owen, became the second staff attorney. A native of Logan, Anderson was educated at the University of Washington and the University of Utah, then completed an acting apprenticeship at the Alley Theatre in Houston, Texas. After living two years in New York City, she attended the University of Utah Law School and interned with the Utah Legal Services' homeless project and their Social Security Disability Task Force. She told the *Tribune* she found the work with the homeless "incredibly satisfying," and she accepted the ACLU post as fulfillment of a lifetime goal.

Carol Gnade's years at the helm were an inspiring reflection on the balance between negotiation and education versus media rhetoric and litigation. Given recent frustrations, she now understood Michele Parish's willingness to bang heads in order to get things done. While negotiation was more pleasant and often appropriate, she concluded, sometimes it went nowhere.

The pace in the affiliate office had always been demanding; but in early 1996 two perennial ACLU issues caught Gnade in the hectic whirl experienced by certain of her predecessors. The first dealt with the ACLU's national and ongoing concern with prisoners and capital punishment. The second rose from Utah's continual tensions around lifestyle. Both gained intensity, impetus, and widespread media interest due to the state's predominant religion and culture.

FRIENDLY FIRE

John Albert Taylor faced execution for the 1989 rape and murder of eleven-year-old Charla King of Ogden. He was the first condemned man since Gary Gilmore to choose death by firing squad rather than lethal injection. Every detail of the execution on January 26 drew local media interest; national reporters honed in mainly because of the rarity of the firing squad and its roots in the old Mormon tradition of blood atonement. Once again the ACLU protested the death penalty. Gnade's involvement, however, mixed memory and emotion with principle.

"When people tell death penalty protesters . . . [such as] Carol Gnade they just don't understand how it feels to lose a loved one to murder, they have an unexpected response," began a January 24 *Deseret News* article by Amy Donaldson. "'I do know how it feels,' said Gnade . . . Her sister was abducted and killed more than twenty years ago. The killer was never caught."

Gnade's opposition to the death penalty had preceded her sister's murder and remained absolute. As she led the ACLU's opposition to an execution even Taylor refused to fight, that loss compelled her to do something unusual. She reached out to Sherron King, Charla's mother. "I wanted her to understand our commitment to human rights," Gnade told the *News*. "We're both mothers, we're both grandmothers, and we really love our children and want them to live in a world that's safe. My heart goes out to her."

The women talked for about an hour.

Gnade drew not only on her personal background but her years in social work. "I feel the system failed these people who kill—it failed them all the way along the line, maybe even at trial," Gnade said. "Then we kill them."

She summoned national clout in an attempt to educate the legislative leadership regarding the abolition of the death penalty. Flanked by Nadine Strossen and Dr. William Schultz of Amnesty International, Gnade arranged a meeting with minority house leader Frank Piganelli, senate president Lane Beattie, speaker of the house Mel Brown, and senate minority leader Scott Howell. Before the meeting began, Gnade related, the visitors chatted about Utah's attractions. An avid skier, Strossen praised the resorts until Carol said, "Gosh, Nadine, you sound a bit like our Chamber of Commerce ads."

After Gnade opened the meeting, Schultz discussed how rare the death penalty is among developed nations, and Strossen brought up constitutional issues and the disparities inherent in the enforcement of the death penalty. In the silence afterward, Gnade asked for questions. The discussion immediately took a religious bent as Howell defended executions and the Bible's "an eye for an eye" admonition. Schultz and Strossen countered with the New Testament perspective. Then, Gnade related, Brown said, "Well, you know, we as a people believe that death is preferable to life here on earth."

Schultz shot back, "Oh, then you must be soft on crime if you execute people."

Brown did not share Gnade's amusement as he added that his constituents believed the death penalty aided in stopping crime. A crowd of journalists and cameras was waiting when the meeting disbanded, and the civil libertarians expressed hope that the dialogue might continue. The next day when Gnade picked up a newspaper, however, she felt slapped. Brown had dismissed the significance of the meeting, she found, by informing reporters that Strossen had really just come to Utah to ski.

"The whole scene, for those of us working on the abolition [of the death penalty] issue, was a very emotional time," Gnade said. "We really believed we could change a few minds, that we needed to try, that this was our work. To have them minimize that was really a shock." The sense of sadness and futility permeated her days. "You go to bed at night with it, and hope you wake up in the morning with a renewed spirit." She drew comfort from the memorial service following the execution and a bouquet of flowers that arrived with this note: "A beautiful thing in a desolate place is all the more appreciated."

As with Gnade's earlier meeting with LDS church officials and Michele Parish, the significance of the discussion between Utah's legislative leadership and prominent civil libertarians may have been not what was said, but that it took place at all. In Gnade's mind, however, the implacable force of the state represented by the firing squad was giddily underscored by an illegal and irrational meeting in the Senate a few days later.

On January 30 the Utah Senate closed a bi-partisan caucus billed as a discussion of a state education fund. Reportedly those present included about twenty senators, Cecelia Foxley, state commissioner of higher education, Scott Bean, state superintendent of public education, and attorneys from the governor's and attorney general's offices. No vote was taken to close the meeting nor were minutes kept, though both were required by Utah's Open Meeting Act. Behind the closed doors, senators Howard Stephenson of Draper and Charles Stewart of Provo leveled charges that public schools were promoting homosexuality and undermining family values.

"Utah Senators Hold Secret Anti-Gay Meet," the *Tribune* reported. Tony Semerad wrote that Stephenson had "produced a box of children's picture books, including one titled, *Heather Has Two Mommies*, about a lesbian couple and their daughter. He complained the books are in circulation in Utah elementary grades—an assertion a leading school-text expert said was unlikely." According to several sources at the meeting, the article continued, Stephenson had also claimed teachers were "instructing students to have anal intercourse."

Some senators present derided the bizarre content of the meeting, and senate president Lane Beattie initially apologized for neglecting to follow the law. Nevertheless powerful people quickly joined ranks regarding the bedrock issue. The meeting had been arranged after ten students petitioned to use a classroom at East High School for a gay and lesbian support group.

"The purpose of the club would be to increase awareness about homosexuality in high schools, to decrease homophobia, and to help gay, lesbian, and bisexual students feel safe and welcome in their school environment," the students wrote. They did not request meeting announcements or advertising. "We feel doing so would attract unwanted attention. We are extremely concerned for the safety and well-being of our members."

Public attention, however, was immediate and glaring once word leaked of the senate's secret meeting. "I'd hoped all along that this would be quiet and anonymous," seventeen-year-old founder Kelli Peterson told the *Private Eye Weekly*. "Then somebody had to go ask Gayle Ruzicka what she thinks. I thought to myself, 'Oh God, why now?'"

Immediately, the ACLU demanded that the senate provide a full list of meeting participants and a record of its content, threatening a lawsuit if they were not produced. Beattie told the media no minutes nor votes had been taken. He now defended the meeting based on a law allowing state officials to meet privately with attorneys if litigation was imminent. The ACLU then demanded that another meeting be held and the same issues discussed openly, but to no avail. On February 15 the Utah ACLU filed suit against the senate asking the Third Judicial District Court to declare the body in violation of the law and issue an injunction prohibiting further secret meetings.

Meanwhile, it became clear that the banning of gay clubs in high schools was prohibited by a federal equal access law, which had been sponsored by Senator Orrin Hatch, among others, to protect Bible study groups. No club could be banned if any were allowed to meet. Now the debate turned to which clubs might vanish in order to prohibit the Gay and Lesbian Club at East High and a Gay and Straight Alliance formed at West High by Kelli's younger sister, fifteen-year-old Holly Peterson.

Governor Leavitt, whose son was student body president at East High, declared the equal access law an inappropriate extension of federal power. "A decision should be made at the local community level to reflect that community's values and priorities." By February 10, both Leavitt and Hatch insisted that schools ought to ban gay clubs and then battle the federal law in court. Legislator Stewart had another idea— why didn't the state simply give up $100 million in federal aid in order to discriminate between clubs?

In a sidebar to this report, the *Tribune* quoted Holly Peterson, who said she had watched two homosexual friends drop out of school and others become deeply depressed. "It's not about sex. Our club is more about stopping the suicide and the drug use and the dropping out of school," she told Associated Press reporter Kristin Moulton. "It's more about leading a safe and healthy lifestyle than a destructive one."

Cartoonist Pat Bagley pictured a gay club meeting for the *Tribune* with a teacher snoozing in the front of an almost empty classroom. Before an audience of one, the club leader volunteered for all assignments, ending with: "Anyway, our activities chairman (me) says our next club activity will be to stop all serious business in the legislature and give our elected officials hissy fits."

People in power weren't laughing, and their responses propelled Utah's controversy into the national spotlight. With a four-to-three vote, the Salt Lake City school board banned all extracurricular clubs beginning in the fall of 1996. Students quickly petitioned the board of education asking them to reconsider their decision. Meanwhile, senators introduced a bill to prevent teachers from "promoting illegal activities" either at school or in their private lives. The body split along party lines with the more numerous Republicans supporting the bill.

"In one of the 1996 Legislature's defining debates, Republicans and Democrats clashed mightily Thursday over a bill sparked by formation of a gay and lesbian club at a Salt Lake City high school," reported Tony Semerad on the *Tribune*'s front page on February 23. "Senators advanced Senate Bill 246 by an 18-8 vote after a 75-minute exchange that ranged from evocations of the U.S. Constitution and tales of teen suicide to quotations from the Nuremburg trials. Only one Democrat . . . broke party ranks in the final roll call."

"The language is so vague that all it does is make teachers paranoid," Gnade said, "and chill their First Amendment rights." The evening after the bill advanced in the senate, the small ACLU office swarmed with students using the telephones to rally support. The next day hundreds of high school students bolted class to protest the actions of the school board and the senate. Some students favored allowing gay clubs and others resented the removal of their own groups, whose emphases ranged from chess to ethnic culture to Frisbees. The East High principal met students on the lawn, told them he agreed with their cause, and asked them to return to class. Some did. Others headed for the Capitol. As West High students formed a caravan, one fourteen-year-old girl—protesting the end of her Polynesian club—fell beneath the wheels of a car. She underwent surgery and recovered from her injuries.

Immediately, the Eagle Forum charged that "outside agitators" such as the ACLU were using the students politically. "We certainly didn't encourage them to have the rally," Gnade said. "They know the penalty for civil disobedience, and we're not encouraging that. But we are letting them know what their rights are."

Gnade continued to lend the youngsters practical, behind-the-scenes help. For instance, they were refused a permit for another rally at the Capitol. The ACLU had been through a similar skirmish, so Gnade called Brian Barnard and asked him to walk a student through the procedure. Gnade arranged to have an adequate sound system donated for the rally. Concerned for the students' safety, she recruited legal observers from the University of Utah and spoke with Salt Lake City police officers. "We're trying our best to make sure we support them, but letting them make the decisions."

Meanwhile, teachers organized the Utah chapter of the Gay, Lesbian & Straight Teachers' Alliance, which they announced at a rally. Reported the *Tribune*: "Skyline High School teacher Clayton K. Vetter enjoys debating so much that Tuesday he placed himself in the middle of Utah's fiery discourse on morality, human rights, and homosexuality." Coach for an award-winning program, Vetter announced his homosexual orientation "to a throng of reporters, students, and citizens" in the Capitol. "'To not stand up now, when there are so many misconceptions and questions concerning gay issues, would go against everything I have tried to teach,' Vetter said. 'This is why I feel I have to come forward. There is too much hope in the world not to come forward. I owe it to my profession and to my students.'"

Both the ACLU and the National Education Association considered the senate bill—which passed both houses—prime for a First Amendment lawsuit. So did the governor, who vetoed the bill, suggesting that legislators write it more narrowly for a special session.

Meanwhile, Gnade heard that the School Board Association was meeting in St. George; she notified the media, which quickly responded. She also called ACLU supporter Clay Huntsman in Dixie and armed him with a legal brief leaked from the offices of Kirton, McConkie & Poelman, a prominent law firm which represented the LDS church. The document described how schools might circumvent the Equal Access Act without paying $2 million in attorney fees, Gnade said. Huntsman soon found he wasn't the only person distributing the brief, for Brinton Burbidge, representing the law firm, handed out copies, as well. The law firm appeared interested in finding a school district willing to go to court, Gnade said.

Burbidge was bypassed, however, when Senator Hatch and Governor Leavitt enlisted Dan Berman, David Jordan, and Matt Hilton (the last associated with the archconservative Rutherford Institute) to draft a bill for the special session and defend it *pro bono* in the event of a lawsuit. "God knows I hate to say it, but they were very smart in the way they crafted it," Gnade said, for it seemed constitutional on its face.

The bill banned sex clubs, clubs promoting illegal activities, and hate clubs. A gay and lesbian support group theoretically could meet in a high school. However, if the high school refused but allowed other extracurricular clubs, the ACLU could sue under the Equal Access Act. At that point the legislative intent would be clear from the material submitted with the bill and the day spent on speeches consisting of "homophobia, myths, and bad information from radical psychologists and therapists who said homosexuality could be changed with a lot of therapy," Gnade said. Schoolteachers in the gay-straight alliance, who reserved a room at the Capitol to meet with legislators, were visited by only six lawmakers, she said. Some teachers, however, participated in talk shows and media coverage nationwide.

The bill overlooked the fact that no sex clubs, clubs promoting illegal activity, or hate clubs had met in high schools before the controversy exploded. In trying twice to eliminate the gay and lesbian clubs but spare others, the legislature had fired a shotgun. Now Utah's school districts would decide which clubs and activities the pellets hit and which they missed. Then the ACLU would decide how best to return fire. In the Salt Lake City District, however, the school board appeared to comply with the Equal Access Act by banning extracurricular clubs altogether, including ethnic, chess, political, and scholarship clubs, along with gay and lesbian clubs. Athletic and pep clubs escaped the ban. The ACLU sued the senate for holding an illegal meeting and pursued the possibility of suing the state regarding the new school clubs law, or the Salt Lake City School District, or both.

Interestingly, Jim Joy, a former director of the Utah ACLU, was championing a similar equal access question in Colorado. There Louis Farrakhan's Million Men March had applied to rent space in a high school for a youth group and been refused although the school rented rooms to other groups. The same issue could easily arise in Utah, Gnade said, if the Young Republicans, for instance, were allowed to sponsor high school groups but the Gay and Lesbian Alliance at the University of Utah were turned down.

In talking with an *L.A. Times* reporter, Gnade made one offhand remark that would be picked up nationwide and used as the *Salt Lake Tribune*'s quote of the week. After explaining the senate meeting, following Taylor's execution, she said, "I will look back at this as the most shameful time in Utah's history. But then, I said that last week."

By 1996 the Utah ACLU differed markedly from the ad hoc group that had formed forty years earlier. For instance, when Gnade heard that a school district in the Utah portion of Wendover was 71 percent Hispanic and experiencing discrimination, she raised the matter in an immigration group that met monthly. The group included police officers, an immigration attorney, and representatives from La Familia and the Catholic Diocese, who welcomed the ACLU's interest in the border town, Gnade said. The strength and versatility the group offered presented a striking contrast to the affiliate's early efforts to combat racial and ethnic discrimination through educating civic officials one by one.

In 1994 regional director Dorothy Davidson noted the strength of most western affiliates. Her own regional office could probably close its doors and not be missed, she said. Eight of the eleven state affiliates in the region were staffed and strong. In contrast, North and South Dakota and Wyoming struggled with large distances and low populations. Davidson wondered whether the national organization shouldn't now concentrate its resources on organizing within those few states.

Davidson emphasized that from the earliest years on, those leading and participating in the Utah ACLU had built the organization through unique contributions. Many Utahns served quietly on the board of directors, as fundraisers, or as cooperating attorneys, often switching positions as the need arose. The issues, lawsuits, personalities, and politics changed with time, but the essential struggle continued as the affiliate grew in membership and muscle.

In forty years the Utah ACLU transformed from a network of volunteers to a stable, vigorous agency. Some of its founders had remained visible in public life. In March 1993 Adam (Mickey) Duncan received recognition from the National Association for Ethnic Studies. Spencer L. Kimball returned to Utah to accept a professorship at the University of Utah Law School. Stephen Smoot worked in the U.S. Department of Commerce, and Steven Cook still practiced law. Jim Joy, who had left Utah to head the Colorado affiliate, remained in that position, appearing in Utah news reports regarding anti-gay laws that had been passed in Colorado and protested by the ACLU. Shirley Pedler left the Louisiana affiliate in 1993 and took over the New Mexico affiliate in Albuquerque, while Robyn Blumner continued to lead the Florida affiliate.

Michele Parish worked with the state affiliates of the National Women's Political Caucus in Washington, D.C., and astonished Utahns once again by marrying a Mormon—Milton Bisseger, an aide to Utah Democratic congressman Bill Orton. The marriage, however, would be short-lived. In organizing state affiliates for the caucus, Parish drew upon her Utah ACLU experience. "I'm not just talking to you from an ivory tower," she would say. "I know what it's like to be under fire in the states, and I know you can do it." She rallied them with, "If you can raise money in Utah for liberal causes, you can raise it anywhere." In March 1994 Parish returned to Utah to speak at the awards ceremony of the Utah Women's Political Caucus.

Remembering her years as executive director of the Utah affiliate, Parish said, "It was a great time of my life. I felt very alive, in the middle of the action, making things happen. What I'm doing now is very different. It took a while to get used to not being in the newspaper.... My primary role is to empower other people." As executive director of the Utah ACLU, she reminisced, "I was just doing what looked like the right thing to do. If I'd known what I was doing, I don't think I could have done it."

As a matter of record, the major lawsuits brought by the Utah ACLU tended to combine victories and losses. When the affiliate objected to the LDS church requiring employees in church-owned businesses to maintain temple recommends, it won in state courts and lost in the U.S. Supreme Court. Following an ACLU lawsuit, LDS seminaries had been allowed to teach religion during released time, but the classes no longer counted for high school credit. The affiliate had forced Brigham Young University to instruct its cadre of off-campus landlords to cease enforcing university standards for non-students; nevertheless, the landlords' policy of segregation in order to promote the BYU lifestyle was upheld in court. School prayer was found unconstitutional by the U.S. Supreme Court, while prayer in government meetings was deemed constitutional by the Utah Supreme Court—and then found unworkable.

The Utah State Penitentiary was allowed to continue double-bunking some cells, but only after it remodeled to improve prison conditions overall. Medical and mental health care procedures and facilities transformed at the prison as a direct result of the hard-fought ACLU litigation.

Abortion remained legal in Utah, thanks in part to the ACLU efforts, even as the state tightened regulations. Doctors treating infertility and difficult pregnancies were freed from the threat of criminal prosecution.

"I enjoy this kind of practice," said Brian Barnard, the affiliate's best known ally. "I enjoy the idea that people have rights and can assert them against government entities. If there aren't attorneys around to do something about it, the Bill of Rights doesn't mean anything."

The history of the Utah ACLU was unendingly dynamic, founded on a relationship with power rather than in polar opposition to it. Given the state's history and homogeneous population, the will of the majority was magnified as seeming both appropriate and preferable. Thus the rights reserved to individuals in the Bill of Rights gained a unique poignancy when countering the power amassed and sometimes intermingled by the institutions of church and state.

While ACLU founder Roger Baldwin likely did not envision a Utah setting when he predicted that civil rights battles would not stay won, the state's own brand of conflicts proved him accurate. Not only did the same issues resurrect, but they were joined by new controversies such as the questions surrounding homosexuality.

The intent to prevail marked all the battles waged in Utah by and with the ACLU. Sometimes the artillery fired across ideological lines produced a metaphorical body count among those involved. And yet the wins and the losses affected both sides for better and worse, whether they took place in the courtroom, the legislature, the media, or through private correspondence. Although the battles continued, no *outside* enemy truly existed.

The ACLU in Utah had committed itself to the cause of preserving civil liberties—everyone's constitutional rights. Therefore it volleyed and was pelted by only friendly fire.

Notes

1. The Long View

SOURCES FOR THIS CHAPTER INCLUDE:

Author's Interviews: Norman H. Bangerter, Kathryn Kendell, Michele Parish, and Christopher Smart. Also see an oral interview with Michele Parish by Everett L. Cooley, November 30-December 7, 1992, Marriott Library.

Books: Ellen Alderman and Caroline Kennedy, *In Our Defense: The Bill of Rights in Action* (New York: Morrow, 1991); John S. McCormick, *Salt Lake City: The Gathering Place* (Woodland Hills, CA: Windsor Publications, 1980); Samuel Walker, *In Defense of American Liberties* (New York: Oxford University Press, 1990); and Edward L. Kimball and Andrew E. Kimball, *Spencer W. Kimball* (Salt Lake City: Bookcraft, 1977).

Contemporaneous Media: *Deseret News*; *The Progressive*—see "Nadine Strossen," by Claudia Dreifus, March 1994; and *Salt Lake Tribune*, in particular a profile of Spencer L. Kimball by Paul Rolly, August 5, 1990.

Legal Documents: *The Criminal Abortion Statute* of 1991.

For additional information, see: Anthony Summers, *Official and Confidential: The Secret Life of J. Edgar Hoover* (New York: G.P. Putnam's Sons, 1993); Thomas G. Alexander and James B. Allen,

Mormons and Gentiles: A History of Salt Lake City (Boulder, CO: Pruett Publishing Co., 1984); Linda Sillitoe, *Welcoming the World: A History of Salt Lake County* (Salt Lake City: Salt Lake County, 1996) or *Salt Lake County* (Salt Lake City: Utah State Historical Society, 1996); Kathryn L. MacKay, "Equal Rights Amendment," *Utah Encyclopedia*, ed. Allan Kent Powell (Salt Lake City: University of Utah Press, 1994); D. Michael Quinn, "The LDS Church's Campaign Against the Equal Rights Amendment," *Journal of Mormon History*, Fall 1994; and Linda Sillitoe and David Merrill, "Inside the Freemen Institute," *Utah Holiday*, Feb. 1981.

2. Conception in Utah

SOURCES FOR THIS CHAPTER INCLUDE:

Author's Interviews: Steven Cook, Dorothy Davidson, Adam M. Duncan, James H. Joy, Spencer L. Kimball, John Morris, and Stephen Smoot.

Books: Samuel Walker, *In Defense of American Liberties* (New York: Morrow, 1991); Benjamin Roe, *A Blend of the Two*, ed. James M. Rock (n.p.: Friends of the University of Utah Library); and "Blacks in Utah," by Ronald Coleman, *Peoples of Utah*, ed. Helen Z. Papinikolas (Salt Lake City: Utah State Historical Society, 1976).

Contemporaneous Media: *Chronicle*, *Deseret News*, *New York Times*, and *Salt Lake Tribune*, in particular "Mormon's Mission Led Him to Fight for Civil Rights," by Chris Jorgensen, April 19, 1993.

Correspondence: February 25, 1957, letter from Marion D. Hanks to Adam M. Duncan regarding civil rights legislation; July 15, 1959, letter from Adam Duncan to ACLU membership regarding issues and fundraising; September 22, 1971, letter from Michael Rudick to *Deseret News* regarding "moral pollution"; August 18, 1973, letter from Michael Rudick to Susy Post regarding women's participation in ACLU; November 8, 1974, letter from Ruth Bader Ginsburg to James H. Joy regarding *Turner v. Department of Employment*; February 21, 1975, letter from James H. Joy to Melvin Wulf regarding *Turner v. Department of Employment;* March 4, 1975, letter from Kathleen Peratis to

James H. Joy regarding *Turner v. Department of Employment;* March 16, 1976, letter from Michael Rudick to John Gallivan regarding publishing advertisements from homosexual groups; and April 29, 1993, letter from Myron Q. Hale to Chris Jorgensen regarding race relations in Salt Lake City in the 1930s-40s.

Other: "Utah," 1961 Report to the Commission on Civil Rights from the State Advisory Committee, Hon. Adam M. Duncan, chair; December 15, 1964, and January 5, 1965, "Minutes of General Membership Meeting"; February 1972 Utah affiliate newsletter; September 26, 1973, press release announcing a class action suit against the Utah State Prison; and September 16, 1974, press release by James H. Joy regarding draft policy.

3. Coming of Age

SOURCES FOR THIS CHAPTER INCLUDE:

Author's Interviews: Brian Barnard, Kathryn Collard, Steven Cook, Dorothy Davidson, Elizabeth Dunning, Shirley Pedler, and Judith Wolbach.

Books: Norman Mailer, *The Executioner's Song* (Boston: Little, Brown and Co., 1979); and Samuel Walker, *In Defense of American Liberties* (New York: Morrow, 1991).

Contemporaneous Media: *Deseret News; Salt Lake Tribune,* in particular "ACLU Director's Tears Fall for Liberty Violations," Judy B. Rollins, March 26, 1978, and "Utah ACLU Chief Heads to Louisiana," Joan O'Brien, January 4, 1987; and *Wall Street Journal.*

Legal Documents: *Amos v. LDS Church; Van Avery v. Jordan School District; Cable Television Programming Decency Act* voided April 10, 1985, by senior district judge Aldon J. Anderson; *Lanner v. Logan School District;* and *Students Against Apartheid v. Peterson.*

Correspondence: June 30, 1976, letter from Michael Rudick to membership regarding Terrace incident; undated letter from Shirley Pedler to membership regarding Terrace incident; April 12, 1984, letter from Ross Anderson to membership regarding issues and fundraising;

FRIENDLY FIRE

and September 1, 1986, letter from Students Against Apartheid and Coalition to Stop Apartheid to Shirley Pedler regarding ACLU assistance.

Other: Undated ACLU flier for Gilmore rally; spring 1984 ACLU annual dinner program; June 27, 1983, press release by Shirley Pedler regarding *Van Avery v. Jordan School District*; and April 21, 1975, "Executive Director's Report." The Judge Building incident was related to the author by Salt Lake City Police Department detectives Kenneth Farnsworth and Jim Bell during research for *Salamander: The Story of the Mormon Forgery Murders*, by Linda Sillitoe and Allen D. Roberts (Salt Lake City: Signature Books, 1988).

4. Welcome to Utah
SOURCES FOR THIS CHAPTER INCLUDE:

Author's Interviews: Brian Barnard, Robyn Blumner, Dorothy Davidson, Gary DeLand, Boyer Jarvis, Michele Parish, and David Yocom.

Books: Samuel Walker, *In Defense of American Liberties* (New York: Morrow, 1991).

Contemporaneous Media: *Salt Lake Tribune*, in particular "Common Carrier" columns October 4, 1987, David L. Wilkinson, "Who Is the Real Threat?" and October 18, 1987, Robyn E. Blumner, "Let's Meet the Real Judge Bork; *Deseret News; Newsweek;* and *Chronicle.*

Legal Documents: Initial complaint in what became *Henry v. DeLand; Reynolds v. Reynolds.*

Correspondence: October 21, 1987, letter from Ross Anderson to ACLU membership regarding current issues.

Other: "Statement by Robyn E. Blumner" regarding seizure by the Drug Enforcement Agency; "Public Speaking Engagements" for Robyn Blumner 1987-88; April 30, 1988, annual ACLU dinner program; and July 20, 1988, press release by Robyn Blumner regarding a cooperative effort by the ACLU, the Legal Center for the Handicapped, and the Department of Corrections to evaluate medical care.

NOTES

5. To Pray or Not to Pray
SOURCES FOR THIS CHAPTER INCLUDE:

Author's Interviews: Norman H. Bangerter, Brian Barnard, Gary DeLand, Pam Elliott, Boyer Jarvis, John Morris, and Michele Parish.

Contemporaneous Media: *The Cache Citizen, Chicago Tribune*—see Jim Robbins article, October 16, 1990; *Church & State*—see "Whither Zion?" by Rob Boston, December 1992; *Deseret News*, in particular "ACLU Fights for Principles that Will Protect Practices: For Utah Director, Controversy Just Comes with Job," by Dennis Lythgoe, September 15, 1989; *Salt Lake Tribune; Standard-Examiner*; and *Wall Street Journal*—see "When 'Freedom' Becomes Religious Censorship," Dallin H. Oaks, May 23, 1990.

Legal Documents: *Johanson v. Fischer*.

Correspondence: March 1989 letters to Governor Norman H. Bangerter regarding a sweat lodge at the prison from Rabbi Frederick L. Wenger, Father Robert J. Bussen, the Very Reverend William F. Maxwell; March 24, 1989, letter from Danny Quintana to Michele Parish regarding sweat lodge victory; November 6, 1989, Elder John K. Carmack to Michele Parish regarding school prayer; January 10, 1990, Michele Parish to Elder John Carmack regarding school prayer; January 16, 1990, Elder John Carmack to Michele Parish regarding school prayer; June 13, 1990, Michele Parish to *Wall Street Journal* regarding its publication of Elder Dallin Oaks's speech; June 22, 1990, Elder Dallin H. Oaks to Boyer Jarvis regarding Michele Parish's letter to *Wall Street Journal*; June 25, 1990, Boyer Jarvis to Elder Dallin Oaks regarding Michele Parish's letter; June 29, 1990, Boyer Jarvis to Michele Parish, resigning as ACLU president; and July 5, 1990, Michele Parish to Boyer Jarvis, accepting his resignation.

Other: August 1, 1989, press release by Michele Parish regarding hair length of Native American inmates; February 8, 1989, press release by Michele Parish regarding sweat lodge lawsuit; August 31, 1989, press release by Michele Parish regarding *Harding v. DeLand*; September 19, 1989, press release by Michele Parish regarding hair length of Native American inmates; April 25, 1989, press release by Michele

FRIENDLY FIRE

Parish regarding *Johanson v. Fischer*; national and Utah ACLU policies on polygamy; October 25, 1989, joint press release regarding religious services for Jewish inmates; "Notes to File-Prison," by Michele Parish, recounting initial discussion with Scott McAlister; "Tape Transcripts, January 2, 1990" regarding Jolivett incident; and May 17, 1991, and July 26, 1991, press releases by Michele Parish regarding school prayer.

6. Guns Blazing
SOURCES FOR THIS CHAPTER INCLUDE:

Author's Interviews: Norman H. Bangerter, Brian Barnard, Cullen Battle, Kathryn Kendell, John Morris, Michele Parish, Christopher Smart, Kathleen Switzer, and David Yocom.

Contemporaneous Media: *Deseret News*; *Standard-Examiner*; and *Salt Lake Tribune*.

Legal Documents: *Harding v. DeLand*; *Baker v. DeLand*; and *Henry v. DeLand*.

Correspondence: February 28, 1989, letter from Michele Parish to Gary DeLand regarding evaluation of the Utah State Penitentiary; March 31, 1989, letter from Michele Parish to Gary DeLand regarding medical care; May 16, 1989, letter from Michele Parish to Gary DeLand regarding prison budget; September 28, 1989, letter from Michele Parish to Scott McAlister regarding prison policy; October 11, 1989, letter from Michele Parish to Attorney General Paul Van Dam questioning Scott McAlister's dual role; December 8, 1989, letter from Michele Parish to Hon. Scott Daniels requesting a grand jury to investigate prison conditions; January 9, 1990, from Boyer Jarvis to Gary DeLand regarding meeting between executives; January 2, 1990, Gary DeLand to Boyer Jarvis suggesting ACLU investigate Michele Parish; January 18, 1990, Gary DeLand to Boyer Jarvis regarding Michele Parish visiting inmates; April 19, 1990, Gary DeLand to Michele Parish regarding prison visits; June 15, 1990, letter from Michele Parish to Lynn Lund regarding mental health care at prison; March 19, 1991, letter from Michele Parish to Bud Scruggs regarding Department of Corrections chief; and March 20, 1991, letter from Bud Scruggs to Michele Parish regarding new Department of Corrections chief.

Other: June 6, 1989, press release by Michele Parish regarding double bunking; September 28, 1989, press release by Michele Parish regarding lawsuit over conditions at Salt Lake County Jail; June 1990 Department of Corrections newsletter, *The Rap Sheet;* Fall 1992 ACLU *Reporter*; and December 18, 1989, press release by Michele Parish regarding filing of *Henry v. DeLand*.

7. The Scarlet Issue
SOURCES FOR THIS CHAPTER INCLUDE:

Author's Interviews: Norman H. Bangerter, Carol Gnade, Kathryn Kendell, Howard Lundgren, and John Morris.

Books: Samuel Walker, *In Defense of American Liberties* (New York: Morrow, 1991).

Contemporaneous Media: *Chronicle*; *Deseret News*; *New York Times*; *Private Eye*; *Salt Lake City Magazine*; *Salt Lake Tribune*; and *Standard-Examiner*.

Legal Documents: *Jane L. v. Bangerter*, including amended complaints, appeals, and decision.

Other: Governor Norman H. Bangerter's comments on abortion in his January 14, 1990, State of the State speech, as transcribed by ACLU intern Sharon Smith; summer 1992 ACLU *Reporter*; winter 1992 ACLU *Reporter*; and "Temple Spires and Capitol Dome" (postcard), by Frank Jensen (Mountain West Prints).

8. Scene Change
SOURCES FOR THIS CHAPTER INCLUDE:

Author's Interviews: Brian Barnard, Carol Gnade, Kathryn Kendell, Howard Lundgren, and Michele Parish.

Contemporaneous Media: *Deseret News*; *Legal Times*; *Rutherford*—see "Back Page column, September 1993; and *Salt Lake Tribune*.

Legal Documents: *Jane L. v. Bangerter*, i.e. Tenth Circuit Court of Appeals Decision.

Correspondence: March 1, 1993, letter to the Utah State Legislature from Rev. Robert Busssen, Rev. Max E. Flenn, Rev. Roger H. Anderson, Pastor Janet L. Swift, Rev. Donald H. Baird, Rev. Barbara Hamilton-Holway, Rev. Bill Hamilton-Holway, Rabbi Frederick L. Wenger, Rev. Marie Green, and Rev. Lyle D. Sellards regarding the Religious Liberties Amendment; and January 19, 1994, letter from Carol Gnade and Kathryn Kendell to Salt Lake City Council regarding prayer at meetings.

Other: ACLU *Reporter*, spring 1993, summer 1993, winter 1993; and April 12, 1994, Minutes of ACLU Board Meeting regarding number of complaints and cash award from *Henry v. DeLand*.

9. The Prison Medical Ward the ACLU Built

SOURCES FOR THIS CHAPTER INCLUDE:

Author's Interviews: Cullen Battle, Gary DeLand, Carol Gnade, Kathryn Kendell, Michele Parish, and Kathleen Switzer.

Contemporaneous Media: *Deseret News*; and *Salt Lake Tribune*, in particular "Utahns Cry Foul Over Warrantless Search," by Michael Phillips, February 5, 1994.

Legal Documents: *Henry v. DeLand,* including stipulated settlement, affidavits, appeal, and United States District Court decision; *Soto v. Mangleson*; *Fitches v. Mercer*; *TDP v. Leavitt*; and *Valdez v. Samuel McPheters and Greg Littlewhiteman*.

Correspondence: September 23, 1993, letter from Kathryn Kendell to Governor Michael Leavitt.

10. And Justice for All

SOURCES FOR THIS CHAPTER INCLUDE:

Author's Interviews: Jensie Anderson, Norman H. Bangerter, Brian Barnard, Kathryn Collard, Carol Gnade, Dorothy Davidson, Kathryn

NOTES

Kendell, and Michele Parish.

Contemporaneous Media: *Deseret News, Daily Universe*, in particular "Number of Utah Suicides Above National Average" by Jennifer Duke, January 14, 1993; *Salt Lake Tribune*, in particular "S.L. Students Rally, Rail, and Rebel," by Samuel Autman, Jennifer Skordas, and Robert Bryson, February 24, 1996; and *Private Eye Weekly*'s cover story "Club Dread," by Ben Fulton, February 15, 1996.

Legal Documents: *Society of Separationists v. Whitehead*; *Wilson v. Brigham Young University*; *Wilson v. Glenwood Intermountain Properties*; and *Dennis Scott Jolley v. Utah State Senate*.

Other: Memorandum May 4, 1994, from Kathryn Kendell to ACLU Board of Trustees regarding Utah Curriculum Guidelines; Memorandum May 5, 1994, from Kathryn Kendell to ACLU Board of Trustees regarding BYU housing policy; "Injury in Utah 1986-1990" (Utah Department of Health Research and Development Program, 1992), regarding suicide rates and methods; and Branbury Park Apartments contract and letter citing violations by rentees.

Index

A

Abortion, 3-4, 8, 55, 58, 60, 71, 80, 145-68, 171, 173-74, 178-79, 185, 189, 192, 198, 209, 214, 221, 233, 243
Adoption, 95-97
Alderman, Ellen, 7
Allen, Chris, 78, 116, 177
Alta Club, 77-78
American Civil Liberties Union (ACLU), *passim*
American Lawyer, 57
Americans United for Separation of Church and State, 116
Amnesty International, 234
Anderson, Aldon J., 59
Anderson, Jensie, 222, 233
Anderson, Marian, 21
Anderson, Robert, 48
Anderson, Ross, 53, 58-59, 69, 127, 161
Andrews, Richard, 78
Andrews, William, 200-201
Anthony, Susan B., 166
Aryan Nation, 69
Asner, Ed, 215
Associated Press, 131, 143
Atkinson, Kelly, 231

B

Bagley, Pat, 76, 160, 188, 191, 237
Baldwin, Roger, 5-7, 10, 16, 243
Ball, Howard, 80-81
Ballard, M. Russell, Jr., 110, 177, 187
Bangerter, Norman, 2-3, 91, 93, 101, 110-13, 115, 117-18, 120, 129, 133, 140-41, 151, 153-55, 157, 165, 169-70, 177, 198, 228
Barnard, Brian M., 42-44, 46, 51, 63, 73, 77-79, 99-100, 113-15, 125, 130, 161, 185, 224-30, 239, 243
Barnett, Ross, 41
Barney, Dennis, 77
Battle, Cullen, 133, 144, 191-93
Bean, Scott, 236
Beattie, Lane, 234, 236-37
Beech, Joy, 108-109
Beehive Clothing Mills, 56-57
Bendavid, Naftali, 175
Bennett, Michael, 211
Benshoof, Janet, 157, 179, 181-82
Benson, Dee, 140, 182
Benson, Ezra Taft, 26
Bergman, Abner, 52
Berman, Dan, 240
Bill of Rights, 5, 7, 47, 57, 71, 96,

105, 107, 113, 138, 148-49, 176, 243
Bishop, Arthur Gary, 69
Bishop, Rob, 231-32
Bisseger, Milton, 242
Blackmun, Harry, 150
Blend of the Two, 16
Blood atonement, 146-47, 234
Blum, Steven H., 59
Blumner, Robyn E., 63-67, 69, 71-79, 81-87, 90-91, 97, 99, 101-102, 120, 122, 125, 144, 148, 195-97, 242
Boam, Peter, 160
Book of Mormon, 55, 214
Bork, Robert H., 67, 69-73
Boston, Rob, 116
Boyce, Ronald, 125, 181
Brennan, William, 30
Brewster, Harriett, 26
Brewster, Sheldon, 22-23
Brigham Young University, 11, 70, 97, 157-58, 215-23, 243
Brimhall, Maurine, 30, 42
Bronstein, Al, 141
Brossard, Ed, 26
Brossard, Laura, 26
Brown, Mel, 234
Burbidge, Brinton, 239
Burger, Warren, 48
Burnett, Stan, 220
Bush, George, 4, 72, 113, 169-70, 173-75
Bushnell, Lance D., 202

C

Cache Citizen, 101
Cahill, Jerry, 98
Campus Christian Center, 16-17
Cannon, Ted, 43, 73-74

Capital punishment, 47-48, 50, 69, 233-35
Carmack, John K., 103
Catholic church, 91, 145, 164, 187, 241
Catholic Women's League, 33
Censorship, 30-31, 42, 58-59, 69, 81, 86, 162, 210, 215
Central Salt Lake City Council of Churches, 91, 110
Chabad Lubavitch of Utah, 224
Christian Coalition, 174, 176, 212
Church and State, 116
Church and state, separation of, 5, 14, 23, 40-41, 53, 55-56, 59-60, 67, 78-79, 97, 100, 105, 107, 109, 114, 116, 161, 164, 171, 174, 176, 185-86, 209, 223-24, 226-27, 230-32
Church of Jesus Christ of Latter-day Saints. *See* Mormon church
Citizens for Decency Committee, 30, 42
Clark, J. Reuben, 25
Clinton, Bill, 167, 169, 173, 210
Clyde, George D., 22
Coalition for Criminal Justice, 40
Coleman, Ronald, 22
Collard, Kathryn, 51-53, 73, 216
Communism, 13, 25-26, 54
Congregation Kol Ami, 52, 91, 93, 187
Cook, Steven, 29, 31-32, 51-52, 242
Coontz, Pat, 24, 26, 29
Cornaby, Kay S., 133
Corradini, Deedee, 169, 202, 224
Corrections, Utah Department of, 1, 3, 31, 74, 81-82, 91-94, 102, 106, 117-44, 191-208
Cowley, Samuel, 26

Cragun, Marlayn, 124, 149
Creationism, 6
Crockett, Alan, 17
Crump, Gary, 213
Cummings, Annette, 163
Cutler, Roger, 78, 115, 229

D

Dabney, Jinks, 47
Daniels, Scott, 133
Davidson, Dorothy, 24, 37, 53, 57-58, 66, 84, 86, 241
DeLand, Gary, 1-3, 74-76, 82-83, 90-94, 98, 101-102, 105-108, 117-18, 120, 122-31, 133, 135-36, 138-39, 141-43, 191, 193-99, 205
DeLand, Loni, 77, 91
Delgado, Lalo, 48
DeLia, Julian, 158
Deseret Gym, 56
Deseret Industries, 56
Deseret News, 30, 33-34, 43, 78, 81-82, 94, 98, 108, 113-15, 130, 132, 142, 158-59, 164, 183, 186-87, 232, 234
Dewitt, John, 203
Dickson, Mary, 102
Donaldson, Amy, 234
Dorsen, Norman, 46
Douglas, William O., 149
Dukakis, Michael, 4, 72, 175
Duncan, Adam (Mickey), 14-25, 27, 178, 241
Duncan, Timothy K., 75
Dunning, Elizabeth (Terry), 56-57, 60, 69, 232
Dunning, John W., Jr., 75-76
Durham, Christine, 227
Durham, Cole, 185
Dutch Reformed church, 172

Dykstra, Ben, 14
Dykstra, Daniel J., 28

E

Eagle Forum, 186, 211-14, 238
Eastman, Crystal, 5
Eckersley, Dave, 161
Edwards, Charles, 24
Eisenhower, Dwight D., 17-18, 24
Ellett, Albert H., 36
Elliot, Pam, 93
Emery, Alfred, 14, 27
Episcopal church, 177
Equal Rights Amendment (ERA), 14, 34-35
Evans, Bill, 105, 177, 188
Evolution, organic, 6
Executioner's Song, 49

F

Fagg, Ellen, 158
Families Alert, 108-109
Farley, Frances, 48, 80
Farrakhan, Louis, 240
Firmage, Edwin B., 113
First Presbyterian church, 187
Fischer, Sharene, 95-97
Fischer, Vaughn, 95-97
Fisher, George, 130
Fitches, Robert David, 207
Flynn, John L., 28
Forbes, Richard, 126
Ford, Gerald, 33
Fowler, William G., 24, 26
Foxley, Cecelia, 236
Francis, Steve, 45, 68
Francke, Michael, 132
Frederick, J. Dennis, 114, 226
Freeman, Alexa, 144
Freeman, David, 219

Freeman Institute, 26
Fritz, Albert, 24

G

Gallivan, John, 31
Gandhi, Mahatma, 70
Gay Community Center, 31
Gay issues, 31, 55, 58, 174, 189, 210-12, 214, 236-39, 241, 243
Gay and Lesbian Utah Democrats, 213
Gibbons, Harry, 77
Gillespie, James, 201
Gillilan, Hugh W., 28
Gilmore, Gary, 47-49, 51, 53, 146, 234
Ginsburg, Ruth B., 34-36
Glasser, Ira, 6, 72-73, 174-75
Gnade, Carol, 160-62, 166, 170-73, 176-77, 183, 186-87, 189, 195, 199-200, 205, 207, 209-10, 223, 230-35, 238-41
Goodnight, Rosa, 152
Graham, Jan, 169, 180, 183
Grant, Paul, 18, 42-43
Greene, J. Thomas, 55, 92, 113, 159, 164, 166-67, 170, 179-80, 182, 184-85
Grondahl, Calvin, 94, 112-13, 167
Grossman, George S., 30

H

Hale, Myron Q., 20-21
Hanks, Marion D., 19-20, 178
Hanson, Stewart, Jr., 30
Harding, Kyle, 126, 129
Harker, Brent, 217
Harlan, John Marshall, 149
Harper, Lee, 42
Harrie, Dan, 179
Harrington, John, 139

Harris, Leslie, 174
Harward, Byron, 226
Hatch, Orrin, 26, 150, 237, 239
Hayward, Pete, 129
Heineman, Robert, 144
Hendricks, Madeline, 218
Henry, Sandra, 134, 193
Hershey, Lewis B., 28
Heywood, E. Reed, 159
Hill, Joe, 10
Hilltop United Methodist church, 99
Hillyard, Lyle, 186
Hilton, Matt, 240
Hinckley, Gordon B., 177
Hinckley, Stuart, 82
Hodgson, Allen L., 24
Hofmann, Mark, 201
Holtzman, Elizabeth, 65
Homosexual. *See* Gay issues
Hoover, J. Edgar, 5, 26
Hotel Utah, 20-21
House, Dawn, 106, 155
Howell, Scott, 234-35
Huey, Henry L., 28
Huntsman, Clay, 239

I

In Defense of American Liberties, 4, 72
In Our Defense, 7
Industrial Workers of the World, 6

J

Janesch, Michael, 68
Jarvis, Boyer, 84-85, 102-103, 105-108, 135-36, 141
Jefferson, Thomas, 166
Jenkins, Bruce, 57, 195, 198-99
Jensen, Marlin, 187-88
Jewish Community Center, 26
John Birch Society, 26, 34-35

Jolivett, David, 135, 138
Jones, James, 199-200
Jones, Maurice, 18
Jones, Robert, 193
Jones, Tia, 199
Jordan, David, 240
Joy, James H. (Jim), 32-33, 35-37, 39, 120, 210, 240, 242

K

Kadish, Sandy, 14
Kendell, Kathryn (Kate), 115, 161, 170-71, 178-80, 182, 185, 187-88, 192, 194, 197, 199-204, 209, 212-13, 217, 219-21, 223, 225-27, 230-32
Kennedy, Caroline, 7
Kennedy, John F., 231
Kent, Theodore, 75
Kimball, Spencer LeVan, 14-16, 25, 178, 242
Kimball, Spencer W., 14
King, Charla, 234
King, Martin Luther, Jr., 70
King, Sherron, 234
Kinghorn, Gerald, 45
Klein, Victor, 30
Knapp, Richard, 218
Konchar-Farr, Cecelia, 163
Ku Klux Klan, 162, 175

L

Lanner, Harriet, 52
Lanner, Ronald, 52
Larson, Maren, 215
Latter-day Saints. *See* Mormon church
LDS Hospital, 159
League of Women Voters, 162
Leavitt, Michael (Mike), 142, 169, 178, 183, 203-204, 209, 232, 237 240
Lee, Rex, 221
Legal Times, 175
Lesbian. *See* Gay issues
Liebler, H. Baxter, 23
Lindsay, Richard, 55, 73, 95
Littlewhiteman, Greg, 206
Lloyd, Sherm, 22
Lockhart, William, 27
Lopez, Mark, 144
Lund, Lynn, 74, 120, 141
Lundberg, Constance, 36
Lundgren, Howard, 152-55, 158, 160, 179, 182-83
Lythgoe, Dennis, 98, 130, 142

M

Mailer, Norman, 49
Mangelson, Paul G., 202
Marcus, Harriet, 47
Marcy, Lisa, 144
Mary Magdalene, 166
Matheson, Scott M., 59
Matthews, Anne, 218
Maxwell, William F., 91
McAlister, Scott, 98, 121-23, 126-27, 130-31, 133-34, 138-39, 142-43, 194
McAllister, LeRay, 156
McCarthy, Dwight, 69
McCarthy, Joseph, 13, 25
McCormick, John S., 9
McCotter, Lane, 141-42, 194
McGovern, George, 65
McKay, David O., 11, 17, 19
McPheters, Samuel, 206
Mecham, Steve, 177
Mercer, Terry, 207
Metzger, Patricia, 59
Milliron, Vaughn, 212

259

Milne, Brent, 53
"Monkey Trial," 6
Montague, Jeff, 61
Montague, Nina Mitchell, 61
Montana, Gary, 91
Moral Majority, 174
Morgan, Nicholas (Nick), 106, 136, 194
Morley, Tony, 207
Mormon church: policy on abortion, 3, 145; LDS prayers, 4, 55, 79, 99; history of, 6, 227; priesthood denial to black men, 11; church/state separation, 14, 23, 100, 227; oppose ERA, 35; fired employees, 56; Articles of Faith, 90; against liquor on "fun buses," 94, 97-98, 105; allowed to lobby, 95; polygamy in, 96, 225, 227-29; sides with ACLU, 164; Special Affairs Committee, 176-77; policy on homosexuality, 210; work for Utah statehood, 225; belief in Mother in Heaven, 229-30; blood atonement, 146-47, 234; employees required to have temple recommends, 242; seminaries lose high school credit, 242
Morris, John, 29, 101-102, 107-108, 117, 141, 168, 171, 177
Moss, Frank, 15, 26, 29
Moulton, Kristin, 237
Moyle, Henry D., 23
Mylar, Frank D., 196

N

National Association for the Advancement of Colored People (NAACP), 17, 47, 201
National Center for Lesbian Rights, 233
National Civil Liberties Bureau. *See* ACLU
National Council of Jewish Women, Salt Lake Branch of, 162
Native American church, 164
Nazis, 46
Nearing, Scott, 16
Nelles, Walter, 16
Nelson, David, 213
Nelson, George ("Baby Face"), 26
Nelson, William, 177
Network, 162-63
New York Times, 32, 36, 156-57, 192
Nichols, Gerald, 66-67, 69, 102
Nixon, Richard M., 32-33, 37
Nolan, C. Dane, 77
Norman, Bonnie, 81, 119, 122, 195-96
Norwood, Roselee, 33

O

Oaks, Dallin H., 70, 103-108, 110, 163, 177, 187
Oberhansley, Curtis, 29
O'Brien, Michael, 91
Ogden Unitarian church, 187
O'Hair, Madalyn Murray, 116
Olsen, Bruce, 98
Olsen, Dennis, 29
Orem Unitarian church, 187
Oritt, Jeff, 152, 154, 160, 179, 182
Ortega, Ruben, 203
Orton, Bill, 242
Our Savior's Lutheran church, 187
Owens, Wayne, 33

P

Parashonts, Travis, 91
Parish, Michele, 1-4, 68-69, 76-77, 89-114, 117, 120-24, 128-32, 135-36, 138, 141, 143, 147-49,

153, 157-58, 161, 164-66, 168-70, 173, 176-77, 186, 191-92, 195-96, 198-99, 201, 233, 235, 242
Parish-Pixler, Wesley, 89, 97
Parmer, Lynnell, 43
Pedler, Shirley, 39-41, 44-56, 58, 60-61, 63, 79, 84, 97, 102, 120, 125, 210, 242
Peoples of Utah, 22
Peratis, Kathleen, 35-36
Peters, Megan M., 78
Peterson, Chase, 60, 177, 187
Peterson, Holly, 237
Peterson, Kelli, 236
Pevar, Steven, 205
Phillips, Michael, 179, 205, 218
Piganelli, Frank, 234
Planned Parenthood, 151-52, 155, 162, 164
Plenk, Bruce, 220-21
Pollak, Walter, 16
Polygamy, 10, 17, 95-97, 225, 227-29
Pornography, 5, 8, 30, 32, 46, 108, 140, 162, 171
Post, Susy, 34
Powell, John, 67
Prayer, public, 3-4, 10, 15, 53, 55, 71-72, 78-79, 89, 99-101, 103-105, 108-16, 146, 167, 170, 176, 178, 185, 187-89, 198, 209, 224-26, 228, 230, 233, 243
Prisoners, rights of, 1-4, 14, 31, 41, 67, 73-75, 81-83, 90, 97, 108, 117-44, 146, 161, 167, 191-209, 233, 243
Privacy, 5, 13, 72, 149-50, 154, 164, 184
Private Eye Weekly, 236
Protzman, Grant, 113

Psychology: An Introduction, 213
Punishment, freedom from cruel, 31, 47, 127

Q
Quintana, Danny, 91-93

R
Rampton, Calvin L., 23, 26-27
Rap Sheet, 124
Reagan, Ronald, 4, 118, 170, 173-74
Reid, Stuart, 176-77, 188
Religion, freedom of, 5, 10, 70, 72, 90-91, 93, 95-96, 100, 104-105, 109, 165
Reporter, 160, 163-64, 181, 189
Reproductive Freedom Project, 66
Reynolds, Jennifer Franks, 80
Reynolds, Michael Jon, 80
Right to Life of Utah, 153
Rights of Indians and Tribes, 206
Ritter, Willis, 48
Robbins, Jim, 111
Robertson, Pat, 176
Roe, Ben, 16, 26
Rogers, Roy, 33
Rolly, Paul, 138
Romney, George, 11
Romney, Vernon, 36
Rudick, Michael, 30, 34, 40-41, 45, 48, 97
Rudolph, Mary, 144
Runyan, Marie M., 27
Rutherford Institute, 175, 240
Ruzicka, Gayle, 186, 212, 236

S
Salt Lake City, 166
Salt Lake City: The Gathering Place, 9
Salt Lake Legal Defender Associa-

261

tion, 28
Salt Lake Tribune, 1-3, 17, 21, 20-33, 36, 39-40, 42, 47-48, 50, 52-54, 60-61, 63, 67, 69-71, 76-77, 80, 82, 85-86, 94, 97, 100, 106-10, 113-14, 125-26, 128, 130, 135, 138-39, 142-43, 147, 152-53, 155, 157-58, 163, 167, 179-82, 186, 188-89, 193, 200, 203, 205, 211-13, 215, 217-19, 223-26, 228-29, 231-32, 236-39, 241
Sandack, A. Wally, 14, 26-27
Sano, Roy I., 160
Santerian religion, 86, 229
Saperstein, Hershel, 26
Satan, prayer to, 229
Schlafly, Phyllis, 35
Schultz, William, 234-35
Schwarzschild, Henry, 50-51
Scopes, John T., 6
Scruggs, Bud, 112, 141, 156-57, 177
Selby, Dale Pierre, 69, 146, 200
Semerad, Tony, 236, 238
Sexual harassment, 138-40, 161
Shah, Madhuri, 159
Shane, Barry, 161
Shapiro, Evan, 194
Shared Ministries of Utah, 187
Shepherd, Karen, 169
Sherting, Jack, 52
Sigel, Barry N., 24
Simpson, Debbie, 213
Sisco, Carol, 128
Skousen, W. Cleon, 25-26
Smart, Christopher, 1-3, 82-83, 117, 126-29, 133-35, 138, 140, 142-43, 195
Smith, Joseph, Jr., 10
Smith, Joseph F., 25
Smith, Samuel, 31

Smith, Sharon, 151
Smoot, Reed, 25
Smoot, Stephen P., 24-27, 242
Snow, Ed, 228
Snyder, Tom, 229
Society of Separationists, 78, 114-16, 176-77, 185, 223-24, 226, 231
Soto, Joe, 202
South Valley Unitarian Universalist church, 187
Speech, freedom of, 5-6, 28, 30, 42, 60, 69-70, 81, 95, 159, 161, 175, 212
Spenkelink, John, 50
Sports Illustrated, 216-17, 223
Stack, Peggy Fletcher, 163
Standard-Examiner, 94, 111, 113, 130, 167
Stephenson, Howard, 236
Stewart, Charles, 236-37
Stewart, I. Daniel, 227
Strossen, Nadine, 7, 162, 164, 215, 234-35
Suicide, 210-11, 237
Sweat lodge, Native American, 90-93, 121, 123
Switzer, Kathleen, 133, 144, 191-93, 199

T

Tanner, John, 86
Taylor, John Albert, 234-241
Thomas, Norman, 5, 16
Thompson, Kim, 194-95
Thoreau, Henry David, 70
Threedy, Debara, 163
Tinker, Paul, 85
Torgensen, Kirk M., 196
Tribune. See *Salt Lake Tribune*
Trinity A.M.E. church, 187

Tripp, Mary Lou, 179
Turner, Mary A., 35-36

U

Uintah-Ouray Reservation, 205
Unborn, rights of, 8
Unitarian church, 26
United Council of Churches, 172
United Methodist church, 160
University of Utah, 13, 19, 25, 27-29, 32, 34, 37, 39, 54, 58, 60, 73, 81, 101, 113, 149, 161, 163, 177, 180, 233, 239, 241-42
Utah Legal Clinic, 79
Utah Legal Services, 44, 233
Utah National Organization for Women, 148, 157, 162
Utah Pro-Choice Coalition, 162
Utah State University, 215
Utah Women's Forum, 166
Utah Women's Health Clinic, 155, 159, 162, 182
Utah Women's Political Caucus, 148, 162, 242
Utah Xpress, 229
Utahns for Choice, 162-63

V

Valdez, Raymond, 205
Valdez, Rosanna, 205-206
Van Avery, Marianne, 54
Van Dam, Paul, 100, 132, 153, 155, 193
Vetter, Clayton K., 239

W

Wade, John, 16
Walker, Anne, 220
Walker, Olene, 169
Walker, Samuel, 4-6, 13, 16, 29, 32, 46, 50-51, 72, 149-51

Wall Street Journal, 55, 103-105, 110
Wallace, George, 41
Walles, Albert, 126
Ward, Joseph, 75
Ward, Leon, 24
Ward, Mark, 182
Warner, Kathy, 163
Wasatch Women's Center, 182
Watkins, Arthur, 15
Watkiss, David, Jr., 56-57
Welles, Ken, 55
Wilkinson, David L., 59, 70-72, 85
Williams, J. D., 21
Williams, Nancy, 101
Wilson, Mark, 215, 219-20
Wilson, Ted, 120
Winder, David K., 56, 222
Wolbach, Judith, 44-45
Women, rights of, 8, 14, 34-36, 54
Wood, Mary Anne, 158, 180, 182, 221
Woodruff, Wilford, 227
Workers, rights of, 8, 10, 176
Wright, Ernest, 31

Y

Yanowitz, Betty, 85
Yocom, David, 73-74, 126-27, 129-30, 140, 143, 200
Young, Brigham, 9, 15
Young, David, 80
Young Republicans, 240
YWCA, 162

Z

Zimmerman, Michael D., 226-28
Zippel, Benny, 224